WITNESSES AND SCHOLARS
Studies in Musical Biography

MUSICOLOGY: A BOOK SERIES
Edited by F. Joseph Smith

Additional volumes in preparation

This book is part of a series. The publisher will accept continuation orders which may be cancelled at any time and which provide for automatic billing and shipping of each title in the series upon publication. Please write for details.

WITNESSES AND SCHOLARS
Studies in Musical Biography

_____

Hans Lenneberg

The University of Chicago

Gordon and Breach
New York   London   Paris   Montreux   Tokyo   Melbourne

Gordon and Breach Science Publishers

Post Office Box 786
Cooper Station
New York, New York 10276
United States of America

Post Office Box 197
London WC2E 9PX
England

58, rue Lhomond
75005 Paris
France

Post Office Box 161
1820 Montreux 2
Switzerland

3-14-9, Okubo
Shinjuku-ku, Tokyo
Japan

Private Bag 8
Camberwell, Victoria 3124
Australia

Library of Congress Cataloging-in-Publication Data
Lenneberg, Hans, 1924–
  Witnesses and scholars.
  (Musicology, ISSN 0275-5866; v. 5)
  Bibliography: p.
  Includes index.
  1. Musicology. 2. Musicians—Biography.
I. Title. II. Series: Musicology (New York, N.Y.);
v. 5.
ML3797.L46   1988   780'.01   88-17
ISBN 2-88124-210-3

*To Johanna for enduring many monologues
and for just being there*

CONTENTS

INTRODUCTION TO THE SERIES

The Gordon and Breach *Musicology* series, a companion to the *Journal of Musicological Research,* covers a creative range of musical topics, from historical and theoretical subjects to social and philosophical studies. Volumes thus far published show the extent of this broad spectrum, from *Music and Its Social Meanings* to *Late Renaissance Music at the Habsburg Court* to the present volume, *Witnesses and Scholars: Studies in Musical Biography*. Forthcoming titles will include works on the history of the trombone, the music of Mendelssohn and Stravinsky and a musical *festschrift* honoring Gwynn S. McPeek. The editors also welcome inter-disciplinary studies, ethnomusicological works, and performance analyses. With this series, it is our aim to expand the field and definition of musical exploration and research.

ACKNOWLEDGMENTS

Parts of this book have appeared in *Opera Quarterly,* * *Bach. The Journal of the Riemenschneider Bach Institute, The Musical Quarterly* and *The Journal of Musicological Research* either in different form or different context.

I owe special thanks to David Fallows, F. Joseph Smith and Standley Howell who read all or parts of the manuscript and made suggestions. Since I did not always heed their advice, though undoubtedly very sage, they are blameless for any deficiencies this book may retain.

*Original version of Chapter IX published in *The Opera Quarterly,* Vol. II, No. 1, Spring 1984, edited by Sherwin Sloan, MD, and Irene Sloan. Copyright 1984 The University of North Carolina Press. Reprinted by permission of the publisher.

CHAPTER I
BIOGRAPHY AND HISTORY

At this time there is no history of musical biography and none of the standard musical encyclopedias has an entry under that subject. Whether this is because biography does not have an independent history or merely a matter of snobbery remains to be examined. What snobbery there is might go back to Guido Adler although it is hard to believe that his contempt for the subject could still prevail after the many great achievements in the genre.[1] Just the same, when Adler placed biography low in the hierarchy of the proper subjects for scholarly musical study, dismissing it as an auxiliary endeavor, he may have kept serious historians away at least for a while. Adler's main interests lay in the study of paleography, history, theory, and stylistic analysis. Eventually, however, other scholars must have realized that serious biography makes use of all these categories, that in fact, style analysis is hardly possible without the knowledge of individual techniques of composition. That Adler had such a low opinion of the uses of biography in 1885 is understandable in view of a then rising tide of popular works. Of the early serious biographers such as Friedrich Chrysander, Otto Jahn, and Philipp Spitta, as well as the pioneer, Ludwig von Köchel, only Spitta and Chrysander were still alive and in a position to protest.[2] Instead they became

---

1. Guido Adler, "Umfang, Methode und Ziel der Musikwissenschaft," *Vierteljahrschrift für Musikwissenschaft* 1 (1885): 5ff.
2. Friedrich Chrysander, *Georg Friedrich Händel*, 3 vols. (incomplete) (Leipzig: Breitkopf und Härtel, v.1 1858; v.2 1860; v.3 1867). Otto Jahn, *W. A. Mozart*, 4 vols. (Leipzig: Breitkopf und Härtel, 1856—59). Philipp Spitta, *Johann Sebastian Bach*, 2 vols. (Leipzig: Breitkopf

co-editors of the *Vierteljahrschrift für Musikwissenschaft*, the journal
in which Adler's manifesto was published. We do not really know
what prompted Adler's disdain for biography as a serious aspect of
musicology; perhaps he only meant that other categories of the
discipline should have higher priority. It is now certain in any case
that genuinely scholarly biographies make use of paleography, the
study of manuscripts, as well as printed editions, historical documents, and stylistic analysis; in fact, one might consider these fields
auxiliary to the writing of good biography. That almost mythical
historical creature, *Zeitgeist*, for example, can never be captured
except by means of biography. This applies especially prior to the
nineteenth century when the interests of musicians were much
narrower than later. To demonstrate that the Enlightenment touched
composers in their work, or that *Sturm und Drang* resulted in an
increase in music in minor keys, requires finding some evidence
showing how composers absorbed such trends.

Thirty-five years after Adler another great scholar, Hermann
Abert, was quite unashamed to acknowledge the rôle of biography as
a part of musical scholarship. Abert even devoted his inaugural
address upon taking the chair of musicology at the University of
Leipzig to the subject.[3] "It would pay," he said, "to clarify and
examine whether musicology has anything more to gain from biography," and thus launched into a survey of past biographies and into
recommendations for their future. To consider biography passé, he
concluded, is only thinking of its outdated methods, not its essence.
As a special category of research, biography is not only possible, it is
even essential. To do without it would leave a painful gap in our
knowledge.

A skeptic might consider Abert's defense of biography special
pleading, since he was then in the process of rewriting Otto Jahn's
Mozart.[4] Such a suspicion, however, is dispelled by reading his work,

---

und Härtel, 1873—80). Ludwig Ritter von Köchel, *Chronologisch-
thematisches Verzeichnis sämtlicher Tonwerke Wolfgang Amadeus
Mozarts* ((Leipzig: Breitkopf und Härtel, 1862).

3.   Hermann Abert, "Über Aufgabe und Ziel der musikalischen Biographie," *Archiv für Musikwissenschaft*, 2 (1920). Reprinted in *Gesammelte Schriften und Vorträge von Hermann Abert*, ed. by Friedrich
Blume (Tutzing: Schneider, 1968): 562.
4.   Hermann Abert, *W. A. Mozart*, 2 vols. (Leipzig: Breitkopf und Härtel,
1919—21).

actually an entirely new biography rather than just an edition. Abert's is a truly great biographical study that reads as if it had been intended to be a response to Adler. Carefully weaving Mozart's life and personality into his time, Abert wrote a comprehensive history of music in the eighteenth century. In order to set Mozart's accomplishment off against a background and to show how and by what Mozart may have been influenced, his biography presents studies of the sonata, symphony, opera, and other forms in such great detail that one can read these sections for their separate value.

In his essay on the aims and the mission of biography the only argument Abert does not present is the need of the public to place the work of art in a context. Adler had chosen not to address in his low ranking of biography the inability of the listener to hear (or to look at or read, for that matter) a work as if it were an object of nature; to leave out of account who created it and when. Until the end of the eighteenth century it had mattered little. As long as the artist was primarily a craftsman and all the works to be heard or seen were primarily contemporary, neither personality nor historical circumstances had been important. But as art became some sort of personal statement and the past was no longer dismissed, the public rightly began to take the creator and his time into account. The public's curiosity grew, in fact, as this knowledge seemed ever more essential, and it was also applied retrospectively. Josquin des Prez's contemporaries may not have been sufficiently interested in him to create and preserve a portrait of the master. We, however, are not happy with the absence of virtually any knowledge of the man and his life. (His contemporaries did not lack respect for Josquin's work; in fact it was highly admired far and wide.) Nor are we incapable of perceiving the power of his music without knowing the composer. Were we to discover that Josquin had a highly dramatic life, full of amorous escapades and all the other trappings of a modern script, would it really affect how we hear his music? In which sense does it matter whether or not Bach was as devout as his devotional music leads us to believe? The aesthetic implications of these questions are very profound, too profound to be addressed in this context. But whether they are answered or not, there is no question that biography has seized our imagination; and that it cannot be ignored. To pretend that modern man's compulsion to find out about the artist is a childish irrelevance would do away with more than half of the criticism of the last two hundred years, since we would have to pretend that iconographical, symbolic, psychiatric, and other types of interpretation in the arts are possible without knowing anything about artists.

To acknowledge biography as a valid topic of aesthetics and history, on the other hand, does not mean that it is necessarily a separate field of historiography; it is part of it. It can be considered either as part of the history of biography in which it is a latecomer, or as part of the history of musicology, another young discipline. In the context of musicology it reflects the advances history and analysis have made in the last one-hundred years even if biography has special problems some of which may remain unsolved. The most obvious question, one so far not satisfactorily answered, is the relationship between life and work. Another consists of the difficulty of writing and reading musical description. More serious is the problem of what kind of musical description truly illuminates what composers were doing, what they were trying to say. Even the great biographers sometimes take recourse to metaphor. Is there anything wrong with Abert's description of the opening of Mozart's Quintet in G minor (KE 516) other than possibly its late romantic hyperbole?

> Its main theme immediately expresses in all its aspects the basic mood of the work; a half-nervous climb and descent, first as stabbing pain, then in sobbing sorrow. In its second half comes a stronger charge bordering on despair followed by a fatalistic plunge.[5]

As the youngest branch of biography the description of musical lives hardly existed before the middle of the eighteenth century. The earliest accounts of musicians not intended as eulogies upon their death, are factual resumés listing the basic data about family, child-hood, teachers, and travels. In the main, they concern themselves with their subjects' professional accomplishments by merely recount-ing positions and works, with an emphasis on those works that were printed. Near the end of the eighteenth century the tone changes. That change is manifested chiefly in the generous interweaving of anecdotes and the personal recollections of relatives and acquain-tances. While this hints at the interest in personality that soon flourished, it also marks the beginning of a new era, visible at first in the lives of Haydn and Mozart. Haydn's earliest biographies consist of little more than anecdotes, most of them designed to show him as a warm and humorous man without affectations, anecdotes that were

---

5.   Ibid. 7th ed., ed. by Anna Amalia Abert, 1955. 2: 321f.

in part ultimately responsible for his nickname, "Papa." Since his development had been relatively normal, the Haydn anecdotes are quite unlike those about Mozart which deal mainly with his incredible facility. Few are about Mozart as a person and he is certainly not depicted as especially warm and humorous. A kind of apotheosis of personal recollection, Nissen's Mozart of 1828 makes one wonder whether he married Constanze because he admired Mozart, or whether she married Nissen because she needed a biographer for her late husband.[6] What is new in Nissen is his extensive use of letters, unprecedented in earlier biographies. (Yet Otto Jahn criticized Nissen for the use of so many letters, accusing him of not supplying a proper narrative.) What had made Forkel's earlier biography of Bach (1802) pioneering was his attempt to deal for the first time with a subject's music.[7]

It is Guiseppe Baini, however, who should get the credit for the first scholarly biography.[8] His life of Palestrina (1828) made a virtue of necessity. To write about a composer of the distant past meant to use archival sources for the mute testimony to be found there. Baini is thus the first successful student of a much earlier composer and his musical environment. Nissen and Baini published in the same year. Nissen's use of letters was a kind of documentary approach, but since he otherwise relied on personal recollections, his is still the old kind of biography; Baini's represents the new.

As the nineteenth century advances, the romantic interests in history as well as in personal development merge in the learned biography which also now always relies heavily on documentation to recapture the past. In popular as well as in scholarly biographies the genius is now regarded as an extraordinary person in whom the historian sees the personification of progress, while popular biographers are inclined to turn artists into romantic heroes. The degree of romanticizing varies. The best popular biographers always tended to adhere closely to reality. Thus in the last third of the century we

---

6.   Georg Nikolaus von Nissen, *Biographie Wolfgang Amadeus Mozarts nach den Briefen* (Leipzig: Breitkopf und Härtel, 1928).

7.   Johann Nikolaus Forkel, *Über Johann Sebastian Bachs Leben, Kunst und Kunstwerke* (Leipzig: Hoffmeister und Kühnel, 1802).

8.   Giuseppe Baini, *Memorie storico-critiche della vita e delle opere di Giovanni Pierluigi da Palestrina*, 2 vols. (Rome: Societa tipografica, 1828).

encounter the first full-fledged professional biographer in the person of La Mara whose real name was Ida Maria Lipsius.[9] Although her biographies catered to growing popular demand, La Mara never stooped to excessive sentimentality. Her biographies were competent, literate, musical, and highly responsive to the facts. While her descriptions of musical works remained on a superficial niveau, this worked well when she was writing about living composers, those whose music she could assume her readers had heard. The scholar, on the other hand, became more concerned with the work of art. In fact, for want of much personal information about Bach, Spitta deduced Bach's personality from his music, something Forkel had also done. This may also have been a result of personal prejudice. Spitta could hardly have failed to see Bach's truculence or his pettiness in financial matters.

An almost opposite approach was taken by Alexander Wheelock Thayer whose biography of Beethoven placed most of the emphasis on the life rather than the music.[10] By the time Thayer began his work, Beethoven's life had already been encrusted with so much mythology that it was Thayer's primary task to get at the true story. There was no need at the time to deal with the music in detail. For the most part it belonged to the repertoire of public as well as private performers. It would be there for more detailed study later. Gustav Nottebohm was in fact at work on more technical musical studies at the same time.

Not until recent times have we begun to understand that an artist's work does not necessarily have much in common with his character or personality. We can be fairly certain at this point that Mozart was not as warm, wise, and orderly as his music suggests, or that Beethoven was not the flaming revolutionary one might take him to be on the basis of his departure from classical composure or on such a work as *Fidelio*. That we now find it easier to accept the schism between some lives and their works is only partly due to the greater realism of recent decades; we also owe it to having come to know such a man as Wagner. Between the idealism of Wagner's music and the shabbiness of his personality lies a seemingly unbridgeable gulf.

---

9.   La Mara's many biographies were collected under the title *Musika-lische Studienköpfe*, 5 vols. (Leipzig: Schmidt, 1868—82).
10.   Alexander Wheelock Thayer, *Ludwig van Beethovens Leben*, 5 vols. (Leipzig: Breitkopf und Härtel, 1866—1908).

The rise of psychoanalysis, whatever else it teaches, or whether its applicability is controversial or not, has shown us that nobody lives perfectly, that purity does not exist, and that absolute evil is as rare as absolute goodness.

It was precisely when general interest in the lives of artists of all kinds surged toward a climax at the end of the nineteenth century that Adler in effect dismissed it. In his own biographical studies Adler was quite consistent, so consistent that his monograph about his close friend, Gustav Mahler, contains little that is personal.[11] While he thus tried to remain "scientific", Adler seemed not to have noticed to what an extent it was Ludwig von Koechel who had carried the impersonal scientific biographical study as far as one could. What else was his catalogue after all, but the use of documentation, biographical information, and stylistical analysis, put in the service of a chronology that would be the ultimate Adlerian biography, a preliminary study for Mozart's purely artistic development? (How decisively our attitude has changed may be inferred from the biographical work of Alfred Einstein who saw no contradiction between revising the Koechel catalogue and his own neo-romantic biography of 1945 in which the glassy surface of Mozart's music is forever being ruffled by "daemonic" undercurrents.)[12]

The logical compromise between Adler's implied view and subsequent biographies was eventually reached in the now common compartmentalization of biographies into separate sections: first the life, then the work. That division has not often been integrated with complete success. Hermann Abert's radical revision of Jahn's *Mozart* is one of the true successes because Abert manages to blend life, history, environment, and analysis so convincingly that we accept the totality as a vivid portrait of Mozart in his time. This is due at least in part to Abert's almost novelistic talent by means of which he recreates a person even when his means include the detailed scholarly procedures of the most pedantic historian. Perhaps no more than two-thirds of his work is still factually acceptable, as Abert would have been the first to admit, but his work is to biography what the Ninth is to symphonies.

---

11.   Guido Adler, *Gustav Mahler* (Vienna: Universal, 1916). See also Edward R. Reilly, *Gustav Mahler und Guido Adler: zur Geschichte einer Freundschaft* (Vienna: Universal, 1978).
12.   Alfred Einstein, *Mozart. His Character, His Work* (New York, London: Oxford University Press, 1945).

A more recent achievement of the scope of Abert's is H. C. Robbins Landon's *Haydn* which differs, however, in its more restricted historical depth and in its somewhat lesser emphasis on Haydn as a person.[13] Instead Landon recreates the various social settings in which Haydn moved and the musical environments in which he functioned. He too separates his sections; in fact, he makes distinctions between the cultural background, the "chronicle," and the chronology of Haydn's compositions, from detailed discussions of his music. The amount of detail his book digests would be unmanageable in any other way.

Landon's work could not have been conceived before Otto Erich Deutsch invented the documentary biography, yet another impersonal approach that Guido Adler would have found acceptable.[14] It is the achievement of Deutsch to have gathered those documents that would be permanently available for ever new interpretations. His kind of book can never become dated; it can only be supplemented or emended.

Abert had insisted that a biography ought to be rewritten every fifty years, a proposal, Walther Vetter writes, that was met with some coolness in scholarly circles at the time.[15] Inevitably, says Abert, we are so conditioned by our own times, our biases and fads, that we cannot ever be entirely objective. Mozart's life and work is an ideal example of changing views, since in two-hundred years his image has gone from that of an amazing prodigy, to superlative craftsman, to somewhat passé master of purity and serenity, to poverty-stricken and misunderstood tragic genius, to his present popularity as perhaps the greatest — though not the most lovable — composer who ever lived.

Biographical dictionaries and other forms of collective biography also had their beginning in the eighteenth century, a fact that should surprise us only when we compare it with the visual arts. Earlier on, musicians seem to have been of little interest as personalities. Their status grew over the centuries along with that of other artists, but not necessarily always at the same pace. Why should the composer of

---

13. H. C. Robbins Landon, *Haydn: Chronicle and Works*, 5 vols. (Bloomington, Ind.: Indiana University Press, 1976—80).
14. See, for example, Otto Erich Deutsch, *Franz Schubert: Die Dokumente seines Lebens und Schaffens*, 2 vols. (Munich and Leipzig: G. Müller, 1913—14).
15. Walther Vetter, "Gedanken zur musikalischen Biographik," *Die Musikforschung* 12 (1959): 132.

chants have had any greater right to an identity than the master-builders of Romanesque and early Gothic churches? When composers' names were at last attached to polyphonic works (albeit not always reliably) and architects identified, one would expect a parallel growth in status from then on. Instead, the visual artist found a chronicler of his work as well as his personality in Vasari as early as 1550, while musicians had to wait nearly one hundred fifty years for similar recognition.[16] What is even more remarkable is that in the meantime, Vasari enjoyed several new editions and that Benvenuto Cellini rightly assumed that there was enough interest in him for an autobiography.

The question of why artists should have had biographers earlier than musicians is of course a very interesting one (see Chapter 3). In the absence of an overview of the history of biography other than Abert's brief essay, it seems not to have been noticed. And Abert, like many of his contemporaries, was inclined to look to Germany and Austria first. To our scholarly grandfathers and fathers, it looked for a while as if all the significant musical developments were coming from Germany and Austria. In his view of the history of biography and autobiography Abert was able to see clearly the influence of Herder and Goethe. Since he did not look abroad, however, Abert failed to see that Jean-Jacques Rousseau must have affected such men as André Grétry and Christian Friedrich Daniel Schubart.[17] The latter's memoirs come closer to the turbulence of Benvenuto Cellini than any other musical autobiography.

Relatively few musicians have left us formal memoirs or autobiographies although many of them were avid correspondents. Not surprisingly they usually have an ear for language and are often well informed. That they were not professional writers makes their letters all the more revealing. As most artists became aware of posterity and worked with an eye to the future, musicians on the whole assumed that it was their music that would speak to future generations. They tended to be much less self-conscious in their letters than were professional writers.

---

16. Giorgio Vasari, *Vite de' piu eccellenti architetti, pittori e scultori italiani* (Rome: [Lorenzo Torrentino], 1550).
17. André Ernest Modeste Grétry, *Mémoires ou essais sur la musique* (Paris: Author, 1789). Christian Friedrich Daniel Schubart, *Schubarts Leben und Gesinnungen von inhm selbst im Kerker aufgesetzt*, 2 vols. (Stuttgart: Gebrüder Mäntler, 1791—93).

With the rise of greater subjectivity and greater stylistic differences among composers in the nineteenth century came the view that music is autobiographical. We anthropomorphize absolute music, as it were. In popular biographies, journalism, even in scholarly monographs, writers about music have often linked the mood of a work to an event in the composer's life or to secret programs. This is so pervasive a trend that some composers have even succumbed themselves. While one modern memoirist, Stravinsky (1936), denies that music can say anything, Shostakovich, in the somewhat dubious memoirs smuggled out of Russia, reproaches his audiences for not seeing through wartime propaganda.[18] The public, Shostakovich says, continues to believe that his seventh symphony was about the battle of Leningrad, whereas it was really about good and evil as well as being a part of his own requiem. In fact, as one reads Shostakovich, it becomes clear that not one of his abstractly titled works was free of literal and autobiographical meaning and that he thinks we have consistently failed to understand him.

The difference between the attitudes of Stravinsky and Shostakovich is quite apparent in the tone of their respective memoirs. Stravinsky's are so devoid of personal elements that, except for certain modern touches and for his acerbity, it might as well be an eighteenth-century autobiography. Stravinsky is entirely preoccupied with composition and performance. Shostakovich carries nineteenth-century emotionalism to its extreme in a melancholy response to a twentieth-century society in which he lived with fear and hatred. His is a paradoxical success-story since he received immediate recognition for the right reasons, but by the wrong people at the wrong time. If he carried the idea that music is message to an extreme, his audience, at least the official part of it, went even further, treating it as propaganda for or against the establishment.

While professional scholarly biographies were characteristically divided into two sections, the life and the work, the biographies intended for laymen also split into different directions. One traditional approach was novelistic although very few biographies went so

---

18.   Igor Stravinsky, *An Autobiography* (New York: 1936), also published as *Chroniques de ma vie* and *Chronicle of My Life*. Dmitri Shostakovich, *Testimony: The Memoirs of Dmitri Shostakovich*, ed. by Solomon Volkov and trans. by Antonia W. Bouis (New York: Harper and Row, 1980).

far as Möricke's.[19] The newer, the psychoanalytical method, presumes that the reader will gain a deeper understanding via a category of biography called "psychohistory." The term is relatively new but the method goes back to Freud's monograph on Leonardo da Vinci and his *Moses and Monotheism*, studies that carry conviction because Freud either separated the work from its creator or wrote about character in terms of the various causes of a historical legend.[20] Freud did not write under the illusion that the uncovering of Leonardo's possible latent homosexuality explained his work, but he theorized about the psychological causes of his relatively small output of paintings. Freud's interest lay in recreating Leonardo on the basis of what seemed hidden in his work. His controversial work on Moses digs at the roots of mythology, historical timeliness, peoples' perception of their leaders, as well as the psychological foundations of a modern religion.

In music a superficial relationship between psyche and creative work sometimes seems obvious. We tend to accept the notion that Mahler, for example, alternated between banal tunes and tragic passages because he heard a barrel-organ on the street while his parents were engaged in a (to him) traumatic quarrel. But it does not explain why Shostakovich uses similar juxtapositions, or the humor of the silly tune that emerges at the end of Bartók's fifth quartet, or the dramatic use of lullaby, march, and folk-song parodies in *Wozzek*. All of these later composers were probably very much influenced by Mahler without knowing the psychic basis for his contrasts which they most likely took to be an extreme form of romantic irony. "Romantic irony" gains little from psychiatric insight although psychiatry may make other contributions to our under-standing of the composer. Maynard Solomon has written an admir-able work about Beethoven, analyzing his ambivalence toward the changing social order and telling us that Beethoven's story of royal descent, so clearly in conflict with his general views of either egali-tarianism or intellectual aristocracy, is a typical "family romance," not at all uncommon in psychiatric case histories.[21] But Solomon can

---

19.   Eduard Möricke, *Mozart auf der Reise nach Prag* (Prague, 1856).
20.   Siegmund Freud, *Leonardo da Vinci*, trans. by A. A. Brill (New York: Random House, 1922). *Moses and Monotheism* (New York: Knopf, 1939).
21.   Maynard Solomon, *Beethoven* (New York: Schirmer, 1977).

hardly explain the appeal Beethoven's music has had for about two-hundred years, i.e., how even the most extreme conflicts of the great man could have found expression in the non-verbal language of music and communicated them to the listener. It is quite likely that the suspicion that his "father" was Jewish led to Wagner's antise-mitism and we may find this fascinating. What does it contribute to our understanding of his works, however, since there the subject of anti-Semitism is completely absent?

That Schumann's insanity was caused by syphillis becomes doubt-ful as one reads the letters of his associates, his own journals, or early biographies. Hints of manic-depressive tendencies are visible very early in Schumann's life. (Recent scholarship has confirmed that he probably did not have syphillis.)[22] The process of examining Schumann's life, however, makes clear how difficult it is to speculate about the artistic psyche in isolation from a generalized view of artis-tic personalities and their socio-cultural environment. The obverse side of this question is that of timeliness. How much does the tem-perament of the individual artist contribute to his "success"? Could a composer of a classicistic temperament succeed in a generally romantic era or would he simply have to choose another area of endeavor? If an individual vacillates between jubilation and depres-sion in a society in which equanimity is the norm, he will certainly be misunderstood, perhaps even confined to a madhouse. As an artist he would most likely be considered merely eccentric. To the reader of many biographies and autobiographies, manic-depressive tenden-cies seem common to all creative persons. Artists tend to crash from the heights of creative exultation to the depths of self-doubt and temporary sterility. And when Mario Praz shows that certain aspects of romanticism constitute a kind of collective neurosis, he implies that the individual madness the biographer sees may actually represent relative normalcy.[23] Psychohistory does not usually see the individual artist of the past in the same way as a patient, i.e., in a social context. No therapist would apply anachronistic standards when evaluating an actual patient. The psychohistorian should ask, for example, why the public of the last century and a half has come

---

22.   See Peter Ostwald, *Schumann. The Inner Voices of a Musical Genius* (Boston: Northeastern University Press, 1985).
23.   Mario Praz, *The Romantic Agony*, trans. by Angus Davidson, 3rd edition. (Cleveland: World, 1963).

to insist on the martyrdom of the artist and whether this does not affect the self-image of the composer?

Perhaps the above bird's-eye view demonstrates that musical biographies cannot be seen as separate from history and music-historical methods. But if they cannot be separated, neither can their separate values be dismissed. Guido Adler may have realized only the former aspect of biography as a sub-discipline.

In yet one other sense, biography is history. The reader who becomes addicted to biographies, whether for scholarly or less exalted reasons, soon discovers that the documentation involved in reconstructing a life has bearing on other lives as well as on social and cultural history in addition to its original, its primary function. While in the early eighteenth century, for example, each autobiography by itself stubbornly resists our gaining any profound insights, as Alfred Einstein already pointed out, reading the surviving fifty or so autobiographies as fragments of a whole is enlightening.[24] There emerge common elements: how, for example, musicians fit into society; what their lives were like; and why, in Germany at least, the work of Bach's contemporaries was so rarely published. The picture is of course incomplete until one investigates the various facets of the individual story by corroborative means, but the questions themselves become vividly apparent in the process. One begins to see the real status of Sebastian Bach, for example, uncolored by later romanticization; and one understands why he was one of many candidates for his position in Leipzig seriously considered only after Telemann, Graupner, and Johann Friedrich Frash. It was no reflection on the esteem in which he was or was not held at the time. The Council first asked three composers who had previously worked in Leipzig, musicians they knew and respected. It was simply an example of what we would now call the "old-boy network" in early operation.

In the nineteenth century, as musicians become more literate and more aware of their environment and their position in it, letters and journals reveal ever more of their attitudes toward what was around them. Read in the aggregate the various correspondences and other writings from, say, 1830 to 1860 (which include the memoirs of Berlioz and Spohr as well as the letters of Friedrich Wieck,

---

24. Alfred Einstein, "Die deutsche Musiker-Autobiographie," *Jahrbuch der Musikbibliothek Peters für 1921* (Leipzig: Peters, 1922): 58ff.

those of the publisher's agent, Heinrich Probst, the recollections of Mendelssohn and Schumann by such contemporaries as Ferdinand Hiller and Wasielewski, Mendelssohn's own letters, Wagner's autobiography, and Meyerbeer's correspondence) which tell us much about that time.[25] A revealing and neglected source about both Clara and Robert Schumann's lives and personalities can be found in Brahms' letters to such friends as Otto Grimm and Joseph Joachim.[26] Eduard Hanslick knew virtually everybody and his autobiography has more information about others than about himself.[27]

Who could guess that Mendelssohn's correspondence with Ignaz Moscheles tells him (and us) precisely what it cost to live in Leipzig, thus casting light on Schumann's contention that he and Clara could live together in modest comfort in spite of what Friedrich Wieck might say.[28] Heinrich Probst is not only full of information about publishers' fees, contracts, and concert-life in Paris, but he also claims that it was he, Probst, who "christened" Chopin's *Preludes*

---

25.   Hector Berlioz, *Mémoires de Berlioz* (Paris: Lévy Frères, 1870); Louis Spohr, *Selbstbiographie*, 2 vols. (Cassel: Wigand, 1860—61); Käthe Walch-Schumann, *Friedrich Wieck Briefe aus den Jahren 1830—1838.* Beiträge zur rheinischen Musikgeschichte, 74 (Cologne: A. Volk, 1968); Wilhelm Hitzig, "Pariser Briefe. Ein Beitrage zur Arbeit des deutschen Musikverlags aus den Jahren 1833—1840," *Der Bär*, 1929—30 (Leipzig: Breitkopf und Härtel, 1930) 27ff. (trans. by Hans Lenneberg in preparation); Ferdinand Hiller, *Mendelssohn. Letters and Recollections*, trans. by M. E. von Glehn, 2nd ed. (London: Macmillan, 1874); Joseph Wilhelm von Wasielewski, *Robert Schumann* (Leipzig: 1858), Felix Mendelssohn, *Briefe*, ed. by Rudolf Elvers. Veröffentlichungen der historischen Kommission zu Berlin (Berlin, 1968). Richard Wagner, *Mein Leben* (first published: Munich: List, 1963); Giacomo Meyerbeer, *Briefwechsel und Tagebücher*, ed. by Heinz and Gudrun Becker, 3 vols. (Berlin: de Gruyter, 1975).

26.   *Billroth im Briefwechsel mit Brahms*, ed. by Aloys Greither (Munich: Urban und Schwarzenberg, 1964). Johannes Brahms, *Johannes Brahms im Briefwechsel mit J. O. Grimm*, ed. by Richard Barth (Berlin: Deutsche Brahms Gesellschaft, 1912), *Johannes Brahms im Briefwechsel mit Joseph Joachim*, ed. by Andreas Moser, 2 vols. (Berlin: Deutsche Brahms Gesellschaft, 1921).

27.   Eduart Hanslick, *Aus meinem Leben*, 2 vols. (Berlin: Allgemeiner Verein für deutsche Literatur, 1894).

28.   Felix Moscheles, ed. and trans., *Letters of Felix Mendelssohn to Ignaz and Charlotte Moscheles* (Freeport, N.Y.: Books for Libraries, 1970; Orig. 1888).

with the opus number 28.[29] Clara Wieck found the action of Erard pianos so awkward that she wrote to Robert Schumann from Paris that it would take three weeks to prepare a concert.[30] She retained her dislike of such actions; twenty years later she warns Grimm via Brahms not to get her another hard-to-play instrument for a concert in Hanover for the same reason.[31]

While Louis Spohr's autobiography was published in 1860, it is an extraordinary eyewitness account of earlier musical life in Germany and Austria, as well as in Italy and England. As such it is not unknown, of course, but neither has it been fully explored.

Few scholars have so far taken much interest in Engelbert Humperdinck, whose letters and diaries are another primary source if for no other reason than that he worked with Wagner in Bayreuth beginning in 1881.[32] His letters contain, among other things, one of the few extant descriptions of Wagner's sense of humor. (Wagner had humor, patronizing though it was.) In general, the literature about Wagner places the master on so high a pedestal or in so low a pit that one scarcely realizes he was human and so his jokes with Humperdinck in Saxon dialect come as a surprise. Humperdinck timed all the "numbers" of *Parsifal* at a performance on July 26, 1882, thus leaving a valuable piece of evidence for modern performers.

These are samplings taken from documents the primary function of which is biographical, of course, although they might not be found by any but the most assiduous historian. Even more interesting is the use of these sources as social and cultural history. As such they are still unexplored territory. Only recently Carl Dahlhaus suggested that we consider past attitudes in the formulation of our own.[33]

---

29. Hitzig, "Pariser Briefe."
30. Berthold Litzmann, *Clara Schumann, an Artist's Life*, 2 vols., trans. and abrd. by Grace E. Hadow (London: Macmillan, 1913).
31. *Brahms-Grimm Correspondence.*
32. Engelbert Humperdinck, *Briefe und Tagebücher*, 2 vols. Beiträge zur rheinischen Musikgeschichte, 106 and 114 (Cologne: 1975—76).
33. It is implied in the introductory pages of Carl Dahlhaus, *Die Musik des 19. Jahrhunderts*. Neues Handbuch der Musikwissenschaft, vol. 6 (Wiesbaden: Akademische Verlagsgesellschaft Athenaion, 1981). Dr. Dahlhaus believes that historians cannot reconstruct how it really was (p. 2). While this is probably true, it seems to me necessary to come as close to such a reconstruction as we possibly can. If all musical

This seems understated, especially since Dahlhaus realizes how major an element of nineteenth-century history biography was. Elsewhere, Dahlhaus says that the history of the period would lose its "local color" if it was confined to a history of structures.[34] At the same time he is not calling for a revival of nineteenth-century methods. Yet in view of its past importance, biography should be retained as a more important factor in the reconstruction of a period than it generally is at present.

While documents before the nineteenth century are scarce and not very revealing, they begin to accumulate after 1800 at about the same pace at which music gained in popular interest. The nineteenth was a century in which the commercial, the intellectual, and the compositional aspects of music flourished with a far greater complexity than we have allowed ourselves to see. Musicologists today are inclined to sneer at history based on "great men," but they still virtually exclude many secondary musicians from consideration. Perhaps many of them were commercial hacks or virtuosos writing bravura pieces for their own concerts. On the other hand, those great composers we so revere had considerable respect for such names as Zelenka, Onslow, Spohr, Johann Nepomuk Hummel, Sterndale-Bennett, Hiller, Ferdinand David, and others, musicians whose music, in spite of our voracious appetite for recordings and radio programs, is still largely unheard.

One of the reasons why autobiographies in the twentieth century are less satisfactory than older ones is that we are still so close that their documentary value has not yet become apparent. Another is our dismay when we realize that esteemed composers are not inevitably profound thinkers or, conversely, that some composers whose music has not made a deep impression on our century write the better memoirs. In many autobiographies we get mainly gossip, often very partisan. Since in the twentieth century so many "schools" of composition exist side by side, the practioners often indulge in sniping; many fail to understand that a composer's stature is not necessarily a matter of the idiom in which he choses to write. For the

---

history is eclectic, as Dahlhaus puts it, the reconstruction of the contemporary scene must be one of the most important choices we should make (see p. 3).

34.   Carl Dahlhaus, *Between Romanticism and Modernism*, trans. by Mary Whittal (Berkeley: University of California Press, 1980).

most part, however, the autobiographies of the last thirty or forty years will have conspicuous documentary value when they are read together. It will hardly matter that all the contributors were very biased.

A few of the great retrospective biographical accomplishments of our century have used contemporary documentation of the widest range, often going far beyond the obvious sources in order to reconstruct the times in which their subjects lived. Abert's merit was his ability to direct the history of a form or genre into paths leading directly to Mozart. Landon's *Haydn* contains remarkable reconstructions of the social and musical environments in which Haydn moved. The tireless combing of newspapers, official documents, letters, and reminiscences of persons who moved in the same environment was gathered in increasingly large tomes by Deutsch and his successors. Curiously, however, it seems to have occurred only to biographers that such sources can be used to recreate a former time and place for us. The idea that the documentation used in biographies can be used independently of a subject, that one need not place a figure in the landscape, has not often been realized.

The following essays reflect some fascination with the subject of musical biography and its various uses. That this fascination did not produce a straightforward history may disappoint some readers. The decision not to write one, however, has the same roots as the question asked at the outset of this chapter, i.e., why has biography not been dealt with before? As one reads one biography and autobiography after another, one realizes that their linear history is difficult to trace. One might perhaps deal with the scholarly and popular treatments of composers over the years, but it is a subject one cannot separate from general historiography. There simply are not enough autobiographies from any one period to allow us to generalize about them. They too tend to complement what we already know about music. Perhaps, in other words, we are seeing what Adler must also have seen; biography as such is an adjunct to general musical history, however essential it may be to scholarship and documentation.

This is not to say that biography is beyond the pale. The subject lends itself to various investigations which are in themselves interesting and valuable. It is possible to single out some of these aspects while also preserving the historical outline.

CHAPTER II

COLLECTING MUSICAL BIOGRAPHIES IN THE EIGHTEENTH CENTURY

When Johann Mattheson's *Grundlage einer Ehrenpforte* appeared in 1740, it was the first collection of biographies devoted to musicians.[1] Giorgio Vasari's *Vite* published one hundred ninety years before, was an entirely different work, one that might have served as Mattheson's model, assuming he knew it.[2] Vasari's book seems to have sprung from his personal enthusiasm for art of all kinds; his style is vivid and direct. The work still serves as the basis for biographical information about many artists and, since Vasari listed the works of each artist he knew, it is still of use in authenticating the art of the Renaissance. Mattheson's style, on the other hand, combines pomposity, moralizing, and pedantry, and *Ehrenpforte* is not even as relatively reliable as Vasari. The tradition of scholarship in Germany probably encouraged Mattheson's sort of writing. It had been only a comparatively short time since Latin was the language of scholarship, and even if now, approximately a hundred years later, books in German addressed a new kind of reader, it was still usual to write pompously and to use as many Latin and Greek terms as possible to impress the public with one's learning. Perhaps

---

1. Johann Mattheson, *Grundlage einer Ehrenpforte, woran der Tüchtigsten Capellmeister, Componisten, Musikgelehrten, Tonkünstler, etc. Leben, Werke, Verdienste etc. erscheinen sollen* (Hamburg: Author, 1740).
2. Giorgio Vasari, *Le Vite*.

Mattheson also hoped to gain respect for a profession that in Germany still had very little status. Musicians were not as well established in the social ranks as most other professions in spite of their special qualifications, a fact of which Mattheson was quite aware. Perhaps that is why he set moral standards for the musicians to be included in his work. His enterprise was undertaken under a kind of subliminal duress; it had to demonstrate that musicians deserved better. Within the covers of *Ehrenpforte* the autobiographical contributions of some musicians, Johann Conrad Dreyer and Georg Philipp Telemann, for example, are written in fresh and simple language.

But why is Johann Dreyer included in a book in which Bach is missing? The fact that Bach did not respond to Mattheson's invitation to submit an autobiography was hardly reason enough to ignore him. Surely any of Bach's several admirers who are included in *Ehrenpforte*, or one of the contributors from Leipzig such as Johann Gottfried Walther or Lorenz Mizler, could have been prevailed upon to supply the missing biography for a musician whose reputation, even if he was known chiefly as an organist, was second to none and whose name is mentioned by several of the autobiographers who are found in *Ehrenpforte*.[3] The great name is invoked once by Johann Francisci, who on page 79 says: "Anno 1725 I wanted to see the famous city of Leipzig again and went there in the company of a local merchant, having duly received permission. I arrived in time for the Easter Fair and had the good fortune of meeting the famous *Kapellmeister* Bach and to learn from his facility." Another entry, that of Johann Balthasar Reimann, has a similar reference on page 291: "During this time [c. 1726] a noble patron here in Hirschberg paid my way to Leipzig to hear the famous Johann Sebastian Bach. This great artist hospitably [*liebreich*] took

---

3.   It is an oversimplification to believe that Bach's reputation was merely that of a virtuoso. While it is clear from contemporary evidence that his dexterity was much admired, it is equally clear that to be a virtuoso on the organ was to be an instant composer of choral preludes, fugues, and bass-realizations. Much evidence points to the esteem in which Bach was held as a master of harmony and counterpoint, i.e., as a composer. (See Hans Lenneberg, "Bach, Handel and Comparative Reputations," *Bach, The Quarterly Journal of the Riemenschneider Bach Institute*, vol. 12: 22ff. and 13: 17ff.)

me in and delighted me so much with his rare talent [*ungemeine Fertigkeit*] that I never regretted the trip."

Even if the modern reader did not see it as an obligation for Mattheson to have included Bach among the subjects of his biography, it is difficult to understand how he could have paid homage to so many obscure musicians and "*eruditi*" and left out the greatest musician of the time. Comparison of Mattheson's biographies with the entries in Johann Gottfried Walther's *Musikalisches Lexikon* of 1732 can only lead to the conclusion that one of Mattheson's criteria was exclusivity.[4] The more obscure names in *Ehrenpforte* are usually not found in Walther, thus justifying Mattheson's book. More difficult to understand are Mattheson's famous exclusions versus some equally famous inclusions. Thus, Lassus and Goudimel can be found, but not Josquin, whom Mattheson mentions elsewhere. Nor do we find any of the myriad other composers of what used to be called "earlier times." In a random sampling of some early names, the following are in Walther, however briefly: Lassus and "Gaudimel," Gombert, both Gabrielis, Jacobus Gallus, Gardane, Gesualdo, Ghiselin, and Glareanus among the G's. Dufay, Josquin, Palestrina, and Victoria are there, though the author had probably neither heard nor seen their music himself. Guillaume de Machaut is missing in Walther as well as in Mattheson unless he is disguised as Guilhelmus de Marscandia about whom Walther says, "a *musicus* frequently cited [*allegiret*] by Franchinus [Gafurius]." Among French luminaries Mattheson included Lully and "Lande, Mich de la," but he found no room for Rameau and Couperin in his pantheon. The article on de Lalande is, properly speaking, not a biography at all. Ostensibly a correction of an error in Walther, it is a two-page essay on the distinction between the titles, *maître de la chapelle-musique* and *maître de musique de la chapelle*, combined with two new facts, namely that the king paid de Lalande's widow 4,000 French "pounds" to buy her late husband's "motets," and that these motets were still being performed at court as late as 1736. It is this sort of entry which makes one wonder if the articles in *Ehrenpforte* truly constitute a biographical dictionary. Aside from Mattheson's innate pedantry and the pleasure he took in one-upmanship, it must be understood that it was common practice to regard books as mutually

---

4.   Johann Gottfried Walther, *Musikalisches Lexikon* (Leipzig: W. Deer, 1732).

complementary. Even late in the eighteenth century reference books rarely repeat what earlier books had already contained; they tend to supplement earlier works apparently on the assumption that their readers owned a library of the few "standard works" then available.

From our point of view, another, earlier book in the genre deserves to be called "the first" collective biography, although Evrard Titon du Tillet's *Le Parnasse françois* (1732) was published as a plan for a public monument to the great of France and included poets, writers, and philosophers as well as musicians.[5] Du Tillet may have been one of Mattheson's sources. On the other hand, a comparison of Mattheson's Lully biography with the one in *Parnasse* reveals that Mattheson's scurrilous suggestiveness is quite foreign to du Tillet, whose biographies are entirely laudatory. The hint of scandal lurks in Mattheson's way of telling his readers that Lully was brought to France from Italy because a traveling courtier was asked by a niece of Louis XIV to "bring her back any nice [*artig*] Italian boy he deemed good for something."

The almost complete absence of Englishmen is the most surprising of Mattheson's omissions, not only in view of his well-known Anglophilia, but more especially because *Ehrenpforte* was dedicated to his employers at the British legation to Hamburg. Apparently Mattheson's interest in things English did not extend to music, which in recent times, he said, "flatfootedly imitated the Italian style."[6] In 1725, in *Critica musica*, he disagreed with a critic of his earlier *Neu-eröffnete Orchestre* (1713) who had insisted that Purcell was English, not French. The anonymous correspondent had cited as proof the inscription near Purcell's tomb in Westminster Abbey.[7] Mattheson insisted that Purcell was French regardless of his place of birth in the same way that Handel would always be German. He based his rebuttal on nothing more than Purcell's name. The name, he says, must have been anglicized from *Pourcel*, which in England would have to be pronounced *Paurcel*. Not content with this proof

---

5.   Evrard Titon du Tillet, *Le Parnasse françois* (Paris: J. B. Coignard, 1732. Supplements, 1743 and 1755).

6.   Johann Mattheson, *Das neu-eröffnete Orchestre* (Hamburg: Author, 1713), as quoted by Beekman Cannon in *Johann Mattheson, Spectator in Music* (New Haven: Yale University Press, 1947): 131.

7.   Johann Mattheson, *Critica musica*, 2 (Hamburg: Author, 1725): 147ff.

he then attacks his critic's English, making his own mistakes in the process.

Only two English musicians survive in *Ehrenpforte*: William Heather has a brief entry in the main body of the book, while Henry Symonds appears in an appendix. Referring once again to Walther, we find "Bird or 'Vogel,' an English composer and lover of canonic writing," and four lines for "Thomas Tallisus." There are no entries for Dunstable, Dowland, or *Henry* Purcell. John Bull gets four column-inches. Clearly there is considerable question about the sources available to both compilers as well as a question of reputations. Walther, who had the right lexicographical instincts, always gives his sources although not adequately. Mattheson usually tells us only that his material came either from a book, a manuscript, or an autobiographical letter. Sometimes he refers to a source in the body of a biographical entry. One cannot rely on such citations, however; several times I have followed them up only to find that there was no mention of Mattheson's information in the source cited.[8]

If it is puzzling that Mattheson did not inscribe more English composers on his portal of honor, one must also wonder why he did not include more theorists. If we postulate that it was one of Mattheson's aims to make music more respectable, he should have welcomed learned writers among his biographies. In 1725, in his *Critica musica*, Mattheson had commented on Brossard's listing of nine-hundred authors (the number given by Brossard himself).[9] There Mattheson augmented Brossard's list by an additional four- to five-hundred names. (Brossard had excluded biographies, but he appended a table of musical authors, that is, all those he knew had written something about music. Typically for an age which suffered

---

8.   Hunting for biographies in Walther is made complicated by the compiler's often idiosyncratic spellings. One finds Purcell by looking under Pourcel. Walther also has two entries for Quantz, the first under the correct spelling, the other under Quoüance where he is described as "a Frenchman who published a *suite des pièces à deux flutes, his first work.*" (See Edward Reilly, *Quantz and His Versuch*, New York: Galaxy, 1971; 109 ff.) One cannot be sure that one has found all the entries because of Walther's spellings. Lexicography in the eighteenth century left a good deal to be desired. Thus Walther did not notice that under *Daniel* Purcell he cites the inscription in Westminster Abbey which reads, "here lies Henry Purcell."

9.   Sébastien de Brossard, *Dictionnaire de musique* (Paris: C. Ballard, 1703).

from what Curt Sachs used to call the *furor classificationis*, Brossard divided them into categories not only by the languages in which they wrote but also by whether he had seen their works himself, whether they were easily available although he had not seen them, and whether he thought them difficult to obtain. (Perhaps Brossard had intended to compile some sort of bio-bibliographical work himself.)

Mattheson's list (in *Critica musica*) contains names of composers who are not generally known to have written about music. He printed his supplement to Brossard with abbreviations for the sources. Unfortunately, he does not explain his abbreviations, which he says are "for my information so that today or tomorrow I can find my *fontes* again." And with his usual air of superiority he takes Brossard to task. "I must remind [the reader] of two things. First, that Brossard could have extended his *catalogum* if he had not made it a rule to cite only *theoreticos*; second, that I not only consider such limits unnecessary, I consider them wrong [*unbillig*] and intend to proceed quite differently."[10] Perhaps when he set to work, he found it more difficult to put together a more complete biographical dictionary than he had thought. He did, however, manage to collect 150 entries (counting his appendix), some of them merely supplements to other sources.

It would be historically naïve to demand that Mattheson should have been able to evaluate musicians correctly. Like all writers up to the end of the eighteenth century, he wrote his books for contemporary readers without considering posterity or permanent stature. Yet it is hard to believe that any evaluation was even attempted unless we accept Mattheson's values. In this work these are often a matter of the high morals he attributes to his musicians even if the full title of *Ehrenpforte* stipulated that the book was to include "the most capable music-directors, composers, performers, etc., their lives, works, merit, etc." The word *Grundlage* — foundation — of course implied that the book was to be further developed later; whether by him or someone else is not specified. Mattheson was aware of his limitations and built a hedge against criticism of his selection as well as against possible errors. In the preface he elaborates by stating that he will "include the best and most *virtuous* [my itals.] music-masters, those who in the name of God arouse to piety and worship, and tame the naturally undisciplined flesh and its

---

10.   *Critica musica*, 2: 109ff.

instincts, thus contributing to the moderation of the soul's excesses and even to the taming of beasts. . . . It is such select persons who shall be memorialized on this portal." He hoped further that his biographies would serve as models to budding musicians and help overcome the low esteem in which musicians were still being held in Germany. "As far as I know," he writes, "there is not one miser like Taffi, no murderous Castagno, no bull-like Raphael to be found in these pages, rather [these musicians] (allowing for human weakness), are capable, god-fearing, honorable, pious men in whose respective styles one can see how far-removed they are from vice." [11]

The modern reader may be taken aback by the absence of terms such as greatness or genius in *Ehrenpforte*. The latter never occurs and greatness is used only once in a poem eulogizing Reinhard Keiser, "the greatest composer of operas in the world, the emperor of opera." Mattheson has praised Handel so often elsewhere, he says, that it is unnecessary to praise him again and Telemann is referred to as being beyond praise. Thus, although Edward Lowinsky traced the concept of genius to the Renaissance and found it again in 1722 in Rameau's *Traité de l'harmonie*, the term is still absent from Mattheson's vocabulary. [12]

Most valuable in *Ehrenpforte* are the numerous autobiographical contributions Mattheson solicited. Before the last third of the eighteenth century, these are generally models of self-effacement. Alfred Einstein called them *Berufsbiographien*. [13] Such biographies confine themselves to the chronology of the author's career, his parentage, travels, teachers, accomplishments, and publications; they are as devoid of feeling as a modern entry in *Who's Who*. The only personal element in these autobiographies is the recurrent story of the early discovery of a compelling need to make music, often against parental wishes and against other odds such as poverty. It is evident from early autobiographies, most of which share this one "romantic" trait, that the compulsion to make music is not limited only to great composers.

Comparing du Tillet with Mattheson shows us that while Matthe-

---

11.   *Ehrenpforte*, Preface: viiif.
12.   Edward Lowinsky, "Musical Genius — Evolution and Origins of a Concept," *The Musical Quarterly* 50 (1964), nos. 3 and 4: 321ff. and 476ff.
13.   Alfred Einstein, "Die deutsche Musiker-Autobiographie," *Jahrbuch der Musikbibliothek Peters für 1921* (Leipzig: Peters, 1922).

son was making an effort to improve the social position of musicians in Germany, du Tillet took their status for granted. His composers stand side by side with the greatest minds in France without apology. At least at court, the position of composer and performer was apparently more highly regarded in France than in Germany. Du Tillet's biographies are quasi-official, none contains any of the spicier facts later historians have unearthed, and none is critical or hierarchical. *Le Parnasse* was dedicated to Louis XV but it is clear that du Tillet was writing about the glory of the court of Louis XIV; only later appendices bring his biographies up to date. Predictably, du Tillet reviews the history of French poetry and philosophy in earlier centuries, but when it comes to musicians, there are no earlier times, since older music was no longer being performed and was not available in modern editions.

Given du Tillet's self-imposed limitation, French musicians of the seventeenth and early eighteenth centuries, his biographical collection has, greater consistency than Mattheson's which lacks all restrictions and therefore juxtaposes composers of stature and lesser ones from different periods in such a manner that the result is virtually random.

Mattheson's longest biographies are those of Wolfgang Caspar Printz with twenty-four pages, Telemann with sixteen, Keiser with ten, Handel and Lully with nine pages each, and Mattheson's own with thirty-six. Major or minor status seems to have had less impact on Mattheson than how much information was available, how highly he personally rated his subjects, or how long their autobiographical contributions came out to be. Any historian, is of course interested in finding patterns and coming to some conclusion about what such a collective biography has to tell us. Other than the cliché that eighteenth-century appreciation was almost exclusively for contemporary music, we learn little. And *Ehrenpforte* does not lend itself to any generalizations but that its author thought highly of himself.

Mattheson's entry for Wolfgang Caspar Printz, transmitted by his son Christopher Peregrin, is partly autobiographical. Like most contributions it is of far greater interest as a document of contemporary attitudes to music, society, and self than it is as biography. Mattheson did little editing, apparently accepting autobiographical contributions as they came even if they contained grammatical peculiarities such as Printz' ". . . Here [in Waldthurn] I was conceived and born . . . on October 10, 1641." Because Printz was the author of thirteen books about music, Mattheson appended a postscript about "musical textbooks," an aside which laments the present state of musical theory when musicians consider themselves too good to write textbooks for students, even though they now ought to know so much more than such ancestors as Printz.

Mattheson's complaint about the lack of good books on music — his own voluminous effort notwithstanding — is echoed fourteen years later in Friedrich Marpurg's introduction to *Historisch-Kritische Beyträge zur Aufnahme der Musik*.[14] It was partly to rectify the dearth of modern musical literature that Marpurg founded this periodical which dealt with new music, summaries and selections from current books, translations of foreign books, etc. *Lebensläufe.* "Lives," were to be a regular feature, but they begin to diminish already in the second volume of 1756. While there are eight biographies in the first volume, the second has only one, the third five, and the last two volumes contain none at all. In the second volume of *Beyträge* we find a number of what might be called incidental biographies. These are part of an article the title of which can be translated as "Chronological Table of Operas Performed in Paris between 1645 and 1745 Including the Lives of Several French Composers."[15] None represent primary biographical sources, since Marpurg took his information either from du Tillet or another dictionary, that of Jacques Lacombe, the *Dictionnaire portatif des beaux-arts*. (This little book was later translated into Italian.)[16] Lacombe himself took much of his information from *Le Parnasse françois.*

Marpurg's later periodical, *Kritische Briefe über die Tonkunst* (1760—64), begins a new venture in Volume II, a series of articles entitled "Beyträge zur Historie der Musik," which include several

---

14. Friedrich Marpurg, *Historisch-Kritische Beyträge zur Aufnahme der Musik* (Berlin: Lange, 1754—78).
15. Ibid., 2, no. 1: 232ff.
16. Jacques Lacombe, *Dictionnaire portatif des beaux-arts* (Paris: La Veuve Estienne et fils, 1752) and *Dizionario portatile delle belle arte* (Venice: Remondim, 1768). Neither version of this book is well-known. Coover (*Music Lexicography*, 3rd ed., Carlisle, Pa.: Carlisle Books, 1971) lists the French original although he does not enter it as a biographical dictionary in the index. This is no serious omission, since Lacombe is of marginal value as a biographer. Of interest to us is that Lacombe limits himself to French and Italian musicians and that the Italian version is identical with the French, except for grammatical and terminological changes required by the difference between the languages.

full-fledged biographies or autobiographies. Here we find the life of Jacob Adlung as well as short entries for Jacob Lustig (1706—96) and Franz-Joseph Meyer von Schauensee (1720—96). Marpurg also corrects several entries in Walther. Perhaps he was planning to compile a biographical dictionary himself.

How haphazard the compilation of biographical dictionaries must have been for the pioneers of the genre only gradually becomes clear to the modern reader. However laboriously these men pieced together the earliest histories and bibliographies in order to give us an overview, they also perpetuated errors from book to book, since they relied rather too heavily on other compilations. The process becomes very visible in a biographical dictionary which in its modernity belongs to the nineteenth century. Since, on the other hand, it was a direct descendant of Walther and Mattheson, one naturally wants to deal with it in this context.

Ernst Ludwig Gerber's *Historisch-biographisches Lexicon der Tonkünstler* for the first time attempts to be a comprehensive historico-biographical source as well as a "Who's Who" of the music business.[17] It is a major achievement, laying the foundation for all subsequent works in the nineteenth century. It is particularly interesting in comparison with its models by Walther and Mattheson and in comparison with its own second version, *Neues historisch-biographisches Lexicon,* which appeared twenty-two years later.[18] For the later edition Gerber had had the benefit not only of more recent historical books, but also of many letters pointing out errors of omission and of fact.

That Gerber seems to us so much more modern may be due less to the romantic *Zeitgeist* than to his practical experience and to his knowledge of reference books. He was a man who in the course of his own research became entangled in conflicts of fact or orthography. Instead of being merely annoyed by inadequate documentation, he took matters into his own hands. He may have been premature in

17.   Friedrich Wilhelm Marpurg, *Der kritische Musicus an der Spree* (Berlin: A. Haude, 1749—50), and *Kritische Briefe über die Tonkunst* (Berlin: Birnstiel, 1760—64). Ernst Ludwig Gerber, *Historisch-biographisches Lexikon der Tonkünstler* (Leipzig: Breitkopf, 1790—92).

18.   *Neues historisch-biographisches Lexikon der Tonkünstler* (Leipzig: Kühnel, 1812—13). The two works will be referred to as Gerber I and II, respectively.

the assumption that his own interest was shared by a large public and that there was consequently a large market. Breitkopf und Härtel willingly published the first edition, but Gerber had great difficulty finding a publisher for the second version.[19]

Gerber did not include his own biography in the first edition (Gerber I), though in Gerber II, "in response to many requests," he consented to give the reader considerable detail about himself. His autobiography reveals that he was a kindly and warm-hearted man who was also a born scholar and bibliographer. Before he had gone to study in Leipzig, he writes, he had managed to find C. P. E. Bach's *Versuch* which

> enlightened me on many [musical] questions.[23] But more than this book, Adlung's *Anleitung zur musikalischen Gelahrtheit* captivated me when it accidentally came into my hands later. The other books mentioned by Adlung reminded me of my father's library. I checked and found to my delight that I was in possession of a considerable collection. . . . The only works [lacking in his father's library] Walther's dictionary, Mattheson's *Der Vollkommene Kapellmeister* and Marpurg's periodicals were acquired. And now I sat so transfixed by my books that my brother had to remind me not to neglect the keyboard.[20]

Gerber's autobiography hardly mentions his legal studies and subsequent legal work, it is so dominated by his love for music. He played and composed as an avocation at first but on receiving an appointment to succeed his father in Sondershausen as a court-musician of the reigning duke he was freed from other occupations. When musical life in his city declined, Gerber turned his primary attention to his hobby, the literature about music. He undertook to collect and study all the portraits of musicians he could find. Hunting for references in books, he amassed so much biographical data that he was eventually able to compile his own dictionary. He then resolved to standardize the spellings of names according to the subject's nationality, a resolution he carried out with fair consistency. (There had been a good deal of musical migration in the eighteenth century after all.) He also determined to use only material he could

---

19.   See Friedrich Rochlitz, *Für Freunde der Tonkunst*, 3rd ed. (Leipzig: Cnobloch, 1868, originally published in 1824—32), 2: 23ff.
20.   Gerber II, col. 293ff.

document. On the other hand, the idea that only original sources could provide true documentation was not yet clear to him or anyone else. Gerber's achievement as a lexicographer is a milestone in the history of musical scholarship and as such ought to be taught as consistently as Eitner's still is, since without Gerber the work of both Fétis and Eitner would have been considerably more limited in scope.

How long before Gerber I appeared did the author finish his manuscript? The question is of interest because Gerber lists works of Mozart that were completed in 1788 and Gerber fully appreciated Mozart's stature. He even went so far as to credit Mozart with a position he had never held and with payments greater than we know Mozart to have received. The new edition, Gerber II, which the author had effectively completed in 1801, relies on Mozart's own systematic catalogue for the years between 1784 to 1791 and contains the following evaluation: "Mozart was one of the first geniuses known to musical history. Instead of quoting all the eulogies he earned, we shall content ourselves with Haydn's judgements." Here follows the oft-repeated endorsement Haydn had given to Leopold Mozart as well as Haydn's letter of 1787 to Franz Roth in Prague, "If I could impress on every music lover, especially great music lovers, the depth and great understanding which I perceive and feel [in Mozart's works] nations would vie to have such a gem within their walls."[21] Gerber's own musical insight is documented by his capsule summary of Haydn's style in the first edition. To quote a section should illustrate Gerber's modernity.

When we invoke the name Haydn, we mean one of our greatest men, great in small things and even greater in large ones. ... Every harmonic artifice, even those from the gothic age of the grey-bearded contrapuntists is at his command. But instead of sounding stiff the devices take on a pleasing character in his hands. He possesses the great art of making his music sound familiar. And although he uses the most artificial contrapuntal devices, he remains accessible [*populair*] and pleasing [*angenehm*] to every music lover. His themes have the stamp of originality and are instantly recognizable as his to

---

21. Gerber II, I, col. 493. Gerber, however, continues with his own appreciation for several pages and wonders how much more Mozart would still have achieved had not his premature end made the further "unfolding of his genius" impossible.

the attentive listener. . . . He carries us along! One experiences alternately anxiety and pleasure [listening] to the complications and resolutions of his ideas.[22]

Reading terms like "greybeards" and "gothic age" sends the curious reader straight to Gerber's article on Bach, since at the end of the eighteenth century several writers about music, Burney among them, considered contrapuntal music hopelessly passé. Clearly, however, Gerber did not share this assumption since his appraisal of Johann Sebastian Bach as a composer — almost entirely taken from Hiller — describes him as a master who knew "the inmost secrets of harmony. . . . His melodies may have been peculiar [*sonderbar*] but they were always different, very inventive and unlike the melodies of any other composer." There is no suggestion that Bach had been old-fashioned, "gothic," rather, Gerber emphasizes that the formalistic devices of counterpoint at Bach's disposal came alive in his hands. In Gerber's use of the term "gothic," he may actually have been referring to the Middle Ages although not necessarily with derogatory intent. He calls Dufay one of the oldest greybeards among polyphonists.

Gerber deemed the time ripe for a biographical dictionary. In the sixty years since Walther, music had reached its apogee, a golden age which was now threatening to go into decline because musicians were catering to the whims of amateurs and to fashion. They were getting further and further away from basic principles (*Grundsätze*), and no longer allowed critics to apply their great knowledge and insights to current production.[23] Among Gerber's list of new masters who arose during the intervening years between Walther's dictionary and his own, were the Germans, Bach (presumably C.P.E.), Benda, Gluck, Graun, Handel, Hasse, Haydn, Hiller, Kirnberger, and Marpurg, and abroad, Galuppi, Jomelli, Piccini, Sacchini, etc.

Gerber's point of departure was Walther's own copy of the *Lexikon* in which Walther had made many additions and corrections. It is therefore of interest to look at those entries in which Walther had been especially deficient to see what had happened to them. Walther's most flagrant error was the entry for "Pourcel," in which Daniel and Henry had become confused and which Mattheson

---

22.   Gerber I, I, col. 610.
23.   Ibid., Preface, p. iv.

had made worse by insisting that Purcell must have been a Frenchman. Gerber I still has him under "Pourcel" although he says that he is also known as Purcell, and that, according to Mattheson, he was born in France around the middle of the seventeenth century. Gerber calls him the greatest English composer before Handel and reports an essentially correct biography. In the second edition, Gerber finally has the name right and says Purcell was born in London. His source is Burney. There is no longer an entry for "Quoüance;" and "Gaudimel" is now correctly spelled Goudimel. Josquinus Pratensis is briefly entered as Jacobus Pratensis in the first edition; he is given his full due in the second edition with an article of three pages, the sources for which were Forkel's and Burney's histories. Guilhelmus de Marscandia still has a brief entry in the second edition as a teacher of music from before the fifteenth century often cited by Gafurius. Gerber wonders if this refers to St. Guillaume, but there is also an entry under "Machaut (Guillaume de), one of the oldest contrapuntists who flourished around 1350, according to Burney."[24] Gesualdo, who is now entered under Venosa, has a biography that has grown from half a column in the first edition to one and one-half columns in the second.

It becomes obvious that one of the main sources for Gerber II was Burney's history, the first three volumes of which should have been in time for Gerber I, but which, Gerber writes, had become only partly available in Germany via a translation of the section on the

---

24. Gerber II, II, col. 282f. The rediscovery of Machaut, first as poet, later as composer, is a story so far not reported in the literature. As late as 1789, when the second volume of Burney's *History* appeared, Machaut was only a name. Burney's correspondent had not been able to make much sense of his music. A few years earlier, La Borde (1780) had included Machaut in his chapters on "lyricists," devoting a special section to his poetry while saying nothing about his music. The first to offer a substantial reference to his music were Choron and Fayolle (1810—11), a reference later expanded by Fétis in his *Biographie universelle*. Fétis speaks of Machaut's "mauvaises successions d'harmonie," which, he says, were endemic until they were finally overcome by the generation of Dufay, Dunstable, and Binchois. Fétis credits François-Louis Perne as the first to have transcribed the music in 1817 or thereabouts. Perne is given a long biography by Fétis. My colleague, the late Professor Vincent Duckles, helped me try to find a supposed article by Perne in the Bibliothèque Nationale in Paris. Neither of us succeeded.

"music of the ancients by Hofrath Eschenburg published in 1781."[25] While Gerber cites Burney and Hawkins in both editions, he apparently preferred Burney; most of the later entries give Burney as his source.

The works Gerber consulted are listed very informally at the beginning of his book, so informally, even by eighteenth-century standards, that one cannot call the list a true bibliography. One of his sources was La Borde's *Essai sur la musique* (1780), another was Forkel's *Allgemeine Geschichte der Musik* (1788—1801).[26] Neither of these books is referred to as often as Burney. In Forkel's case this is especially understandable considering that he was much more interested in the history of style, harmony, and notation than in individual composers. Forkel's work, in fact could be considered a precursor of Riemann's *Geschichte der Musiktheorie*; it is a "great-man" history concentrating on theorists. Such chapter headings as "Von Guido bis auf Franchinus Gaforious [sic]" take the reader by surprise even if he realizes the extent to which early historians were dependent on theoretical writings in order to decipher old notations and to understand the contrapuntal context in which the notations functioned.

La Borde's work, on the other hand, contains a biographical dictionary in its own right in his third and fourth volumes. While La Borde excluded Germans and Englishmen, he covers composers, performers, and lyricists (i.e., poets whose texts were set to music) from ancient Greek times to his own in separate sections divided by nationality. An occasional German is admitted to this pantheon because, rightly or wrongly, La Borde considered such theorists as Martin Agricola, Michael Praetorius and "Athanase Kirker" "*écrivains latins*" (presumably because he had never read Praetorius whose abominable language cannot be called either German or Latin).[27]

The browser in La Borde realizes that his *Essai* is not reliable by

---

25.   The reference is to Johann Joachim Eschenburg's *Dr. Karl Burney's Abhandlung über die Musik der Alten* (Leipzig: ?, 1781).
26.   Jean Benjamin de La Borde, *Essai sur la musique ancienne et moderne* (Paris: P. D. Pierres, 1780). Johann Nikolaus Forkel, *Allgemeine Geschichte der Musik*, 2 vols. (Leipzig: Schwickert, 1788—1801).
27.   Martin Agricola (1486—1556) wrote treatises in German as well as in Latin.

any standards. Nevertheless it is a valuable source which modern scholarship should not continue to disregard, especially in tracing back "lyricists" or uncovering contemporary attitudes to various musics. La Borde, for example, gives the perfect illustration for Lowinsky's historical distinction between the two uses of "genius," *être un génie* or *avoir de génie*, in a single sentence. Speaking of Corelli he says, " . . . *son génie, sa science et son goût . . . lui ont assuré à jamais une des places les plus distinguées parmi les génies qui ont influés sur le progrès des beaux-arts.*" (The incidental hint at posterity seen for the first time in biographical references is also noteworthy.)

It is one of the delights of tracing the history of biography that the compilers sometimes write their own history. One is bound to look up Gerber's entries for both Burney and Hawkins in order to discover his attitude toward them. In the first edition Gerber respectfully summarized Hawkins but he had not yet seen most of Burney's volumes. In Gerber II, Hawkins' biography is briefly supplemented, incidentally making clear that Gerber did not repeat entries from the first edition; he often just brought them up to date and corrected errors. Burney's work of history is discussed and compared to Hawkins'. To summarize what Gerber says about Burney: he was the first to write a history of. the art rather than of artists, unlike Printz and Hawkins and others before them. Of course, he includes artists in his history but only those who had some impact on it. One could see with what enterprise he deciphered and scored old musical works in order to show "the gradual progress of harmony and its enrichment." Gerber goes on to praise Burney's style and the humor with which he presented the driest topics, always "treating his readers as if they were spoiled children."

Gerber apparently read English with some facility. There are only hints that he preferred Burney to Hawkins although he shared Burney's notion of progress in music. Gerber too believed that recent music was to be considered better than that of the past. On the other hand, there is nothing to show that he actively disapproved of Hawkins' antiquarianism. If he had strong feelings about it, his entry on Hawkins constitutes a model of editorial objectivity.

What is also clear is that such terms as genius and greatness have crept into the lexicographer's everyday vocabulary. In considering the history of the term genius, it is probably less important to find early uses than it is to find it now transformed into a standard term applied with the same connotations it still has today. Apparently genius and great man or great artist are terms used interchangeably. Gerber calls Paisiello an extraordinary genius, Piccini is merely a genius, and Tartini is "*ein Originalgenie*," a term without an idiomatic English equivalent. Bach and Mozart are referred to as a great artist and a great master, respectively, with a quote from Marpurg about Bach, namely, that he was a man who combined the perfection and the gifts of several great men. Most touching is the comment about Mozart, who was still alive and still considered quite young when Gerber finished the manuscript of the first edition. "This great master became so deeply intimate with harmony, due to his early familiarity with it, that the unpracticed ear has difficulty following him. Even sophisticated listeners must hear his works several times. It is fortunate for him that he has reached perfection while young among the gracious and playful Viennese (*gefälligen und tändelden Wiener*) or he might have shared the fate of the great Friedemann Bach whose flights of fancy very few mortals could still follow."[28]

That Gerber could be critical as well as admiring is easily illustrated in his comments on Mattheson: He says that at Mattheson's funeral the composer's own funeral music was played. "It is reported to have sounded very sad. This is all the more plausible, since the old man who had been deaf for forty years had musically been left behind by forty years. For the same reason one must blame his [literary] style on his times rather than on Mattheson himself."[29]

Just where one should draw lines to limit the subject of eighteenth-century collective biography at either end is not easy to decide. While Gerber II properly belongs to the beginning of modern musical scholarship, a contemporary work, Alexandre Choron and François Fayolle's *Dictionnaire historique des musiciens*, which heavily depended on Gerber I, is regressive to the extent that it did not heed Gerber's determination to have consistent spelling depending on the subject's nationality.[30] Gerber acknowledged in his new biographical dictionary that the French work was largely derived from his own earlier effort. Apparently not offended, he only regretted that the Frenchmen could not have had the benefit of his revisions and additions before rushing into print. Choron and

---

28.   Gerber I, I, col. 976.
29.   Ibid., col. 908.
30.   Alexandre Choron and François Fayolle, *Dictionnaire historique des musiciens* (Paris: Chimot, 1810—11). Hereafter referred to as Choron.

Fayolle have some new entries as well as other additions and emendations. On the whole, however, we should be inclined to call their work more than two-thirds "plagiarized," plagiarized, moreover, from an already outdated source in a manner that had already been improved upon in 1792. Fétis and Eitner took Choron into account in their respective bio-bibliographies as they did every other work accessible to them, but the line of true ancestry is clear from Walther, Mattheson, and Titon du Tillet to Gerber who added a host of other sources, musical and non-musical, a complex process of cross-breeding difficult to reconstruct. Gerber is the last of a line, as it were, as much a lexicographical genius as Eitner. While one cannot diminish Fétis' accomplishment, his little dishonesties and his charlatanism may just be sufficient to keep him out of that musicological heaven to which he undoubtedly aspired.[31]

At least as difficult as it is to decide where nineteenth-century scholarship begins, is it to establish the proper beginning as well as the limits of collective musical biography. The earliest bibliographies, those of Adlung, Forkel, and Becker, list a number of works containing biographies of musicians in sections entitled "Biographie" or "Lebensläufe."[32] Many of these are collections of sermons or eulogies. Sometimes they are works dealing with a musician or two among other illustrious men. They represent a field in which there is still much to be gleaned. This is equally true of the earliest general collected biographies which began to flourish midway in the eighteenth century.[33]

---

31. Somewhat suspicious of Fétis' glib critical comments about obscure composers, I had students in several of my classes in bibliography and methods of research track down music Fétis considered deficient. They found that his evaluations, some of which accuse composers of incompetence and contrapuntal ignorance, did not bear close scrutiny. One Renaissance *Kleinmeister* after another was innocent of parallel fifths and similar sins. As a leading scholar of his day, Fétis had little to fear from critics retracing his steps.

32. Jacob Adlung, *Anleitung zu der musikalischen Gelahrtheit* (Erfurt: Jungnicol, 1758), Johann Nikolaus Forkel, *Allgemeine Litteratur der Musik* (Leipzig: Schwickert, 1792). Carl Ferdinand Becker, *Systematisch-chronologische Darstellung der musikalischen Literatur von der frühesten bis auf die neue Zeit* (Leipzig: R. Friese, 1836; Supplement, Leipzig: 1839. Reprint, Knuf, 1964).

33. For example, Johann Georg Meusel, *Teutsches Künstler-lexikon* (Lemgo: Meyer, 1788), Angelo Fabroni, *Vitae italorum doctrina*

At least two manuscripts should probably be considered. That by Pitoni from about 1740 was not rediscovered until Baini mentioned it in 1828 and is therefore of greater relevance to nineteenth-century historiography than to the century treated here.[34] The other, an even earlier work by the historian of Oxford, Anthony à Wood, was cited by Burney. H. Watkins Shaw briefly discussed the Oxford scholar, dating his manuscript as circa 1690.[35] As a source of factual data Anthony à Wood may be of some value. In the present context there is not much to say about him. Both works, if one can call them that, fall outside the historical mainstream.

Two reasons account for Johann Adam Hiller being left to the end in spite of his chronological place before Gerber. First, he was not a genuine lexicographer, having selected his relatively few subjects because they were "famous and esteemed men"; second, probably a related reason, his work is critical and appreciative rather than biographical. From the beginning of the biographical century, from Walther on, one sees an almost mindless gathering of biographical data being gradually replaced by growing discrimination. Walther's allocation of space was a response to the listing of published works, the only reason why Bach received fewer columns than Telemann. A few years later Mattheson printed as much or as little as he had available. Keiser, the composer Mattheson seems to have admired most, received less space than Printz and Telemann, both of whom had themselves submitted the material he printed. All

---

excellentium . . . (Rome: imprint varies, 1778—1805), and the enormous *Grosses vollständiges Universal-Lexikon* published by Johann Heinrich Zedler (Halle and Leipzig, 1732—54), to name a few conspicuous ones. Also still awaiting exploration is the *Mercure de France* in which many obituaries may be found. Joannis Guigard's *Indicateur du Mercure de France, 1672—1787* (Paris, 1869), gives neither the first names nor the professions of his "indexees" and is therefore of little help.

34.   The Pitoni manuscript said to be in process of publication by Othmar Wessely is entitled "Notizia de' contrappuntisti e compositori di musica dagli anni era christiana 1000 fino al 1700."

35.   H. Watkins Shaw, "Extracts from Anthony à Wood's 'Notes on the lives of Musicians,' Hitherto Unpublished," *Music and Letters* 15 (1934): 157ff.

36.   Johann Adam Hiller, *Lebensbeschreibungen berühmter Musikgelehrten und Tonkünstler neuerer Zeit*, Part 1 (Leipzig: Dykische Buchhandlung, 1784).

of them were dealt with in fewer pages than those for the compiler himself, a subject about whom Mattheson knew most of all. One has no sense that Mattheson felt any obligation to assign space on the basis of merit; morality is not necessarily related to artistic genius. Du Tillet included composers ~t court who by virtue of their position had automatically attained a certain status. Except for his anti-German bias (or ignorance of the language), La Borde is comprehensive as well as critical. He singles out composers he thought especially deserving. Gerber is the first *true* lexicographer, not only comprehensive but prepared to exercise value-judgment.

Hiller included only seventeen composers from Adlung to Tartini but expressed his willingness to add more living musicians if they would send him their autobiographies.[37] This would have played havoc with his alphabetical scheme, and one wonders how many more famous and esteemed men he could have found in the last remaining letters of the alphabet had the planned second part of his collection ever appeared. He included living musicians and some who had died in the second half of his century but was not rigidly committed to the last criterion.

What one sees in Hiller is the beginning of a new spirit. A kind of egalitarianism among craftsmen had once considered any employed master-musician basically as good as any other, assuming he had mastered his craft. Hiller's criterion "most esteemed" and subsequently Gerber's free use of terms such as "great" and "genius" mark the beginning of an aristocracy of talent and intellect clearly foreshadowing a new class to which one could belong only by virtue of outstanding ability.

A similar change of attitude can be seen in autobiography which changes from the cool description of facts to greater introspection and to far greater willingness to discuss political and moral ideas. Although many of the entries in the collected biographies surveyed here were autobiographical, autobiography deserves more extensive analysis.

---

37.   Besides Adlung and Tartini, Hiller chose the following for inclusion: J. S. Bach, Georg Benda, Georg Heinrich Bümler, Johann Friedrich Fasch, Georg Gebel the Elder, Graun, Handel, Johann Christian Hertel, Ernst Christian Hesse, Jomelli, Pisendel, Quantz, Felice Salimbeni, and Gottfried Heinrich Stölzel.

CHAPTER III

GIORGIO VASARI AND MUSICAL BIOGRAPHY

If musicians are frequently considered suspect characters and music-making in history has sometimes been frowned upon by society, especially religious society, there is no doubt that as an intellectual endeavor music has enjoyed great prestige. While musicians may have been suspect making music, as long as they only theorized about it, they merited high academic standing. In fact, we musicologists, their heirs, have taken for granted that composers enjoyed greater respect than artists whose work is more physical, often dirty, and less cerebral, if cerebral at all. Curt Sachs· used to joke that the Greeks had no equal to Apollo, no proper god of art. In view of this, it must give us pause that in 1550, at a time when little is known about the lives of even the most admired individual musicians, there appeared a large collection of biographies of Italian artists. Its title, quite long even as I abbreviate it, was *Le Vite de piu eccelenti architetti, pittori et scultori italiani da Cimabue insino a' tempi nostri. . . .*[1] It is now usually just called "Vasari's Lives." Whether or not it was a best-seller we can no longer tell; a normal printing in those days ordinarily consisted of one to two thousand copies although there could be more. However many were issued, they sufficed for Vasari to prepare a new and enlarged edition that saw print in 1568. (It is the revised version that forms the basis for the innumerable reprints and translations that have come out since Vasari's day.)

---

1. Giorgio Vasari, *Le Vite de piu eccelenti architetti, pittori et scultore italiani da Cimabue insino a'tempi nostri descritte in lingua toscana* (Florence: Torrentino, 1550. 2nd ed., Florence: Giunti, 1568).

As we know, it took some time for musical biography to catch up. With the possible exception of Johann Mattheson's *Musikalische Ehrenpforte* of 1740 and the two versions of Gerber's biographical dictionary of 1790 and 1812, respectively, there was nothing like Vasari's *Lives* until the first volume of the first edition of Fétis came out in 1835.[2] We are bound to ask ourselves whether it was the artists' prestige as seen by Vasari, who was himself an artist, or their popularity that made the work such a success. In a sense it hardly matters. But it must strike anyone as odd that neither theorists, fellow-musicians, nor literati saw it as an example for a similar collection of composers. There were certainly enough prestigious musical names at mid-century to have provided the material. That they were not natives for the most part made the adjective *italiani* unlikely for a title-page, but was nationalism a factor in this case? A biographical collection of composers, even if merely esteemed in Italy, ought to have sold just as well, one would think.

Comparison with any collection of musical biographies of the eighteenth and early nineteenth centuries is misleading. Even Fétis is so unlike Vasari that we can use him only as a measure of Vasari's modernity. Fétis wrote what was basically a straightforward reference book and all his interesting judgments and chatty or controversial asides notwithstanding, that is what he achieved. Vasari's *Lives* can take its place as a reference source, whatever the author's primary goal may have been . But it deserves its success first of all as an original contribution that is erudite and perceptive as well as entertaining. A musically equivalent work would have required a sixteenth-century Burney with a great deal of Hawkins, i.e., equal doses of entertainment and erudition. And like this imagined Burney/Hawkins, Vasari has to be read with caution. Much of what he tells us is hearsay or legend; many works he describes are now lost or were misattributed in the first place. Yet the comparison with the two histories is on the whole more telling than comparison with biographical dictionaries, since Vasari writes more like a historian than a lexicographer, always keeping generational continuity in the

---

2.   Johann Mattheson, *Grundlage einer Ehrenpforte* . . . , Ernst Ludwig Gerber *Historisch-biographisches Lexikon der Tonkünstler. Neues historisch-biographisches Lexikon der Tonkünstler.* François-Joseph Fétis, *Biographie universelle des musiciens et bibliographie générale de la musique* 1st ed. (Paris: Firmin-Didot, 1835—44).

foreground. (Vasari even digresses into theoretical matters with some frequency.) Both Burney and Hawkins, in their turn, may have been historians by predilection or intent but they rely heavily on what biographical sources were available in their day.

To carry the resemblance still further, at least when it comes to Burney, Vasari is a modernist, ultimately preferring the masters of his own day to those of the past. At the same time Vasari has a strong sense of relationship with the past while Burney seems to regard history as an obligation, a duty that has to be borne. It seems he can hardly wait to get to modern times. Vasari's ideal is Greek antiquity and the spirit of this antiquity that was being revived in the thirteenth century, though Vasari skipped over all the dark centuries in between. His earliest modern masters, Cimabue and Giotto, have his full esteem, while Burney regarded their musical contemporaries as primitives or even barbarians. Once Cimabue and Giotto set art on its right path again, there began, according to Vasari, a steady development culminating in the divine Michelangelo, with, moreover, plenty of heroes in between.

There is of course an inherent difference betwen art and music, namely, that art endures while music exists only when it sounds. It is therefore quite plausible that Vasari is always able to cite old masters as models for the new. (He goes so far as to suggest that Coreggio would have been a greater artist had he paid more attention to his predecessors, something that would never have occurred to Burney.) When music theorists and composers pay heed to their ancestors at all, it is usually only to the immediately preceding generations who were their teachers. Art, on the other hand, as long as it is not placed in storage or destroyed, remains visible everywhere, while old music was then in effect stored. It remained in storage until the late eighteenth century began to dust it off. It is true that in the meantime many schools of art had gone in and out of fashion, as they still do. Murals were painted over and lost forever and buildings adapted to modern tastes, but the art of the past never disappeared completely; it was selectively ignored. While some old works fell into the hands of junk-dealers, for example, others were purchased by such patrons as Lorenzo da Medici who simultaneously also commissioned new ones.[3]

---

3.   A survey of the situation on which I base my statements is contained
      in Joseph Alsop, *The Rare Art Traditions.* Bollingen Series 27,
      Princeton University Press (New York: Harper and Row, 1982).

Old music survives only rarely, as, for example, in the gentlemanly interest in catches, glees, and madrigals of eighteenth-century England. But the humanist revival of Greek drama by sixteenth-century poets, literati, and musicians was only an abstract ideal. Had a performable repertoire really survived intact, it is unlikely that it would have been staged. Tinctoris' statement that music written more than forty years ago was no longer worthy of performance may have been a new idea in 1477, but it was an idea that prevailed for just about three-hundred years or to about the time Carl Philipp Emanuel, among others, was beginning to rediscover the vitality of older music, his father's as well as that of others.[4]

All these reflections come to mind when one tries to find explanations for Vasari's *Lives* in an era in which potential musical biographers sat on their hands. To explain why there was a Vasari and no musical biographer may elicit some protest, since his work appears to be an isolated phenomenon needing no explanation. But how isolated is an event that requires a thousand readers, perhaps more, and enough demand for a second edition? And this is not all; there is some related evidence pointing to the same question, the nature of comparative status at the time. Consider, for example, that at Michelangelo's Florence funeral — it was not his first — a crowd gathered in the church and overflowed into the street. How large a crowd we do not know; it may have numbered in the thousands. But we do not hear of a similar act of public homage to a musician until it happened to Beethoven in 1827. Where is there a composer who could be said to have lived like a prince, as Raphael did, previous to the stars of opera and virtuosodom of the nineteenth century? While we know of several earlier composers such as Handel, Telemann, Carl Philipp Emanuel Bach, and Haydn, to name a few who lived in middle-class comfort, and while we suspect that Willaert, Monteverdi, and Lassus were among those similarly well off, I doubt that anyone would use the term princely for a single composer before 1800. It is

---

4.   The often-cited phrase of Tinctoris from *De Arte contrapuntis* comes to me via Edward Lowinsky, "Music of the Renaissance as Viewed by Renaissance Musicians," in *The Renaissance Image of Man and the World, ed. by Bernard O'Kelly: 132* (Athens, Ohio: Ohio State University Press, 1966).
      See Ernst Suchalla, *Briefe von Carl Philipp Emanuel Bach an Johann Gottolb Immanuel Breitkopf und Johann Nikolaus Forkel* (Tutzing: Hans Schneider, 1985) Letter 189: 241.

conceivable that calling the above eighteenth-century composers middle-class is using an unusual adjective. It is appropriate because of their transitional position as men finding their way from servitude to free-lance status. As long as composers had served court or church, the best they could ever hope for was a benevolent master or group of masters.

Artists had never been in a similar position of servitude. While it was the normal lot of musicians until the middle of the eighteenth century, the artists' norm was much more like that of tradesmen whose studios were comparable to workshops in which they employed apprentices and journeymen. This may not have been either a financially secure or very respectable social position, but it prepared them for the good times of the fifteenth century. Thus as the wealth of princes and merchants increased in the fifteenth century and cities grew, the demand for all kinds of artists grew proportionately. They now tended to travel from commission to commission, a factor causing local guilds to lose control over them. Perhaps artists in the past had not enjoyed intellectual equality with musicians but they were making up for it in wealth and freedom. Humanist thinkers, moreover, began to accept theirs as another liberal art. No doubt they were helped by the fact that apprentices now went to school to learn proportion, anatomy, and perspective, i.e., theory. With that last gain, artists were now the equals of composers in every respect but one — they were wealthier.[5]

It is possible that without theory Vasari might not have considered his colleagues worthy of a book although their high visibility must have caused them to be of great interest to the general public. Composers, on the other hand, held their reputations almost entirely among colleagues and discerning patrons. Josquin des Prez' situation in Ferrara is a classical example of the plight of the composer before the middle of the eighteenth century. Brought to the Este court because of his "fame" within a limited circle, he never, then or later in his life, achieved even enough "popularity" to find a biographer. The next few generations of composers did not do much better in that sense. Willaert, Lassus, and Monteverdi received considerably more pay and even enjoyed somewhat wider reputations but the true

---

5.   My overview is based in large part on Arnold Hauser, *The Social History of Art*, 2 vols. (London: Routledge & Kegan Paul, 1957), 1: 311ff.

popularity of artists was never theirs. Nor can Josquin's salary at Ferrara compare with that of artists although for a musician it was quite good, amounting to two hundred ducats and a benefice.[6] The benefice probably brought in an additional one hundred ducats. (Willaert and Monteverdi were paid considerably more at San Marco.) But a single work of art usually cost more than the salary of a musician. Of course the cost of music at court and in the church was not limited to the salary of a composer. Added on must be the entire establishment of anywhere up to about twenty musicians, depending on wealth and ostentation, the cost of acquiring and maintaining instruments and copying manuscripts. Music, in other words, might cost three thousand ducats per year to maintain. This amounts to what some sources say Michelangelo was paid for the Sistine Chapel murals which, however, took him the better part of four years and required an uncertain number of assistants. (Comparing salaries is not easy because of the variety of currencies and the different values for the same currencies.) According to at least one source, however, Filippino Lippi was paid two thousand ducats for a mural at St. Maria sopra Minerva in Rome and Da Vinci's salary paid by Lippi Perugini in Milan came to two thousand ducats per year. Compared to even Willaert and Monteverdi's pay in Venice, this was astronomical.[7]

In places such as Ferrara, music was essentially private. It took place for the most part at court and in private chapels. If the general public had no access to the music of Josquin, then how could he have become popular? But Ferrara had public churches as well, and in places like Venice the music at San Marco must have been heard by thousands. Yet the composers there, no less "divine" than Michelangelo and Raphael, never achieved the popularity of the latter.

Are we missing something here? Is it possible that there is another factor acounting for a Vasari without a musical equal? In an oblique way Nino Pirotta also raises the question. Writing in a different context, he asks why there were no major polyphonic composers

---

6.   The several references to Ferrara are all taken from Lewis Lockwood, *Music in Renaissance Ferrara, 1400—1505* (Cambridge, Mass.: Harvard University Press, 1984).
7.   Arnold Hauser, *Social History of Art*, 1: 311ff.

produced in Italy after about the middle of the fifteenth century. "It would still remain to be explained," writes Pirotta, "why the age that saw an enormous display of native ingenuity in architecture, the fine arts and all minor artistic crafts should have leaned so heavily on foreign talent for music."[8] He echoes my own nagging sense that there is something wrong when a place as music-loving as Italy pushes music so completely into the background in even one artistic area. Is it possible that fifteenth- and sixteenth-century Italy regarded its serious music, polyphony we assume, the way our time regards its? Nowadays there are obviously several audiences for several genres of music. Sometimes they overlap but often these publics exclude almost completely music that is not their first choice. We have art-music, old and new (often for different listeners), jazz, country-music and folk-music, disco, rock and roll, etc. It would be absurd to try to guess what public accepts which, but we can safely say that there is no such thing as a general public. Why should there have been one in the Renaissance? Even among the people who by virtue of their class and wealth had access to the best, there were probably highbrow and middlebrow tastes, possibly corresponding to polyphonic and homophonic music, respectively. The suspicion that such might be the case arises when one speculates why a Borso d'Este got rid of most of the polyphonists in his employ when he came to power in Ferrara in 1450. In their place he engaged vocal and instrumental improvisors who left no written music.[9] The best-remembered among them, though only by reputation, was Pietrobono dal Chitarrono. Borso's may be only one case but he clearly demon-strats that such types existed. Other improvisors in other places, described in the literature in the warmest language, show that musical improvisation was something to be reckoned with elsewhere too.[10] The traces of what improvisors played or sang, though prob-ably only the traces, survive in such forms as *strambotti* and *frottole*. That the oral tradition can ever be reconstructed except through

---

8.   Nino Pirotta, "Music and Cultural Tendencies in Fifteenth-Century Italy." *Music and Culture in Italy from the Middle Ages to the Baroque* (Cambridge, Mass.: Harvard University Press, 1984): 84.
9.   See Lewis Lockwood, *Ferrara.*
10.   A thorough survey of the literature is included in William F. Prizer, "The Frottola and the Unwritten Tradition," *Studi Musicali* 15 (1986): 3ff.

literary sources, is highly questionable. We shall probably never know how it sounded[11].

My goal is much more limited, however. At the beginning of this essay I questioned why there was a Vasari in the absence of an almost total blackout of musicians' biographies. We have at least a conjectural answer if we postulate that the musical tradition of which we are proudest may have meant very little to the "general public" of the sixteenth century. This may be only an academic point but it gains strength when it is reinforced by the opinions of another scholar who arrived at it via a different path in a different context. In his essay, "Novelty and Renewal in Italy, 1300—1600," Nino Pirotta again seems to come to my rescue when he says that in fourteenth- and fifteenth-century Italian musical society, among its humblest as well as its most exalted members, "Italian taste was essentially answered by other [than polyphonic] types of music and musicians, by singers, players, dancers and mimes of whose music we have no direct knowledge."[12] Pirotta believes that this changed in favor of a more homegrown polyphony in the sixteenth century and it is obvious that there was a more homegrown polyphony. Still, when all is said and done, it can also be conjectured that the *seconda prattica* was at least in part a rationalization, an excuse for the practitioners of the new style to overthrow polyphony. Such conjecture can do no harm; it may even help us keep our eyes open for signs of another musical reality than the one we grew up with.

---

11.   I believe that the above paper by Mr. Prizer overestimates the resemblance between *frottole* and other more popular genres and the improvisational actuality and still think that we can never reconstruct improvisation except as a vague approximation. I should also mention an article by Hiroyuki Minamino entitled "Conrad Paumann and the Evolution of Solo Lute Practice in the Fifteenth Century," *The Journal of Musicological Research* 6 (1986): 291ff. I cite the latter only because it has bearing on the question of Paumann's responsibility for German lute-tablature which both writers accept although Minamino does so much more cautiously. None of this affects the position of my essay in any fundamental way.

12.   Nino Pirotta, in *Music and Culture*: 165.

CHAPTER IV

TOWARD A COMPOSITE PORTRAIT OF THE EIGHTEENTH-CENTURY MUSICIAN

When Alfred Einstein published an article about the autobiographies of German musicians in 1921, he was not very explicit about his sources.[1] Since he found most of the autobiographies very disappointing, he reviewed them rather casually although what he wrote is still entirely valid. Einstein took only one non-German autobiography into account, that of Lodovico Zacconi of 1620, recently described by Hermann Kretzschmar, but found it similarly uninformative.[2]

That there were any autobiographies at all we owe to Johann Gottfried Walther and Johann Mattheson who solicited them for

---

1. Alfred Einstein, "Die deutsche Musiker-Autobiographie."
2. Hermann Kretzschmar, "Lodovico Zacconi's Leben auf Grund seiner Autobiographie," *Jahrbuch der Musikbibliothek Peters für 1910*, 17 (Leipzig: Peters, 1911): 45ff. Kretzschmar's article, written because he considered Zacconi's autobiography undervalued, was based on a publication of Friedrich Chrysander published in the *Vierteljahrschrift für Musikwissenschaft* (10 [1894/5]: 531ff.). Although derived mainly from a manuscript in the library of the Liceo Musicale (now Conservatorio di Musica G. B. Martini) in Bologna, Chrysander's version is a conflation of the manuscript and sections of the second volume of *Prattica di musica* (Venice, 1622), an entirely legitimate enterprise, since Chrysander clearly explained his insertions. That it was an undervalued account is due to the fact that Zacconi ignored the musical changes going on around him. He was a musician of the sixteenth century.

their reference books; there was not yet the self-expressive urge that would later find its outlet in letters as well as in music. Walther limited his entries to the bare facts. We do not know whether he received them in that form or reduced them to essentials himself.[3] Mattheson, on the other hand, seems to have incorporated whatever he received without much if any editorial intervention. In effect, Mattheson began a tradition in music that in other fields, artistic, scholarly, and scientific, already existed.

If Einstein found Zacconi disappointing, he would not have been impressed by an even older autobiography. Thomas Whythorne, a musician and one of the earliest autobiographers of any kind, says little of interest about music that is not already known although one would call him garrulous in every other respect.[4] Whythorne's memoirs date from 1576, approximately the same time as the more famous verbal self-portraits of Benvenuto Cellini and Girolamo Cardano. Studded with proverbs and sayings, partly in verse and in an orthography invented by Whythorne himself, his manuscript is of great value to historians of pronunciation, of proverbs, and, of course, of autobiography. Yet he tells us little about music even though he journeyed to Italy at a time still of burning musical interest. The only composer he mentions is Adrian Willaert, and while he has much to say of the drinking habits of the Dutch and Germans he encountered on his travels, he seems to have shunned musicians. The musical history that he recounts can be found elsewhere. As for England, he says,

> In time past, music was chiefly maintained by cathedrals abbeys and churches . . . but when they were suppressed, then went music into decay . . .
>   To speak of music in houses, you shall understand that divers noblemen and women in times past, imitating the prince, would have organists and singingmen to serve God.[5]

What Einstein called a *Berufsbiographie*, a short factual account of the subject's life containing little in the way of feeling or opinion,

---

3.   Johann Gottfried Walther, *Musikalisches Lexikon*, and Johann Mattheson, *Ehrenpforte*.
4.   James M. Osborne, *The Autobiography of Thomas Whythorne* (Oxford: Clarendon, 1961).
5.   Ibid.: 243f.

predominates in the early eighteenth century. A few decades later writers became sentimental, even flamboyant, as well as more observant. While there can be found in early biographies touching asides about childhood, the death of parents, illness, and other woes, they are passed over rather dryly; such troubles are taken for granted. But in spite of the generally factual tone of the early authors, their style often tells us a good deal about them.

Previous writing about autobiography had as its primary focus autobiographies for their own sake. Both Einstein and Kahl treat the form as literary or psychological documentation.[6] As a result they both found the earliest examples of the genre rather bland. Kahl wondered if autobiographies are not inherently suspect as documents, since there is always a chance that the writer may have confused "inner experience with external fact."[7] While such reservations are necessary when dealing with self-portraits of any kind, they would seem to be more appropriate to romantic memoirs than to the early ones. Pre-romantic autobiographies are so impersonal that there is little risk of their authors confusing *Dichtung und Wahrheit*, fiction and truth. Kahl also had reservations about seeing musicians as types rather than as individuals.[8] Looking at their lives collectively, however, makes them far more provocative without diminishing the individual. Together they are not only more revealing, but they also supplement each other in such ways that one ultimately gets to know each individual better.

As a collection of documents the autobiographies of the early eighteenth century confirm one of Mattheson's critical comments about the low state of German church music in the provinces, for example.[9] Many of the musicians he invited to be in *Ehrenpforte* were self-taught. Some might even be considered primitives although since in most cases their music is not available, we cannot confirm this.[10]

---

6. Willi Kahl, *Selbstbiographien deutscher Musiker* (Cologne: 1948; reprinted, Amsterdam: Knuf, 1972).
7. Ibid.: 10.
8. Ibid.: 14.
9. Johann Mattheson, *Das neu-eröffnete Orchestre* (Hamburg: Author, 1713): 11ff.
10. A list of the autobiographies consulted is appended to this article. Page references and dates will be given in that appendix. All translations are free paraphrases except when the exact wording of the original is important, in which case the original is quoted in German.

To begin with an example: Johann Georg Hoffman had his first musical experience under Johann Heinrich Quiel. In order to improve the local church service, "which was in a very bad state, Quiel twice weekly held 'singing-lessons,' in part to practice ordinary chorales but also to rehearse motets and cantatas [*Oden*] which were to be sung on a coming Sunday or holy day."[11] Nine-year-old Hoffman at first just attended these lessons but soon joined in, feeling the urge to learn more about music. He learned "notes and how to sing them," and in spite of his family's poverty was given a cheap violin. Gradually he had opportunities to read books by Werkmeister and Printz, Niedt, Heinichen, and Mattheson, and acquired music by Reinhard Keiser which he played and sang so often that he soon knew it by heart.[12] Working out figured basses he noticed that some pieces had their subjects sometimes in the upper voice, sometimes in the lower, and sometimes in the middle (though he does not use the word "subject"). The secret of what we now call invertible counterpoint, he discovered, lay in the avoidance of vertical fifths in certain parts of the measure when the subject was in the highest voice.

Although he never did find a proper teacher, he continued to buy music, taught himself French and Italian, and learned to transpose in order to reconcile organ pitches with accompanied voices. In 1720 he became assistant organist in one of the churches at Breslau (now Wrocław, Poland), his apprenticeship obviously finished. In Breslau, he says, he wrote several years of cantatas, some Passions, and occasional works for weddings and funerals, etc., at least four-hundred compositions.

Aside from the inherent fascination with such a portrait of a self-made musician, it is revealing that he mentions rehearsals which, as he explains, were made necessary by the low state of the local music, thus implying that they were not normally required.

Hoffman's teacher, Quiel, tells how he discovered meantone

---

11. The word *Ode* was used so loosely at the time that it seems possible to translate it in a number of ways, depending on the context. Walther says that in the then-customary usage it usually meant a poem with several stanzas in the same meter and with the same rhyme-scheme, a song.
12. The reference to books by Heinichen and Mattheson is one of those instances in which the author confused fact and imagination. Hoffmann could not have read these authors as a young man, since they had not yet been published.

temperament when he found that certain chords did not sound good on a harpsichord or clavichord unless he tuned the fifths a little lower than perfect.[13] Not until years later did he find out that this was a standard recommended method of tuning.

Leafing through Mattheson's collection of autobiographies one can form a composite image of a generation of composers. Such a portrait reveals trends and helps to highlight the biographies of the great. In drawing a portrait of the composers approximately contemporary with Bach, one is somewhat handicapped by Mattheson's imprecise indications of his sources. When is an autobiography genuine? When its source is given as "*ex autogr*," or only when that indication is matched by an account in the first person? (In general Mattheson indicates the origin of a biography as "*ex ms.*," from a manuscript, "*ex oper.*," presumably from the preface to some music or a didactic book, "*ex libr.*," from a book, sometimes, "*ex notit.*," from some sort of notice, possibly an obituary, *ex lit.*, from a letter, and once or twice from "*ex autogr. fil.*" from the autograph of a son. Some of those headed by "*ex autogr.*" may have been reported in the third person and some may have been paraphrased by Mattheson, although the latter's own autobiography is also in the third person. What makes one uncertain about this is that several of the third-person narratives have editorial asides casting doubt on the others. I shall assume that all those identified as coming from autograph sources indeed have their origin in a self-description. This expands considerably the group of autobiographies discussed by Einstein.)

The lives of Bach's contemporaries tend to illustrate how upwardly mobile the German worker and artisan class was in the early eighteen century. Many autobiographers came from poor families and although musicians as a group were not highly regarded (in spite of the distinction made in several autobiographies between "beer-fiddlers" and cantors), there is a strong sense that musicians were more educated and more respected than weavers or shoemakers, having had to learn not only their complex craft, but also several languages. A fair number of the authors attended lectures at a university and several wrote learned books.

Occasionally someone like Georg von Bertuch or Bertouch, a gentleman-composer of high military rank, boasts of his ancestry. Johann Anton Coberg's father was mayor of the little town of

---

13.   For Quiel's autobiography see appended list.

Rotenburg. Nicolas Deinl was the son of a cantor in Nuremberg and Johann Conrad Dreyer (1672—c. 1742) had a shoemaker for a father. His family lacked the means to allow him to take music lessons, sent him to school for a while, but finally decided he should learn the shoemaker's trade. Several musicians descended from fathers who were minor officials, several from ministers, and a considerable portion had fathers and grandfathers who like Bach's had also been musicians.

If it is impossible to generalize about the parents of our musicians, it is certain that in every case music was not simply a profession or an activity like any other; it was a compulsion to which the child sooner or later succumbed. In what must be one of the strangest entries in any musico-biographical dictionary, a Johann Ulrich Steiner born in Winterthur, Switzerland, in 1698, "is reported to be a respected tradesman there." He had studied Latin, philosophy, rhetoric, and Greek before his father took him into the family's gold and silver business at the age of eighteen. He married a lady who was a keyboard player.

> In 1726 he had a shooting accident in which he injured the index-finger of his left hand which ended his pleasure in hunting. In place of this pastime he chose music, studying violin, oboe, bassoon, horn and even the trumpet as well as voice.
>
> In 1730 he took the liberty of writing to Mattheson to ask if it was possible to learn how to play keyboard instruments at the age of 32. He received a sensible and encouraging reply. . . . Finally he reached a level at which he frequently played the organ at Costnitz and even wrote a ten-part Mass which for such an old student is pretty good. (In a footnote Mattheson says he sent him an inscribed copy of the *Kleine Generalbass-Schule* but that must have been later, since the book was not published until 1735.)

Bach's *Wanderjahre* have their parallel in many of the autobiographies. Only a few musicians went as far as Italy, among them Friederich Georg Dieterich and Conrad Friedrich Hurlebusch, the latter subsequently finding his way to Stockholm. Georg Motz managed to visit most of the major cities of Italy with a subsidy from his employer. Treu (Fedele) studied with Vivaldi and Biffi. Gottfried Heinrich Stölzel traveled only briefly.[14]

---

14.   Stölzel's autobiography is very terse. Johann Adam Hiller combined

If we hope to learn something about these musicians' observations, however, we are destined to be disappointed. There is scarcely a word about the state of music, about landscapes or cities. *Berufsbiographien* assume that only personal history is appropriate.

Most traveling took place during Lent when musical activity was usually reduced or eliminated altogether, and the weather made traveling feasible. One has the impression, reading a collection of biographies, that in Lent the roads of Germany were full of musicians trading places. Often traveling is also mentioned when some other local period of mourning caused music to be suspended.

Those musicians who provide chronological information usually began their formal studies between eight and twelve and generally held their first appointments by the time they were eighteen to twenty years old. In those respects Bach's or Handel's lives are by no means unusual. If we had nothing but their biographies to tell us who they were, we should think them two of the many ordinary composers whose lives were quite similar. Or, reversing this suggestion, what of the hundreds of compositions mentioned by composers which have never been heard?

One composer, Daniel Gottlieb Treu, alias Daniele Teofilo Fedele, who came from a family of printers, reports that he engraved his first compositions, *Ouvertures sur les violons avec les quatre parties d'instruments*, at the age of 12, and that he wrote four "German operas," two to his own text, that had not yet been performed. He considered them too difficult for any but the most virtuoso performers. While in the employ of the Duke of Württemberg he also wrote "sonatas *a* 4 or *a* 6 and every morning worked on a violin concerto."

He claims to have been popular in Italy. In addition to operas he wrote many German and Italian cantatas, arias, *Sinfonien*, and multi-voiced instrumental works.

Tobias Volckmar is more modest.

My small musical powers produced the following. One year of arias for two voices, 2 violins, viola and continuo, 1 printed little occasional work [*Festwerk*] entitled *Gottgefällige Musik-Freude*, 15 sacred vocal compositions *a voce sola*, 2 violins, 1 viola, 1 wind and a bass for organ, etc., etc. . . . I shall mention only one of my keyboard works

---

what he found in *Ehrenpforte* with the obituary in Mizler's *Neueröffnete Bibliothek* to make a more complete story for *Lebensbeschreibungen*, Part 1: 236ff.

which I had intended to be printed, since it consisted of fugues based on our ordinary chorales written in oblong quarto. No publisher has so far been found to take it. One printer . . . to whom I sent it replied that he would like to undertake publication but since in many places the chorales were sung to different melodies . . . , it was too risky an enterprise.

Georg Gebel, also from Breslau, after describing his many sacred and secular works, says, "Although I was occasionally asked to publish my keyboard pieces . . . I have been prevented from doing so by the following observation, namely that one cannot please every-one. . . . To want to do so is presumptious . . ." He concludes, "ill will and envy have kept me in my present station."

"I also invented a clavichord with quarter-tones [at which Mattheson shudders in a footnote] as well as a large harpsichord with a manual of six octaves and pedals."

Repeatedly musicians mention their works and say at least something about publication. Anton Englert in a third-person "auto-biography" reports that he studied theology at the University of Leipzig in 1693 and became cantor in Schweinfurt in 1697. "Since his office required it, he set several 'years' as well as many other mostly sacred pieces with enough skill to mark him as not just another amateur composing for a hobby . . . In 1729 he became rector and a professor of the gymnasium in his city where he still plays the organ in the main church." He seems to have published nothing.

Valentin Bartholomäus Hausmann, who like Bach was often asked to test organs, set several "years" for a variety of churches and was about to have some chorale-variations engraved in copper when his "engraver" died. He "also completed three different treatises, one on composition, one on proportions and tuning . . . and a third on the examination, inspection and building of organs." He appends a list of the books and manuscripts he owned to his autobiography, several of them otherwise unknown.[15]

Conrad Friedrich Hurlebusch mentions a number of works in his

---

15. No biography mentions the supposed treatise by Orlandus Lassus and Christian Clementius Hausmann says he owned it? It was supposedly entitled "Principia de contextu et constitutione cantilenarum." Neither have I found Hermann Schein's "Manuductio ad musicam poeticam." Eitner's *Quellenlexikon* (2: 468) lists the former under the otherwise unknown Clementius.

third-person autobiography. At the end he — or perhaps Mattheson
— reports that among his compositions was "a most beautiful and
precious engraving dedicated to the King of Sweden and entitled,
Compositioni musicali per il cembalo ... , *stampate a spese
dell'autore in Hamborgo*," i.e., they were, as appears to be typical,
printed, at his own expense.

Johann Theile says that he regularly sent sonatas to Leipzig to be
sold at the Fair, sonatas that had already been played for his majesty
the emperor in Vienna, "who as a connoisseur of counterpoint
esteemed them highly."

Almost invariably musicians mention their compositions for the
church and sometimes their operas without reference either to
intended or actual publication. Printing, most frequently at the
composer's expense, seems to have been reserved for keyboard
music, for organ compositions based on chorales, for songs, or for
books.[16] Evidently the few works of Bach published while he was

---

16. Martin Ruhnke has shown that all one could find in publishers'
catalogues of the time were compositions for keyboard, organ, or
songs. (See his "Telemann als Musikverleger," in *Musik und Verlag;
Karl Vötterle zum 65. Geburststag*, edited by Richard Baum and
Wolfgang Rehm [Kassel: Bärenreiter, 1968]: 502ff.) While Protestant
church music was rarely published (it was not even mentioned very
often), there was some publishing of Catholic liturgical music in
southern Germany. One can see this reflected not only in the catalogues of the firm of Lotter in Augsburg, but also in the brief
biography of Meinrad Spiess which appears in Mizler's *Bibliothek* [3,
1752: 168ff]. Until 1750 the publisher Lotter listed 133 titles of
which only a very small portion was instrumental music. Apparently
there was a market for Catholic liturgical music at the smaller courts
and perhaps in monasteries, while the Protestant churches prided
themselves on employing their own cantor-composers. See Hans
Rheinfurt, *Der Musikverlag Lotter in Augsburg (1719—1845)* (Tutzing:
Schneider, 1977).

Horst Heussner in "Nürmberger Musikverlag und Musikalienhandlung, im 18. Jahrhundert" (*Musik und Verlag*, pp. 319ff.), traces
publishing trends in several ways. One of these consists of listing the
works advertised in the Nuremberg journal, *Friedens und Kriegs-
Courrier* [sic] from 1719—70. Up to 1750 there were announcements
for 5 treatises, 34 collections for keyboard instruments other than
organ, 2 collections definitely for organ, 16 titles for small ensembles
of 2 or more instruments, 68 collections of vocal music of a non-
liturgical though sometimes an inspirational nature, and 11 vocal
works set to religious texts. We encounter several old friends among

alive represent more than a typical German composer's catalogue of publications. While in the long view Bach was certainly underappreciated in his day, he cannot be said to have been singled out for an especially harsh fate. We are, in fact, asking the wrong questions when we wonder why Bach published so little and Telemann so much.

The error consistently made in our biographies is to compare our hero-composers with an abstract ideal. The reality of Bach's time was that his few published works are third in number for German musicians of his generation. Of twenty-five composers born within ten years of either side of Bach, only six published anything at all. Of these Christoph Graupner, 1683—1760, Conrad Friedrich Hurlebusch, 1696—1765, Johann Mattheson, 1681—1764, Gottfried Heinrich Stölzel, 1690—1749, Georg Philipp Telemann, and Johann Gottfried Walther, 1684—1748, only Telemann published many works, somewhere in the vicinity of seventy including some reissues. Graupner's three titles were all financed by himself. Four of Hurlebusch's six publications were published with his own money. Stölzel published two works and Walther, one. Of Mattheson's nine publications (of musical works), four were published by the composer and at least forty of Telemann's works were published by himself. (It is difficult to be sure in Telemann's works which sometimes list a dealer where his works were available even if Telemann may have been the actual publisher. The lutenist Sylvius Leopold Weiss, 1686—1750, whose reputation was comparable to Bach's as a virtuoso, seems to have published nothing.[17]

To put Telemann's many publications in perspective at all, one must first deal with his phenomenal productivity and with his ability to produce music of all kinds. According to him, he wrote two-hundred orchestral suites [*Ouverturen*] as well as other works in just two years while employed as music-director by Count Erdman von Promnitz at Sorau. "In Silesia and in Cracow I learned [something] about Polish and 'hanakische' music in its truly barbaric beauty.[18] In

---

these, namely, Bach's *Clavier-Uebung*, Part II, and Sperontes, *Singende Muse*.

17.   A survey of publications by composer is now possible since the *Répertoire international des sources musicales* has completed the series A/I/l, *Einzeldrucke*. Such a survey is not, of course, absolutely reliable but it should suffice for the purpose of an overview.

18.   Probably "*kanakisch*," i.e., primitive.

ordinary inns this music was made by fiddles strapped to the body and tuned a third higher than ordinary violins, a bagpipe [*Bock*], a *Quintposaune* and a regal ... An attentive listener could gather enough ideas from this music for a life-time in just eight days."[19] Telemann traveled widely and became known in many places whereas most of the cantors and organists settled in one place and had only local reputations. The compositions published in his lifetime made up only a small part of his huge output which consisted mainly of music for entertainment, as he said. There were cantatas, arias, sonatas for a variety of instruments, and keyboard music in every style. He himself refers to "Lullyesque suites," "*corellisierende Sonaten*," "*fugierende Choräle*," and Scottish pieces, a veritable delicatessen of music with something for every taste. No other contemporary composer produced such a variety of fare, certainly not on Telemann's level of competence. Evidently Telemann, who was also largely self-taught, had the knack of realizing what was wanted.[20]

The upward mobility of the working class I mentioned above is just one illustration of what we have long referred to as the growth of the bourgeoisie which eventually came to consume music voraciously. In the first half of the eighteenth century few German composers besides Telemann seem to have realized that there was a market for other than keyboard music, though, if they had, it would have availed them little, since Germany's publishing and distribution of music were not well enough organized at that time to make their efforts very profitable.[21] While German-speaking countries had as venerable

---

19.   A *Quintposaune* lies a fifth lower than regular trombones.
20.   Ruhnke shows how Telemann filled a basic need for amateurs and *collegia musica*. Even so he published largely at his own expense. "Telemann als Musikverleger": 511.

  A most revealing title for Telemann's commercial instincts is the following: *Musik vom Leiden und Sterben des Welterlösers, bestehend aus Chören, Chorälen, Arien, Cavaten und Recitativen; in 4 Singstimmen und für mancherley Instrumente, also abgefasst, dass auch eine einzelne Person sich selbige beym Claviere zu Nuze [sic] machen kan [sic]*. Apparently this is a full-fledged Passion for large ensemble arranged so as to be playable by a single performer. (See Heussner, "Nürmberger Musikverlag.")
21.   Ample evidence for the fact that many musicians served as local distributors for each others' publications can be found. In a single book, *Bach-Dokumente II* (Fremdschriftliche und gedruckte Doku-

a history of publishing as Italy, France, and England up to about 1680, something caused the business to decline for nearly one-hundred years. In addition to the low state of the music trade, engraved works were always prey to copying instead of purchase, an ingrained habit Breitkopf still complained about many years later.[22] Telemann's efforts on his own behalf notwithstanding, publishing must have enticed German composers largely by its prestige rather than profit. Even though engraving was so frequently financed by the composer himself, published works never fail to be mentioned either by the contributors to *Ehrenpforte* or, earlier, by Walther who, in fact, lists mainly published works.

Printing was apparently usual only for musicians who had some cash and were willing to risk it. In 1740, when Telemann must have tired of selling music, he advertised in a Hamburg journal that the plates of forty-four of his works were for sale. For a work which cost three guilders a copy, he asked one-hundred guilders for the plates. In that way the buyer would be able to receive a yield of six percent on his investment even if he only sold two copies a year.[23] (To advertise so honestly seems to us incredible now. In our age of hyperbole who would hold out so small an inducement in an advertisement? By our standards, in fact, we are inclined to suspect that there were years when the potential buyer might not sell any copies at all.)

While these autobiographies bring some light into the still dim history of publishing, they also make clear how much music remains to be uncovered. Our tacit, somewhat complacent assumption holds that truth and beauty will out and that all forgotten music must be inferior even to that of those second-best composers with which we are familiar. For that matter, we do not even know very much about the relatively few artists whose works Bach occasionally used. One of

---

mente zur Lebensgeschichte Johann Sebastian Bachs, 1685—1750), Supplement to *Neue Ausgabe sämtlicher Werke*, ed. by Werner Neumann and Hans-Joachim Schulze (Kassel: Bärenreiter, 1969), one can find several references to the practice. See, for example, items 260, 363, and 492.

22.   See ibid., item 381, in which Johann Gottfried Walther bewails the current situation in publishing, complaining to a publisher that for every copy sold to a music-lover, ten are copied by others.

23.   Werner Menke, *Das Vokalwerk Georg Philip Telemanns*, as quoted by Ruhnke, "Telemann als Musikverleger": 510.

them, Gottfried Heinrich Stölzel, corresponded with Mattheson first in 1719 but later supplemented his resumé in 1739. His autobiography in *Ehrenpforte* remains incomplete, nevertheless, and needs Johann Adam Hiller to round it out in 1784.[24] Gerber's biographical entry is an almost exact copy of Hiller's who in turn relied on the obituary in Mizler's *Musikalische Bibliothek.* The latter is almost lavish with praise for Stölzel, while Eitner damns him with very faint praise a hundred years later. Some of Stölzel's trio sonatas available in modern editions and a few other works are comparable in quality to the music of Vivaldi or Telemann, two other composers good enough for us, and for Bach who used it at one time or other.[25]

Although Bach voiced numerous complaints about the state of church music in Leipzig, the problem of income from *Accidentien*, and a certain amount of official deceit, his situation was better than that of most contemporaries. I have not counted the number of autobiographies in which musicians report that they uprooted themselves and their families to accept better positions only to find on their arrival that the position did not exist or had neither the scope nor the income they had been led to expect. One prime example can be found in the autobiography of Johann Francisci who left his position in Pressburg (now Bratislava) with a long list of complaints. Of his sixteen points, some of which concern his housing, his often late paychecks, and the cost of living, I select here only those of direct musical interest. He left because:

> the old and decrepit positive organ prevents worship rather than furthering it;
> because one forces on me arias by [Anton Ernst] Kopp from Chemnitz [sic] who profits by reaping in another's field, something he would not allow anyone to do to him in his own town;[26] because there is a lot of resistance to the performance of my own work;
> because little or nothing is spent on the necessary instruments [performers?] required for *Figuralmusik* in praise of God;
> because choristers cannot make a living here and are forced to move elsewhere;

---

24.   See note 14.
25.   See, for example, "Johann Sebastian Bachs Aufführungen zeitgenössischer Passionsmusiken," *Bach Jahrbuch 1977* (Berlin: Evangelische Verlagsanstalt, 1978).
26.   In a footnote Mattheson says that Kopp was no great shakes as a composer. But why then include him?

because I am not certain whether I am supposed to be a director, cantor or organist,
because I am reproached with every mistake made in the choir-loft, even the smallest.

We cannot tell whether the Pressburg officials had reason to treat Francisci as badly as he says they did. Francisci, whose father had also been a cantor, obtained his first position as cantor and choir director at eighteen upon the death of his father, but continued his musical education by studying the music of others. He himself testifies to his lack of training in composing; nevertheless he produces testimonials regarding his merit which Mattheson omitted for lack of space. That his ability was highly regarded, he says, is attested to by the fact that his chorus performed one of his cantatas on the occasions of his nameday and birthday in 1734.

While we can no longer take sides, Francisci's complaints raise several questions which are also implied in some of the other memoirs. Reading these gradually makes clear that organists and choirmasters were not usually required to compose music. This was the job of the cantor. Francisci's confusion about his job is therefore understandable. As a result of the Pressburgers' lack of fondness for his music, however, it is clear that another musician was paid for the use of his work, a practice not encountered in modern histories. Free-lance composing is also mentioned by V. B. Hausmann. Some of Francisci's complaints, especially those regarding the town's lack of expenditures for music, are echoed in very similar complaints by Johann Heinrich Quiel.[27] Quiel, a very unpretentious man, was organist for both Protestant churches in a town named Nimbtsch. On Sundays and holy days he played under the direction of the cantor; on ordinary days he was in charge. His language is not clear, but he seems to say that the cantor was supposed to provide (*verrichten*) the "choral music with which I had nothing to do and, as I often noted, neither did the cantor." Apparently the cantor did not always provide music, at least not new music, so that Quiel made it his job to ensure there would be some. He resented it, however, when it seemed to grow into his responsibility. "Had I not resisted, I and all my successors would have had this duty without compensation." He copied much music, he says, some of it obtained via the agency of

------

27.   Marpurg, *Beyträge* 2: 547ff.

colleagues at Breslau. It begins to seem that one of the reasons most Protestant church music was not considered publishable by its composers may have been that publication made performance in other churches possible without compensation for the author.

In Nimbtsch, Quiel was at the mercy of unpaid choristers and instrumentalists who came and went as their lives dictated; the community was unwilling to pay for musicians although in 1720 they did finance the building of a new organ.

To discuss Quantz' autobiography in this context is a double departure, since he was neither a church musician nor still representative of Bach's generation.[28] But he can serve as a contrast to the norm in several respects, not the least of which is the nature of his autobiography which marks him instantly as far more worldly than the others. He departs from the typical *Berufsbiographie* not so much by virtue of the depth of his self-portrait as by his observations of the musical scene which are a gold mine of contemporary reporting. Much of what he says about singers and performers is not relevant here, but he too implicitly confirms Mattheson's low opinion of the state of church music. Thus he says that his teacher, an organist named Kiesewetter, did not share the fault of his colleagues "who are in love with the stiff and tasteless music of older composers because they are not capable of playing new and better music. . . . Kiesewetter sent to Leipzig for music by such famous men as Telemann, Melchior Hoffmann, Heinichen and others." Not until Quantz got to Dresden, however, did he learn that the mere playing of the notes was not what music was all about. (Quantz confessed that although he was devoted to new music, he rather enjoyed writing fugues.)

Traveling extensively, Quantz spent three years in Italy from where, when summoned back to Dresden in 1727, he returned via London. In London he had an opportunity to give a "benefit concert" for himself, which, while he did not take advantage of it, he describes in considerable detail. But for all his mobility, he never visited Leipzig only about seventy miles from Dresden. One wonders if Bach's reputation made him fear for his modernity. Perhaps the style he considered *passé* was not quite so sterile as he thought. That he was uncertain seems to me apparent in the description of a performance of Johann Joseph Fux's opera, *Costanza e fortezza*, in Prague with 200 musicians and 100 singers. "[The music] was more

---

28.   Ibid., 1: 197ff.

sacred than theatrical but very imposing [*prächtig*]. Its concertato-style *ritornelli* made a great effect even though they must look stiff on paper. In fact, it came off better than music in a more *galant* idiom with its many short fast notes." Quantz thought this was largely because ensembles do not often play well enough together to bring off the *galant* style. He found this true also for Lully overtures which, he said, were more effective orchestral works than *galant* overtures in spite of their seeming aridity.

It was probably not safe for a "modern" to acknowledge Bach until after he died and took his style to the grave, as it were. After 1750 the stream of Bach's reputation grew rapidly, to use Friedrich Blume's image, even faster than Blume acknowledges.[29] Bach entered the pantheon of Germany's greats long before the revival of the *Passion according to St. Matthew*, probably even before Forkel's biography of 1802.[30]

If Quantz is beyond the scope of the representative composers of Bach's time because of his comparative worldliness, Jacob Adlung does not quite belong there either. Born fourteen years later than Bach he has in common with him that he too was an organist.[31] Just as Quantz's orientation toward secular music is apparent, so Adlung reveals himself as a scholar rather than a musician. Obviously gifted in music and apparently an accomplished organist at an early age, Adlung did not feel the compelling force drawing him to music. Instead he inclined toward scholarship and learning about which he says much more than about music. For that reason he contributes to

---

29. Friedrich Blume, *Johann Sebastion Bach im Wandel der Geschichte*, Musikwissenschaftliche Arbeiten, 1 (Kassel: 1947), trans. by Stanley Godman, *Two Centuries of Bach* (London, New York: Oxford University Press, 1950). Blume showed that Bach was never quite forgotten. In my own article, "Bach, Handel and Comparative Success," *Bach*, 12 (1982), pp. 22ff. and 13 (1983), pp. 17ff., I carried Blume's assumption further, showing that in 1792 Breitkopf und Härtel published pictures of Bach, Handel, Mozart, and Haydn as frontispieces to the four volumes of Gerber's biographical dictionary, a kind of climax to a reputation that had grown rather than died after Bach's death.

30. Johann Nikolaus Forkel, *Ueber Johann Sebastian Bachs Leben, Kunst und Kunstwerke* (Leipzig, 1802). Modern edition edited by Walther Vetter (Kassel: Bärenreiter, 1968).

31. Marpurg, *Kritische Briefe über die Tonkunst*, 3 vols. (Berlin: F. W. Birnstiel, 1760—64), 2: 241ff.

the picture of the position of the German musician from still another angle. He reports, for example, that although he had the degree of *magister*, he did not elect the ministry as a career because he was "physically unsuited to preaching" — perhaps he had a speech defect — and rejected the profession of schoolmaster because it paid less well than that of an organist. When he considered establishing himself as a professor, however, he met with a certain kind of opposition on the part of other professors who thought that an organist could not also be a professor; "a good musician could not be a good scholar." (Was this mere snobbery or a question of temperament?)

The life of Johann Friedrich Fasch indirectly touches on that of Bach, giving us another clue to the process of selecting a cantor in Leipzig.[32] Fasch had been a student in the Thomas-Schule under Kuhnau from 1701—7. Subsequently he attended lectures in the university and organized a *collegium* of students. When it had more than twenty members and had outgrown his own quarters, the *collegium* moved to the Café Lehmann. Fasch was also in charge of opera in Leipzig and was even commissioned to write an opera which, he says, met with great applause even though Fasch considered himself not yet qualified to compose. When in the following year he received additional commissions, he turned them over to Stölzel, thereby, he says, establishing Stölzel's reputation. For his part, Fasch decided to learn the rules of composition and went in search of his former teacher, Graupner, for further instruction. After extensive travels, Fasch came to a small town, Zerbst, in 1722 where as *Kapellmeister* he was in charge of both secular and church music. He had been there only eight weeks when he received a letter from the Mayor of Leipzig asking him to come and audition for the position of cantor. He decided he could not leave his new position.

Fasch is one of the few composers to mention his salary of four-hundred thaler, about the same as Bach's at Cöthen. The number of professional musicians under his charge was similar to the forces in Leipzig, but in Zerbst he was not required to teach. One can readily see why he had no particular interest in leaving Zerbst despite Leipzig's greater prestige.

The fact that Fasch was one of the finalists for Bach's position suggests that the members of the town-council of Leipzig first asked

---

32.   Marpurg, *Beyträge*, 3: 124ff.

musicians they already knew. Telemann, of course, in addition to being an "old boy," had already developed a large reputation. Graupner, another alumnus known to the authorities, probably did not have the "name" of either Telemann or Bach but he was a known quantity. That there was another finalist formerly from Leipzig indicates that the lower ranking of Bach was less a matter of philistinism than practicality. Had Fasch been interested, it is quite possible that he would have been engaged; Bach might never even have auditioned.

In this particular approach to the use of autobiographies to draw a composite picture of the composer of an era, as documents go, Mattheson's self-portrait is nearly useless. His position at Hamburg and his diverse interests make him as untypical as Bertuch, the gentleman-musician, or Adlung, the scholar. In addition to functioning at the opera and in church-music, Mattheson produced more learned words than one has any right to expect from even a full-time scholar. His position as secretary of the British legation in which he served at one time or other as virtually full-fledged *chargé d'affaires* must have been very demanding, since it required extensive reports on all sorts of commercial and political matters. It is understandable that Mattheson's autobiography is almost that of a split personality alternating between musical and other activities, with music coming out somewhat neglected.[33] His memoirs may be of greater interest to historians of Hamburg and England than to musicologists. Although Mattheson was not a great composer, he was obviously a brilliant man. As such he had the vanity of the species, a vanity that can still irritate, especially when it comes to his inability to acknowledge the stature of his erstwhile colleague, Handel. Einstein dismissed his autobiography as *lakeienhaft*, flunkey-like, perhaps largely because of irritation with his air of superiority over Handel and his patronizing comments about Bach elsewhere, rather than because of the language of the autobiography itself. A much more appropriate term for Matteson's style is not servile, but pompous. Flunkeyism and pomposity were both rampant in the period, as one can see in the dedications of musical works as well as in the reverence with which musicians give at least lip-service to all authority, religious, worldly,

---

33. One relevant detail is the fact that although Mattheson was a celebrated theorist many of his theoretical works were also published at his own expense.

and even musical. One wonders how many of the musicians who praised Mattheson's books in their autobiographies were not just making certain that their names would be included in his collective biography. That neither Bach nor Handel was awed by Mattheson seems to me evident in their lack of response to his invitation to submit autobiographies. It is unfortunate for posterity that neither was as servile as lesser contemporaries and that Bach's only surviving autobiographical statement is the brief resumé written at a time when he was most unhappy at Leipzig.[34] Handel left not even that.

Early Autobiographies

ME Mattheson, *Ehrenpforte*, ME, when in the third person, [ME]
MH Marpurg, *Historisch-Kritische Beyträge*
MK Marpurg, *Kritische Briefe*

Adlung, Jakob, 1699—1762	MK II	431
Backhaus, Johann Ludwig, 1715—	MK	
Bertuch (Bertouch), Georg von, 1668—1743	[ME]	23
Coberg, Johann Anton, 1650—1708	[ME]	37
Deinl, Nicolas, 1665—c1730	[ME]	50
Dieterich, Friedrich Georg, 1686—	[ME]	51
Dreyer, Johann Conrad, 1672—1742	ME	52
Englert, Anton, 1674—after 1739	[ME]	58
Fasch, Johann Friedrich, 1688—1758	MH III	124
Fedele, Daniele Teofilo, see Treu		
Fischer, Christian [Friedrich], 1698—	ME Sup	402
Francisci, Johann, 1691—1758	ME	76
Gebel, Georg deu Eldes, 1685—c1750	ME Sup	405
Graf[f], Christian David, 1700	MH III	343
Graupner, Christoph, 1683—1760	ME Sup	410
Hausmann, Valentin Bartholomäus, 1678—	[ME]	103
Höck, Karl, 1707—72	MH III	129
Hoffman, Johann Georg, 1700—1780	ME	110
continued in	MH I	362

---

34.   Reprinted in several places. English translation in Hans T. David and Arthur Mendel, *The Bach Reader* rev. ed. (New York: Norton, 1966), pp. 125f.

Hurlebusch, Conrad Friederich, 1695—1765	[ME]	120
Kellner, Johann Pater, 1705—72	MH I	439
Kirsten, Michael, 1682—1742	ME	137
Krieger, Johann, 1652—1735	[ME]	151
Kuhnau, Johann, 1660—1722	[ME]	153
Lüders, Hans Heinrich, 1667—1750	[ME]	173
Mattheson, Johann, 1681—1764	ME	187
(Written by himself in the 3rd person)		
Mente, Johann Gottfried, 1698—after 1781	ME Sup	414
Mizler, Lorenz Christoph, 1711—81	[ME]	228
	ME Sup	420
Motz, Georg, 1652—1717	ME	234
Pestel [Bestel], Johann Ernst, 1659—	[ME]	255
Printz, Wolfgang, Caspar, 1641—1717	ME	257
Quantz, Johann Joachim, 1697—1773	MH I	197
Quiel, Johann Heinrich	MH II	547
Raupach, Christoph, 1686—1744	[ME]	282
Reimann, Johann Balthazar, 1702—49	ME	290
Rosenbusch, Johann Conrad, 1673—after 1740	[ME]	294
Scheibe, Johann Adolph, 1708—76	ME	310
Scheuenstuhl, Michael, 1705—50	[ME]	316
Schwenckenbecher, Günther, 1651—1714	[ME]	333
Seber, Nicolas, 1680	[ME]	335
Sorge, Georg Andreas, 1703—78	[ME]	337
Steiner, Johann Ulrich, 1698—1741?	[ME] Sup	427
Stölzel, Gottfried Heinrich, 1690—1749	ME	342
Störl, Johann Georg Christian, 1676—	[ME] Sup	351
Tegetmeier, Georg, 1687—	MH III	342
Telemann, Georg Philipp, 1681—1756	ME	354
Theile, Johann, 1646—1722	[ME]	369
Treu (Fedele), Daniel Gottlieb, 1695—1749	[ME]	371
Volckmar, Tobias, 1678—1756	ME	383
Walther, Johann Gottfried, 1684—1748	ME	387
Zeidler, Maximiliam, 168?—1745	[ME]	400

CHAPTER V
COLLECTIVE BIOGRAPHY AND NATIONAL PRIDE

To accept Ernst Ludwig Gerber as the founder of modern biographical lexicography establishes only the beginning of what we now take for granted. It is a truism to aver that interest in musicians was growing very quickly at the beginning of the nineteenth century and that, on the whole, the status of the musician as artist became established once and for all. The signs of this increasing esteem become visible everywhere at the turn of the century. Thus, for example, we find it in Bohemia where at about the same time as Gerber I a certain Bohumir Jan Dlabač was also issuing a biographical dictionary.[1] Very likely national pride was a factor in the new wave of biographical reference books, since the work by Dlabač was only the first of the national dictionaries that came to be issued with greater or lesser competence in England, Italy, Silesia, and America.[2]

---

1. Bohumir Jan Dlabač, *Versuch eines Verzeichnisses der vorzüglichen Tonkünstler in oder aus Böhmen*, Materialien zur alten und neuen Statistik von Böhmen, 7 & 12 (Prague: 1788 & 1794).
2. Giuseppe Bertini, *Dizionario storicho-critico di musica*, 2 vols. (Palmero: Tip. reale di guerra, 1814—15).
    Bohumir Jan Dlabač, *Allgemeines historisches Künstler-Lexikon für Böhmen und zum Theil auch für Mähren und Schlesien*, 3 vols. (Prague: Hasse, 1815—18). John Sainsbury, *A Dictionary of Music and Musicians*, 2 vols. (London: Sainsbury, 1825). The second edition is dated 1827 and I can report with assurance that it was a reissue without changes or corrections. I have chosen not to deal with an earlier English dictionary, William Bingley's *Musical Biography*, 2 vols. (London: Colburn, 1814; 2nd ed., 1834, reprinted New York: Da Capo, 1971), since it is of far less interest from my point of view than

Some of these works were occasionally tainted with a certain degree of chauvinistic (albeit harmless) truculence although their *raison d'être* may have been primarily commercial. Music was becoming a commodity and represented a growing market. According to at least one lexicographer, Carl von Ledebur, local or regional works began to appear because universal compilers such as Fétis were not accurate; they lacked the more specific local sources.[3]

John Sainsbury, or whoever wrote on his behalf, addresses himself quite plainly to the issue of "Englishness" in music. He was motivated, he writes, not only by utility, but also by national self-respect. John Rowe Parker's American collection makes a point of including a large proportion of American artists, but he never openly expresses his irritation at their neglect elsewhere. (At the same time he completely overlooks such a fellow-Bostonian as William Billings.) But if the neglect of the musical art of America troubled Parker, it was not native art, it was the European tradition, as practiced on the East Coast, that he thought was being slighted. Boston, Parker says, was not fertile soil for culture, for the breeding of indigenous artists. Nevertheless, a young pianist, a Miss Alexei Eustaphieve, "will do honour to her town . . . [and] will at no distant time be envied by the first capitals of Europe," in spite of that.[4] By some sort of accident, Miss E. was trained entirely in America. Her father and she had gone to St. Petersburg so she could study with Daniel Steibelt, but the two returned almost immediately; for some reason their mission was aborted.

Parker's envy of European culture is implicit in his comparison of Miss E. with that other prodigy, Mozart, who had had the advantage of living in a part of Europe, "the most celebrated for musical science; his father was an eminent composer and profound teacher of harmony . . . almost the whole community in which he lived . . . [consisted of] more or less zealous cultivators and admirers of music." But whether Boston was a favorable climate for prodigies or

Sainsbury. John Rowe Parker, *A Musical Biography* (Boston: Stone & Fovell, 1825, reprinted Detroit: Information Coordinators, 1975). Carl Julius Adolph Hugo Hoffmann, *Die Tonkünstler Schlesiens* (Breslau: Aderholz, 1830). Carl Kossmaly and Carlo (pseudonym), *Schlesisches Tonkünstler-Lexikon* (Breslau: E. Trewendt, 1846—47).

3.   Carl Freiherr von Ledebur, *Tonkünstler-Lexikon Berlins* (Berlin: Rauh, 1861).
4.   Parker: 198.

not, Parker adds another argument. How does one really know which stories about Mozart are true? They all certainly seemed highly exaggerated.

Giuseppe Bertini seems to have had no feelings of inferiority. His book (published in 1814—15) contains the standard German, French, and English names, as well as an occasional Arabic theorist and such poets or estheticians as Dryden and Gottschedt. Far from belatedly taking sides in the old controversy over the respective merits of French and Italian opera, Bertini relies on one of the pro-French pamphleteers, the Abbé Laugier, for his information about Campra and De Lalande.[5] He is even up-to-date enough to have a short article on "Luigi" van Beethoven, the supposed natural son of Friedrich-Wilhelm of Prussia, born in 1772. But while Sebastian Bach is called immortal in the article about Emanuel, "who founded the Bach schools of Berlin and Hamburg," the article on Sebastian himself is not nearly so lavish with praise. Most of Bertini's information in this case came from Marpurg, Hiller, and Forkel, part of it via Gerber in the form of directly translated passages. Elsewhere Bertini acknowledges his debt to the first edition of Gerber, calling his own work rather too grandly a "*rettificazzione e correzzione*" of the former. Gerber's warm feelings about Bach eluded Bertini, however.

Whatever its symbolic value, Bertini's collective biography is not one of the great accomplishments of the genre. Sainsbury, on the other hand, is very good. His entries for many English musicians are unique, and many are based on autobiographical contributions. It is difficult to tell the autobiographies apart, since their style is relatively homogeneous, not because of editorial work but rather because the contributors seem to have tried to write objectively.

Sainsbury deserves extended discussion here because he has been generally underrated, even maligned. A recent article calls him a plagiarist.[6] Such an accusation could spring only from a lack of familiarity with the biographical dictionaries of the period. Sainsbury's borrowings from all sort of available sources were quite common. Sainsbury usually even acknowledges them. In fact his title page cites

---

5.   Lavgier, Marc-Antoine, *Apologie de la musique française contre M. Rousseau* (Paris: n.p., 1754).
6.   Lawrence Richie, "The Untimely Death of Samuel Wesley; or the Perils of Plagiarism," *Music and Letters* 60 (1979): 54ff.

Gerber and Choron as well as other works. "Plagiarism" was the accepted norm. The American, Parker, says in his preface, that in a work of this kind little originality is to be expected. "It is not the business of the Compiler to form fictitious incidents . . . but merely to present in convenient form, the facts which tradition has preserved." In several cases the musicians whom Sainsbury asked referred him to available biographies already published, i.e., they did not think of this as unethical.[7] Charles Clementi, for example, writing on behalf of his father, Muzio, tells Sainsbury to use the biography available in the *Quarterly Musical Review*; except for one correction his father finds it satisfactory. He then goes on to supply a list of works which corresponds to that published by Sainsbury. Domenico Corri refers Sainsbury to his own book, *The Singer's Preceptor*, for his biography while Charles Dignum cites the December 1798 issue of *The European Magazine* as a source for data to be used by Sainsbury. It appears that Sainsbury's very extensive Beethoven biography is taken from *The Harmonicon*, yet the existence of a draft worded somewhat differently among the letters to Sainsbury indicates that its author, possibly Edouard Schulz, wrote two different versions.[8] Frequently Sainsbury acknowledges as his sources the periodicals where he found them. That Sainsbury irritated the publishers of some of those journals is probably less a matter of his ethics than it is due to commercial considerations. At one stage the publisher of *The Harmonicon* threatened to bring suit against Sainsbury.

The 181 letters to Sainsbury now in the Euing Musical Library in Glasgow have been known since 1931 when Henry George Farmer referred to them.[9] Not all of them are true autobiographies. Some are very detailed, some bare outlines. Sainsbury usually printed them almost as they came, occasionally eliminating some chatty sections or

---

7. Sainsbury's correspondence consisting for the most part of the letters of musicians who had been invited to submit autobiographies has been preserved in the Euing Music Collection in the Library of Glasgow University. I should like to thank the staff of that library for the prompt response to a request for a microfilm of the documents.

8. Mr. Standley Howell pointed this out to me and referred me to Alan Tyson, "Stages in the Composition of Beethoven's Piano Trio Op. 70, No. 1," *Proceedings of the Royal Musical Association* 97 (1970—71): 2ff.

9. Henry George Farmer, "British Musicians a Century Ago," *Music and Letters* 12 (1931): 385ff.

rearranging them; the changes are usually very few. Most of his revisions are quite obvious in the originals, since the eliminated parts are simply crossed out. These letters triple the known autobiographical sources of the eighteenth and early nineteenth centuries. They should be considered in proportion to the so-called plagiarized parts of the dictionary, since they represent a high proportion of original material. A letter to Charles Clarke in the Euing collection states that the dictionary for which Sainsbury is soliciting his autobiography " . . . will embrace everything valuable in the German, French and Italian works together with much original information."

Apparently it was understood that the subjects would subscribe to a copy of the book; many of them pledge to do so, and one writer, a J. Sullivan, apparently writing on behalf of Jonathan Blewitt, orders six copies to be sent to Milliken Bookseller in Grafton Street, Dublin. If Sainsbury was not a truly sincere propagandist for English musicians, his efforts obviously insured a fairly good sale if the subjects bought copies. (This kind of appeal to vanity is still standard procedure today.)

We must fault Sainsbury for not consistently making certain that dates were included in the biographies. In some cases he never even found out what given name a subject's initials stood for. But if a contributor did not give dates, Sainsbury left them out. In one case a musician asked specifically that his name, Clarke-Whitefeld, was not to be spelled Whitefield but that is how it appears in the printed version. The compilation must have been a very hasty one; most of the letters are dated late in 1823, and additional correspondence and verification could not have taken place.[10] (A list of the surviving letters is appended to this chapter.)

---

10.   This may be the place in which to deal with several questions provoked by Sainsbury's dictionary. There is first of all the question of whether or not Sainsbury was the editor or merely the publisher. As far as I have been able to determine, Sainsbury published only one other work besides the dictionary, a collection entitled *Vocal Anthology; or the Flowers of Song being a selection from the vocal music of Italy, Germany, France, Switzerland and England; the whole adapted to English words* (London: Sainsbury and Company, 1825). No bookseller or publisher named Sainsbury has been found in London directories although at 111 Fleet Street there was a tobacconist by that name. Sainsbury's offices were at Salisbury Square (now called Salisbury Court) which is at 81 Fleet Street, in the house, in fact,

Sainsbury's allotment of space for major composers is quite revealing. Sebastian Bach receives ten columns of the most admiring language. The list of Beethoven's works is up-to-date. He receives eleven columns, the same number as Purcell. Clementi gets ten, Thomas Arne, six, Gluck, eleven, Grétry, four and a half, Handel twenty-six, Haydn, twenty-four, Josquin, three, Mozart, twenty-six and a half, Pleyel, two, and Rossini, twenty-one. Clearly Sainsbury found it possible to elevate English musicians without lowering foreigners. That he was defensive about English music is implied in the article on Henry Purcell.

> We shall here conclude our history of Henry Purcell, which, we fear, by many Italianized readers, may be considered already too circumstantial. Had his short life been protracted, we might perhaps have had a school of secular music of our own, which we cannot to this day boast of.[11]

However apologetic the statement seems to be, it is probably quite realistic. Also noticeable is the style of the paragraph. Perhaps its stilted sentence-structure reflects Latin, but it is more likely that some of the contributors were foreigners. We know nothing about Sainsbury's assistants after all. Sainsbury was the publisher of the dictionary and is generally assumed to have been its author. But his work was probably limited to editing, i.e., compiling and preparing copy for the typesetter. Having seen the nearly verbatim copying of many of the autobiographical letters, one must conclude that

---

where Pepys was born. It is conceivable that this is the same Sainsbury or a member of his family who went briefly into the music-publishing business. Sainsbury acknowledges the assistance of "messengers" among whom may have been a J. Sullivan of Dublin, Edouard (or J. R.) Schulz who had spent some time in Vienna, a John Berridge, and a W. Beckwith, all names that come up in the correspondence. At this time I have found nothing further about them.

Virtually all the autobiographies were sent to Sainsbury in the last three months of 1823. The musicians who were asked for autobiographies were given a very short time to comply with the request; at one point it is clear that one person had ten days in which to respond. On October 4 of 1824 one Charles Evans acknowledges receipt of a copy of the dictionary. It was printed in about ten months, a likely explanation for the unchecked facts or for not getting birthdates in all cases.

11. Sainsbury, 2: 320.

Sainsbury's procedure may have been similar when editing the copy submitted by those persons he called "messengers"; some of them at least were probably foreigners. Several of the autobiographical letters sent to him were in French and Italian. These are usually followed by anonymous translations. Quite possibly some contributors resided abroad, a suspicion that grows as one reads the entry on Guillaume de Machaut which contains information not likely to have been available in England at the time. That Sainsbury had the information and mentions Perne cannot be explained, in other words, unless he had a correspondent in Paris who wrote, "François-Louis Perne has reproduced the Mass which is a great curiosity with a modern score." [12] (Again the style is curiously stilted.)

In his article on Beethoven, Sainsbury claims that Burney, obviously still a figure to be reckoned with, defended Beethoven's "unexpected and abstruse modulations." Where Burney made such a statement is not clear. It is possible that Sainsbury extrapolated the claim from Burney's other writings, say, those on Monteverdi or Gesualdo; i.e., Burney defended unexpected modulations in general. Dr. Burney, for his part, had written many of the articles on music in Rees' *Cyclopedia*, the successor to Chambers, but he had no article on Beethoven, understandably, since he was writing in about 1801.[13] In general, Burney's biographies are not distinguished. They were based for the most part on his own earlier work with few modifications. Burney did not even change his opinion about Bach, a composer who was steadily gaining in esteem everywhere else.

Without wishing to derogate the venerable Burney, any defense of Sainsbury is bound to aver that his biographical articles were far superior to those in Rees' *Cyclopedia*. Some of those are downright terrible. In Burney's article on Mozart, for example, total confusion reigns. Burney defends Mozart against distorting performances — here his article digresses at disproportionate length — but his list of works is nothing less than nonsense. When Burney's biographer, Roger Lonsdale, says that, "for various reasons Burney's articles [in Rees] are not easy to discuss and evaluate," it may be that he does

---

12. See, Fétis, *Biographic universelle* (2nd ed., c 1867) 6: 493, for information about Perne.
13. Abraham Rees, *The Cyclopedia or Universal Dictionary of Arts, Sciences and Literature*, 39 vols. (London: Longman, Hurt, Rees, Orme & Brown, 1802—20).

not wish to speak ill of the old gentleman.[14] But whatever his great merit had been in the past, these contributions do not show Burney at his best. On the other hand, Sainsbury looks far less venal, when we realize that similar borrowings from his own and other writings are part of Burney's biographical entries. In any case, it should be clear how much of a contribution Sainsbury made in spite of all the flaws that were still endemic among biographical lexicographers at the time.

On the western shores of the Atlantic, John Parker's little work was far less ambitious. Were it not that his dictionary was a first, it would get even less attention than it has. Parker's work contains a mere thirty-four biographies apparently arranged in some sort of hierarchical order rather than alphabetically. At the end there are some essays on various topics such as the anthem, the metronome, church music, the voluntary, and Logier's system. While we know that Logier's "chiroplastic" device spread with great rapidity in England and Germany, it is a symptom of the wide interest it received that Parker assigned it a special place in his book. Parker gives us a vivid description of Logier's method of teaching in groups, while Sainsbury includes a long biography of the inventor and pedagogue.

How preoccupied Parker must have been with Anglo-American vindication is suggested by the fact that about twenty of his biographies are of musicians not from continental Europe; they are either English or American. The book's subtitle, "Sketches of the Lives and Writings of Eminent Musical Characters," indicates that Parker did not feel any obligation to supply complete data, and in several cases neither birth dates nor first names are given. Some of the articles were culled from journals such as *The Musical Euterpiad* which Parker edited. While this is not exactly "plagiarism," it again illustrates the indifference to exclusivity that was characteristic of the time.

The fact that Parker was not one of the great lexicographers should not deter us from using his book as a guide to his milieu. He says, for example, "that Haydn had scarcely composed his symphonies than they were performed in the U.S.A." Recent writings trying to retrace the performing histories of Haydn's and Beethoven's

---

14   Roger Lonsdale, *Dr. Charles Burney* (Oxford: Clarendon, 1965).

works have ignored Parker's hints entirely.[15] We are obviously not reading old reference books as historical documents.

In the central part of Europe, Dlabač began a lexicographical tradition at about the same time as Gerber. Whether it is justified to consider his book as primarily symptomatic of the rise of nationalism is moot.[16] All it takes to begin an enterprise of this sort is a compulsive type of individual who must pursue his own questions to their logical conclusion. If the work is timely, i.e., if there is sufficient interest, it tends to be published. A less timely effort such as that of Pitoni not only never saw the light of day, but Pitoni seems not even to have planned for its publication.[17] We know that Gerber began his collection of biographical data as a consequence of trying to find out more about the subjects of the portraits he was collecting; the dictionary was a by-product. Dlabač was a librarian, i.e., in the business of gathering information. That such work resulted in early masterpieces of the lexicographical genre is simply our good fortune.

One might surmise that Gerber and Dlabač were men of the Enlightenment infected by romanticism. Apparently the writings of Herder had a good deal of influence everywhere in Europe, and the transfer of Herder's ideas about the relationship between people and their place, about ethnicity, would not be misapplied in a musical dictionary. Bohemian musicians, especially those who moved west in the eighteenth century were after all widely admired.

It is impossible to know how many copies of Dlabač's earlier dictionary sold in central Europe. Perhaps the neglect of Dlabač in contemporary literature was related to the fact that the more centrally placed writers of the time considered Bohemia provincial. On the other hand, the apparently small demand for the much more central Gerber I kept Breitkopf from wanting to publish the second expanded edition. Gerber's advantage was simply that a high proportion of his musicians were more widely known, while most of the subjects of Dlabač's work had much narrower reputations. Why should someone other than a fellow-lexicographer such as Fétis, someone living in Vienna or Paris, want to own a dictionary of

---

15. See, for example, Irvin Lowens, *Haydn in America* (Detroit: Information Coordinators, 1979).
16. Mark Germer, "Dlabač Dictionary and its Place in the Literature," *Fontes artis musicae* 28 (1981): 307ff.
17. See Chapter V.

Bohemian composers? In fact, if such Bohemians as Richter or Stamitz had not come west, they might never have been heard from. A book such as Dlabač's would most likely depend on regional interest for its success.

Whatever the fate of his first attempt at a biographical dictionary, Dlabač's second, much larger work dealt with all sorts of artists and artisans; i.e., it was not a purely musical reference book. As Mark Germer points out, it was old-fashioned in the sense that elsewhere musicians were being treated as superior to other artisans, as people of great talent, even genius. Music was in fact coming to be the foremost art. Gerber was in tune with this trend while Dlabač was not.

None of this has much to do with the quality of either biographical collection. Dlabač was perhaps even more thorough than Gerber. He was certainly better at giving his sources. Realistically speaking, however, we must admit that Prague was relatively provincial and that "the big time" was elsewhere. That Bohemian musicians brought their talents west in the second half of the eighteenth century and became a major factor in the development of instrumental music at the time does not alter the fact that Bohemia itself was not in the mainstream as a place.

The vast increase in musical consumption, the vitality of musical life were felt nearly everywhere. That is most likely the chief cause of the increase in musico-biographical reference works. The demand for knowledge and the interest in musicians became universal. Even Breslau, which one must admit to have been rather special, had its own collective biographies, beginning with Hoffmann's in 1830 and supplemented by Kossmaly in 1846.[18] The latter is a sort of useful curiosity, not so much because of its biographical information, but rather because of its many valuable facts about musical life in Breslau. That the second work was conceived as a supplement to Hoffmann is evident from the fact that it was published in alphabetically complete fascicles. Apparently subscribers were expected to add these fascicles to their Hoffmann. The names contained in its six installments were not primarily those of renowned musicians. But the book describes musical societies and conservatories, lists the members of orchestras, salaries, programs, instrument builders, and similar data of considerable sociological interest. Thus it describes

---

18.   See note 2.

the first public chamber-music concerts, given in 1831 to 1832 after several earlier attempts to get subscriptions had failed. The programs were devoted primarily to Beethoven, Haydn, and Mozart in that order, as well as to Hummel, Spohr, and Moscheles.

We have reached the end of this era in a sense, since in 1835 the first volume of Fétis' *Biographie universelle* appeared, the first modern bio-bibliography that started a tradition continued by Eitner and culminating in RISM.[19] While one may not esteem Fétis' accomplishment at first, considering his many errors, his opinionated approach, as well as his occasional charlatanism, it becomes clear that even such admired works as Dlabač's, Gerber's, and Sainsbury's were not in the same league. Singlehandedly, Fétis brought music lexicography into the mainstream of musical history, making all other attempts, except perhaps that of Gustav Schilling, seem primitive by comparison.[20]

The national biographies, i.e., those that were not meant to be "universal," reached a climax in the Polish dictionary of Sowinsky (1857) which undoubtedly benefited from Fétis' example.[21] Again the question of nationalism arises and again one must conclude that it was probably not as strong a factor as was fashion. French interest in musical Poland may have been largely the result of Chopin's renown. One certainly gets that impression from the fashionable persons who are listed as subscribers. Most of them were aristocrats. Only a few of the 165 subscribers who ordered 220 copies were booksellers, librarians, musicians, or scholars. (Among them were Fétis and Julian Fontana.) Yet the book is far more modern in character than any of the national or local dictionaries before. This is because of its inclusion of a comparatively excellent short history of Polish music, and even more so because of its underlying attitude. Most of the literature about music in Poland written in Western Europe treats early Polish music as an offshoot of Central European styles. This is still the case in Reese's *Music in the Renaissance* or in

---

19. Robert Eitner, *Biographisch-bibliographisches Quellen-Lexikon der Musiker und Musikgelehrten vom Anfang der christlichen Zeitrechnung bis zur Mitte des 19. Jahrhunderts.* 10 vols. (Leipzig: Breitkopf und Härtel, 1898—1904). *Répertoire international des sources musicales.*
20. Gustav Schilling, *Encyclopädie der gesammten musikalischen Wissenschaften*, 6 vols. (Stuttgart: F. H. Köhler, 1835—37).
21. Albert Sowinski, *Les Musiciens polonais et slaves anciens et modernes. Dictionnaire biographique . . .* (Paris: Adrien Le Clère, 1857).

Kurt von Fischer's contribution to *Aspects of Medieval and Renaissance Music*.[22] In an article in the latter, von Fischer cites a manuscript from Cracow as an example of the late survival of organum-like technique "on the periphery of the main-stream of music." Sowinsky on the other hand emphasizes native Polish musical character and treats Central European practices as they are assimilated into Polish music in just the opposite way, i.e., as the Polish adaptation of European styles to Polish taste. Sowinsky includes many musical examples. (These were not always transcribed accurately by modern standards.) Sowinsky was quite aware of the isolation of Polish music. Thus under the entry for Nicolas Gomolka (born in 1539 although Sowinsky says 1564), he complains, "the merit of his Psalm settings are such that he would have become immortal had he been a German or Italian." Among other lexicographers only Fétis had included more than just a few Polish composers, and even in *Music in the Renaissance* Gomolka has one page and one short musical example in a reference basically designed to illustrate the "diffusion of the central language."[23]

Sowinsky is of course too obviously inclined to praise Polish music to be taken at his word. Still his book is an accomplishment of considerable merit, and one is surprised to find that the authors of the article on Poland in *The New Grove* ignore him completely.[24] They limit themselves entirely to works originating in Poland.

It is quite natural that we regard such works as have been described in this chapter as books in which to look up persons, in many cases only because we cannot find them in more recent sources. Summaries in the great encyclopedias tend to look at them from this point of view only, taking into account their coverage and general reliability. A reader who is interested in their cultural and social testimony soon finds himself engrossed in what they have to tell us, incidentally often finding hints of "firsts" or other data that

---

22. Gustave Reese, *Music in the Renaissance* (New York: Norton, 1954). Kurt von Fischer, "Organal and Chordal Style in Renaissance Sacred Music: New and Little-known Sources," *Aspects of Medieval and Renaissance Music*, ed. by Jan LaRue et al. (New York: Norton, 1966): 173ff.
23. Reese, *Renaissance*: 751f.
24. Boguslaw Schäffer and Jan Steszewski, "Poland," *The New Grove Dictionary of Music and Musicians*, 20 vols. (London: Macmillan, 1980), 5: 26ff.

seem to clash with what we know about something. One does not, of course, immediately set out to rewrite history on the basis of such finds and takes the assertions of the likes of Sainsbury with great caution. On the other hand, the generally greater reliability of Eitner over Fétis is gained at the expense of the commentary that supplies considerable atmosphere. Eitner cannot be as interesting a witness to an earlier-musical scene as were Fétis or Sowinsky. Eitner's desire to be objective, while entirely laudatory from the point of view of modern scholarship, also makes him somewhat bland. In the reconstruction of history he can no longer be the direct witness in the sense the earlier lexicographers should now be seen.

Appendix

Autobiographies and quasi-autobiographies in Sainsbury. Square brackets indicate that the "autobiography" was submitted by someone other than the subject or that it is not certain to be by the subject.

Abel, J. L.
Adams, Thomas
Adcock, James
Addison, James
Anderson, Lucy
Ansdell, W. F.
Ashe, Andrew
Ashley, John
Baker, George
Bark, William
[Barthelemon, Francois H.]
Baur, Charles A.
Beale, John
Beckwith, John C.
Begrez, Pierre I. M.
Betts, Arthur
Bissett, Catherine
Blake, Benjamin
Blake, William
[Blewitt, Jonathan]

Blount, J. W.
[Borgondio, (Signora)]
Bottomley, Joseph
Broadhead, John
Burrowes, John F.
Butler, Thomas H.
Calkin, James
Calkin, William [1]
Catalani, Angelina
Challener, Neville B.
Chapple, Samuel
Clark, Richard
Clarke-Whitfeld, John
Clementi, Muzio [2]
Clifton, John Charles
Coccia, Carlo
Cooke, Nathaniel
Cooke, Thomas Simpson
Coombe, William F.
Coombs, James Morris

Corfe, Joseph
[Corri, Domenico]
[Corri, Montague]
[Crevelli, Domenico]
[Crouch, Frederick, W.] [3]
Cudmore, Richard
Cummins, Charles
[Cutler, William] [3]
Dance, William
[Danneley, John F.]
Dickons, Maria
[Dignum, Charles]
Dizi, François J.
Dussek, Sophia Giustina
Eager, John
Ellis, Samuel
Essex, Timothy
Ferrari, Giacomo G.
Ferrari, Victoire [4]
Fish, William
Fisin, James
Foy, James
Frost, Edward
Goodban, Thomas
[Gow, Niel & his sons
    Nathaniel
    John]
[Graef, Johann Georg] [5]
Green, John
[Griesbach, C. J.] [6]
Griesbach, Georg, L. J.
Griesbach, John H.
Griesbach, W.
Guest, George
[Guest, Ralph]
Gutteridge, William
Hamerton, William H.
Harper, Thomas
Harris, Joseph. H.
[Harrison, Samuel]

Hart, Joseph B.
Haydon, Thomas
Heather, William E.
Hempel, Charles W.
Hill, Frederick
Hill, Joseph
Holder, Joseph W.
Horn, Charles F.
Horn, Henry
Howell, Thomas
Hoylan, John
[Huxtable, Anthony]
Huxtable, Christopher
[Huxtable, William]
[Jacob, Benjamin]
Jay, John G. H.
Kellner, Ernest A.
Kiallmark, Georoe [7]
Klose, Francis J.
Knapton, Philip
Knyvett, Charles
Lambert, George
Langshaw, John Jr.
[Langshaw, John Sr.]
Lates, Charles
[Lates, John James]
Latrobe, Christian I.
Liverati, Giovanni
Logier, Johann B. [8]
[Lord, John]
Lord, John Jr.
[Lord, William]
Luppino, T. W.
Lyon, Samuel T.
Mackenzi, Joseph
Marsh, John
Marshall, James
Masi, Girolamo
Mavius, Charles
Meves, Augustus

Meyer, Philip
[Meyer, Philip Sr.]
[Miles, Mrs.]
Monro, Henry
[Nathan, Isaac]
Neate, Charles
[Nielson Lawrence][9]
[Panormo, Ferdinand charles]
Panormo, Francesco
[Parke, John]
Parke, William T.
Parry, John
Patton, Matthew
Perry, Frederick C.
[Petrides, Joseph]
Petrides, Peter
Possin, Johann S. C.[10]
Powell, Thomas
Pratt, John
Prina, J. F.
Purkiss, John
[Randles, Elizabeth]
[Rawlings, Robert]
Rawlings, Thomas A.
[Rawlins, Thomas]
Reeve, Cotton
Reinagle, Joseph
Relfe, John
[Rimbault, Stephen]
Rogers, Robert

Rudall, George[11]
Sexton, William
Sherman, Samuel
[Simms, Edward]
Simms, Edward Jr.
[Simms, John]
Sinclair, John
Smith, Charles
Stevens, William S.
Sutton, William W.
[Taylor, Richard]
Tomlins, Thomas
Townsend, John
Turle, William
Tydeman, Zebedee
Valentine, Thomas
[Vertue, Matthew]
Viner, William L.
Watkins, Thomas P.
[Weippert, Erhardt]
Weippert, John
Weiss, Carl R.
[Wesley, Charles]
[Welsh, Thomas]
[White, John]
Wilde, Henry, Sr.
[Wilson, Marmaduke]
[Wright, Thomas]
[Wright, Thomas Henry]

Notes for Autobiographies

1. Omitted in Dictionary.
2. List of works only, submitted by Charles Clementi.
3. Refers to an autobiography not included but sent by messenger.
4. Madame Victoire.
5. Name given as John in Dictionary.
6. Omitted in Dictionary.
7. His letter dated February and March 1825.
8. Autobiography not included. He says he is returning it with corrections.

9. No autobiography but a request that his name be corrected from "Neilson" in the second edition.
10. Name given as John in Dictionary.
11. Omitted in Dictionary.

CHAPTER VI

WITNESSES, SCHOLARS, AND WOULD-BE SCHOLARS. MUSICAL BIOGRAPHY AT THE TURN OF THE NINETEENTH CENTURY

History has not been kind to Nikolaus von Nissen whose well-intentioned biography of Mozart remains the first such work that can be taken seriously.[1] As Constanze Mozart's second husband, he was close to both kinds of sources, oral and documentary; in that sense he had all the advantages. When Nissen's book appeared, it was basically the draft of a not-quite-completed study, since the author had died before finishing it without having had the opportunity to make revisions. Unlike all the earlier biographies — the exception was Forkel's *Bach* — Nissen's was not just a collection of anecdotes tied together by dates and events.[2] Nissen selected among the letters of the family those that seemed to him most important and produced the ancestor of what we now call a documentary biography with no examples to follow. When Otto Jahn wrote his book about Mozart forty years later he expressed his dissatisfaction with the mass of documentary material Nissen reproduced without proper connections, yet to the modern reader it is remarkable how well Nissen's

---

1. Nikolaus von Nissen, *Biographie Wolfgang Amadeus Mozarts.*
2. Johann Nikolaus Forkel, *Ueber Joann Sebastian Bachs Leben, Kunst und Kunstwerke.* All quotations above are in my own translation.

biography hangs together.[3] Jahn acknowledged that reproducing the many letters was meritorious, but criticized the absence of a proper narrative. Until Schiedermeyer published all known Mozart letters in 1914, there could not be a more complete collection.[4] Nissen was not a musician and he was not qualified to analyze music, but he was the first to put Mozart's life in order. That he was squeamish about certain of Mozart's peculiarities should not surprise us; even Jahn and Schiedermeyer still replaced Mozart's scatology with dashes. Perhaps for the same reason Constanze is rarely quoted directly, and we learn little from Nissen about her intimate relationship with her husband. Nissen seems not to have been jealous of his wife's relationship with her late husband even if Mozart could hardly have been an easy act to follow.

Nissen's Mozart stands at the apex of the old type of biography, standard except for Forkel, a mixture of anecdote, eye-witness testimony, selective documentation, and rather crude attempts to list a composer's works. That Nissen did not have enough musical training for the kind of analysis that makes Forkel's book so much more interesting is no great loss to posterity; Mozart has since been well served in that respect. Personal reminiscences, on the other hand, would have been lost had he not recorded them.

Nissen's Mozart appeared in the same year as a new kind of biography, the life of Palestrina by Baini, which, by force of necessity, was based on archival research and which for the first time attempted to place a composer's work in historical perspective.[5] There had been an earlier attempt to write a "scholarly" biography, that of Guido of Arezzo by Luigi Angeloni. This was possible thanks to the collection of medieval treatises in Martin Gerbert's collection which Angeloni supplemented by his own research in Parisian libraries.[6] Angeloni was a linguist who was totally naïve in matters of musical scholarship as well as historical research. His work was privately

---

3.   Otto Jahn, *W. A. Mozart*.
4.   Ludwig Schiedermeier, *Die Briefe Wolfgang Amadeus Mozarts und seiner Familie*, 5 vols. (Leipzig and Munich: G. Müller, 1914).
5.   Giuseppe Baini, *Memorie storico-critiche della vita e delle opere di Giovanni Pierluigi da Palestrina*.
6.   Luigi Angeloni, *Sopra la vita, le opere, ed il sapere di Guido d'Arezzo* (Paris: Author, 1811). Martin Gerbert, *Scriptores ecclesiastici de musica sacra potissimum*, 3 vols. (Berlin: 1784), reprinted (Milan: Bollettino bibliographico musicale, 1931).

printed and probably had little immediate influence although Baini
mentioned it and some years later Kiesewetter made it the basis of
his own work about Guido. Fétis also took it into account in his
Biographie universelle.[7] Kiesewetter said that Angeloni's book was
very rare and had never been available in the trade. The copy he had
read came from the library of the Gesellschaft der Musikfreunde in
Vienna.

By the time Angeloni elevated him to the status of patron saint of
Italian music, Guido was already a legend, virtually the inventor of
music as well as of several musical instruments, praised by Athanasius
Kircher and Marin Mersenne. Angeloni wrote out of the same kind
of national pride that motivated Forkel's *Bach*. To him, "*nostro
immortal Guido d'Arezzo*" stood at the beginning of Italian musical
glory. Both Kiesewetter and Fétis praised Angeloni's biography but
damned his musical scholarship.[8] Fétis' article summarized all the
contributions Guido had *not* made, while Kiesewetter tried to
correct attributions and assign them to the right theorists. For his
part, Angeloni continually digressed into more familiar territory such
as the beauty of Italian and its suitability for musical setting,
forgetting that Guido had written about music set exclusively to
Latin texts. Angeloni's biography was a belated defense of Italian
music. Still, in his bumbling way, the author documented everything.
His may be the first musical monograph in which on many pages the
footnotes take up more space than the text. Not even the genuinely
learned Kiesewetter had so many citations. There is not in Angeloni
a musical example; he does not reproduce staff notation or a
Guidonian hand, not even the music for *Ut queant laxis*.

Forkel's biography of Johann Sebastian Bach is almost the
counterpart of Angeloni. Forkel seems to have cared little about
documentation. He was far more interested in the life and the music
and he made no effort to ensure that he had recovered all of Bach's
works.

Forkel had corresponded with Emanuel Bach as early as 1774,
indicating that he had thought about this biography for almost thirty
years. He intended his book about J. S. Bach to be the culmination

---

7.   Raphael Georg Kiesewetter, *Guido von Arezzo, sein Leben und sein
      Wirken* (Leipzig: Breitkopf und Härtel, 1840); François Joseph Fétis
      Biographie universelle, (1835—1844).
8.   Fétis, in the article on Guido of Arezzo.

of his history of music, but decided to issue it sooner, since the publisher, Kühnel, was projecting a complete and critical Bach edition with Forkel as editor.[9] This, thought Forkel, was an urgently needed venture, since the increasingly faulty copies of Bach's music then in wide circulation would-eventually lead to his artistic oblivion.

It is true that Forkel's *Bach* is a landmark in the history of composers' lives although not, as is often repeated, because it was the first scholarly and analytical such work to be encountered. While Forkel was concerned with the structure and content of Bach's music — he is a pioneer in that respect — he made no effort to establish a comprehensive list of works or to unearth whatever documents might have contributed to a more accurate biography. On the other hand, Forkel is the first "romantic" biographer. His German nationalism we can almost take for granted. That he regarded Bach as the greatest "musical poet" of all time or that he believed Bach wrote for his own satisfaction rather than to please audiences are elements of biography that came to predominate in the nineteenth century. Forkel is romantic also because he is the first biographer to treat a composer in terms of his development. It may not have been unscholarly to try to establish a precise chronological order of a composer's opus even if the attempt was foolish in this case, but Forkel regarded the works from before 1720 as immature and maintained that Bach achieved greatness only in his later works. Romantic also is Forkel's assertion that there is deeper meaning in Bach's polyphony than the merely clever interplay of equal voices or the complexities of counterpoint. While Forkel is sometimes regarded as old-fashioned because he believed the glory of polyphonic writing to outweigh homophony, the fact is that he found the expression of feeling rather than technique to be the important characteristic of great music. "Speaking of Bach's fugues," he said, "there is freedom, ease and flow in the progress of the whole, an inexhaustible wealth of modulation carried out with irreproachable continuity ... consistency and variety in style ... Finally one gets such a sense of [the music as] a living organism [*Leben*] that it sometimes seems to the performer or listener that all the tones are spirits."[10] Bach invented melodies that were timeless, said Forkel, another romantic idea which could not have occurred to a musician or writer a few decades earlier.

---

9.   Forkel, *Bach*: 7.
10.   Ibid.: 40.

Forkel was not the first to evaluate his subject. There was, as we have seen, a growing tendency in the late eighteenth century to rate musicians in addition to giving the outline of their lives and listing their works. Such collective biographies as Hiller's or Gerber's contain increasingly intelligent commentary about music, and the journals of the period are more and more commonly inclined toward musical criticism. What makes Forkel's work novel is a result of his improvement of such criticism; he was more specific. We are fortunate that Forkel stood in two camps, so to speak. His own musical education was based on the treatises of Bach's time; he was brought up in the same tradition as his subject although, perhaps without being aware of it, he had at least partly outgrown it. Consciously or not, he had been influenced by the romantics who generally were the first to understand the profundity of Bach. The modern tradition of measuring success or failure in past composers' lives is almost irrelevant. Many of them achieved renown and comfort, others remained poor and their works controversial, but the modern perception of how well or how badly they were treated by their contemporaries is a kind of anachronism that may never even have occurred to a composer who thought he was just writing music. Obviously such composers as Bach or Mozart knew that they were superior to most or even all of their contemporaries. Did they know in the romantic sense that they were "timeless," that their music would still have something to say to us two centuries later? Could Mozart have guessed at the increasing fascination *Don Giovanni* would hold for scholars and audiences when he wrote it primarily as musical theater? The relative success of a Bach can only be measured by reputation and income; the veneration of later times is not a factor one can apply as a standard for pre-romantic audiences. To a limited extent Forkel was aware of this. He repeated one of C. P. E. Bach's comments in more elaborate form.

> What the world calls brilliant fortune, Bach did not enjoy. While he had a well-paying position, he also had many children to feed and educate. Other means were not available to him nor did he seek them. He was much too profoundly involved in his work and his art to have taken a path a man such as he might have taken to find a goldmine in his day. Had he wanted to travel, he would have earned the admiration of the entire world as even one of his enemies admitted. . . . Nevertheless, he did not lack either friendship or honor.[11]

---

11. Ibid.: 84.

Forkel maintained that connoisseurs and amateurs gave Bach all the admiration he needed, worth more than medals or golden chains.

Forkel oversimplified, of course. While Bach might have done without medals, he certainly did care about money. But money was already becoming too vulgar a word in Forkel's time to utter before romantic sensibilities. While Mainwaring had been unembarrassed in assigning the crassest motives to Handel, we have entered new territory with Forkel, who, in that respect, too, set the tone for several generations of biographers.

Forkel is sometimes called the first musicologist because he was the first to divide the discipline into several of the sub-categories that still pervade musical scholarship. An article by Wolf Franck calls him the founder of musicology yet old-fashioned at the same time.[12] Forkel was still very much under the spell of the doctine of the affections, writes Franck, and therefore limited in his ability to understand recent music. Perhaps so, but in his writing about Bach there is only one reference to affect, although some other elements of older musical theory remain visible under a veneer of original musical analysis. While, for example, Forkel seems to be the first tacitly to recognize harmonic rhythm by pointing out that harmonic changes occur more quickly in Bach's keyboard music for the chamber than in organ music played in reverberant churches, he was in fact only modernizing what he had learned from baroque theorists such as Mattheson who had long ago made distinctions among operatic, theatrical, and churchly styles on the basis of acoustics. Even in pointing out that Bach's setting of four-part chorales kept to a strict and evenly distributed voice-leading in all the parts, unlike settings by more recent composers who maintained close harmony in the left hand, Forkel was basing his knowledge on a polyphonic tradition that had been more or less discarded by younger minds. Forkel's understanding of Bach's polyphony, a polyphony that always sustained interesting harmonic progressions, was the insight of a performer. Only a musician immersed in the music was able to recognize these stylistic traits. Only a musician who had learned the same theoretical foundations as Bach would have been able to extrapolate from them and develop so rich an understanding. But that Forkel may have been old-fashioned by inclination or training,

12.   Wolf Franck, "Musicology and Its Founder Johann Nikolaus Forkel," *The Musical Quarterly* 25 (1949): 588ff.

seems to be less important than that he was old-fashioned at a time when the older fashion was beginning to come back into style.

We might be inclined to say that Forkel had no business giving us an overview of Bach, since he knew only a fraction of his music. Not only was most of the church music not available to him, but even such major works as the *Brandenburg Concertos* had not been rediscovered. Forkel had heard or seen enough, however, to recognize in Bach the master of logical, concise, and consistent polyphony, a polyphony dominated by harmonic movement, so organically conceived that it was unprecedented. Forkel's view that Bach represented the culmination of a tradition that had taken a long time to develop was remarkably appropriate as well as romantic.

If Baini had any precursors, they were Forkel and Angeloni although that does not in any way diminish his own achievement for which in 1828 the time was finally ripe. Kiesewetter in publishing Kandler's modified translation of Baini made sure that a German version of this fundamental book would be available even if in his preface Kandler deplored the effusiveness with which Italians tended to violate the canons of scholarly sobriety.[13] None of this activity was relevant to Nissen. He was just an admirer who happened to be in the right place at the right time and who had access to the sources.

Between Forkel and Nissen, i.e., between 1802 and 1828, there are a number of memoirs and biographies, accounts which, while of great documentary value, must be read with caution. The autobiographies of Adalbert Gyrowetz or Karl Ditters von Dittersdorf, for example, are for all their seemingly authentic detail the memoirs of old men.[14] (The autobiography of Gyrowetz was published in 1848, but the events that interest us and its general tone belong to an earlier time and shall be treated here.) Gyrowetz frequently reported

---

13. Franz Sales Kandler, *Ueber das Leben und die Werke des G. Pierluigi da Palestrina* (Leipzig: Breitkopf und Härtel, 1834). Kandler's book was a free translation of Baini's with comments and critical remarks. Upon Kandler's sudden and early death, Kiesewetter published the work with further invaluable comments and emendations.

14. Adalbert Gyrowetz, *Biographie des Adalbert Gyrowetz* (Vienna, 1848). The edition I used is that of Alfred Einstein in "Lebensläufe deutscher Musiker von ihnen selbst erzählt," vols. 3 and 4 (Leipzig: C. F. W. Siegel, 1915). Carl Ditters von Dittersdorf, *Lebensbeschreibung* (Leipzig: Breitkopf und Härtel, 1801). Modern edition by Norbert Miller (Munich: Kösel, 1967).

meetings and events that could not have occurred at the time he said they did or which otherwise do not match what we know. Dittersdorf seems to report the events he was party to more accurately, but since his autobiography was dictated and appeared in an edition by Karl Spazier, we have no way of knowing what may have been "cleaned up," changed, or omitted. Still, it is puzzling that historical scholarship tends to overlook this and other such sources.[15] What Gyrowetz reports about his dealings with publishers or his relationship with Haydn in London, not to mention his eyewitness account of the French Revolution, is of considerable interest even if taken with a grain of salt. Gyrowetz refers to himself as apolitical in his memoirs, so naïve that when he first heard of the Revolution in 1789 when he was traveling from Italy to France, he did not even know what the word meant. He had been hoping to sell some of his compositions in Marseilles to publishers to whom he had letters of recommendation. "In these confused times, however, it was not likely that one could do business with music, although he had heard that several of his symphonies had already been successfully performed in Marseilles, and that others of his works had been printed in Paris." This was news to Gyrowetz and we should expect him to have been angry, since he had not been paid. He had no idea which works had reached Paris or how, but rather than fret, he was eager to get there. (His lack of anger is significant. Why rage at a fate every successful composer must then have taken for granted?) Music, Gyrowetz continues, was in great favor at Marseilles where church-music and string-playing were very good but music for winds and military music was behind the times.

Gyrowetz traveled on to Lyon. To paraphrase his account: he saw gallows in villages along the way, some of them "occupied." When he stopped in the evenings he found young people playing fife and drum, dancing and singing, and generally satirizing the aristocracy. With all this excitement going on around him, he searched out a music store at Lyon to ask for new works that might be available. Imagine his surprise when told that there were some quartets by one

---

15.   H. C. Robbins Landon is a notable exception. He not only makes use of Gyrowetz' autobiography in his work on Haydn, but he also quotes from it extensively in his article on Gyrowetz in *Die Musik in Geschichte und Gegenwart* ([Kassel: Bärenreiter, 1956]), 5, cols. 11 ff.) and points out how valuable a source it is.

Gyrowetz which were selling so well that they had already been reissued several times. On his arrival in Paris, his first call was on the publisher Imbault who was completely unembarrassed by his piracy and offered to buy whatever other works of Gyrowetz he might have with him. Since Gyrowetz had no money, he obtained an advance of six hundred francs never once demanding to be paid retroactively. Some days later he went back with his music and found that Imbault had gathered enough musicians from the Opéra to play through it. One symphony of his was known to the musicians to be by Haydn. It took Gyrowetz some effort to convince them that he was the composer. Again he was flattered rather than angry although he asked that the proper composer should from now on receive credit. But, he writes, to this day (1848) it was still generally being credited to Haydn.

It is tempting to continue this account. It should be enough, however, to demonstrate the narrative's interest to historians. Gyrowetz' report on the London scene is equally fascinating although more problematic. After a short stay in Dover, he continued by "maill-kotch" to a hotel in London. Soon he was introduced to the "Prince of Wallis." (He had taken some English lessons while in Paris but they obviously had not included writing.) His description of the musical life of London is as interesting as what he reported from France. It becomes especially intriguing when he describes the arrival of Haydn and says, ". . . Gyrowetz helped Haydn greatly by introducing him to the right people." Gyrowetz claimed that London society did not take to Haydn at first. "They found him too old and, while they wanted to hear his symphonies, they were not eager to meet an old man." Gyrowetz says he was annoyed by this and made it his business to talk to the most influential people. If Haydn was aware of any initial coolness toward him, he did not report it in his letters.[16]

Stendahl or Louis-Aléxandre-César Bombet, an earlier pseudonym of Henri Beyle, produced a very derivative biography of Mozart. He reports, on what evidence we cannot tell, that the Emperor Joseph I's famous Philistinism, "too many notes, Mozart," was withdrawn by

---

16.   See H. C. Robbins Landon, *The Collected Correspondence and London Notebooks of Joseph Haydn* (London: Barrie and Rockliff, 1959).

his majesty after the actual performance.[17] This story and Stendahl's characterization of the emperor as a man who had no opinions of his own is indirectly confirmed by Dittersdorf's autobiography.[18] Dittersdorf's stilted conversation with the emperor has been reported in the literature about Mozart or the documentary supplements to the complete works.[19] It is of enough interest to bear repeating. Here is the relevant excerpt:

Emperor: Have you ever heard Mozart play?
Dittersdorf: Three times till now.
E: Have you also heard Clementi? Some prefer him to Mozart. What do you think?
D: Clementi possesses only art. Mozart has art as well as taste.
E: What do you think of Mozart's compositions?
D: He is without doubt one of our greatest original geniuses. I have never heard such an astonishing wealth of ideas. I wish he were not so wasteful with them. He hardly lets the listener catch his breath. One can barely reflect on one idea when another comes along. In the end one cannot remember any of them.
E: In his pieces for the theater his only flaw is that the singers complain they are being overwhelmed by his full accompaniment.
D: That surprises me. It is possible to write harmony and accompaniment without spoiling the vocal line [*Kantilena*].[20]

---

17.   Alexandre-César Bombet (Henri Beyle), *Lettres écrits de Vienne en Autriche, sur le célèbre compositeur Haydn, suivies d'une vie de Mozart, et de considerations sur Métastase et l'état présent de la musique en France et en Italie* (Paris: 1814). I have relied primarily on the translation entitled *Haydn, Mozart and Metastasio*, by Richard N. Coe (London: Calder and Boyars, 1972).
18.   Dittersdorf, *Lebensbeschreibung*: 227 ff.
19.   Otto Erich Deutsch, *Mozart, die Dokumente seines Lebens*, Neue Ausgabe sämtlicher Werke, ser. 10, suppl. (Kassel: Bärenreiter, 1961). Joseph Heinz Eibel, *Addenda und Corrigenda zu Mozart, die Dokumente seines Lebens*, Neue Ausgabe, ser. 10, suppl. (Kassel: Bärenreiter, 1978).
20.   It is not clear to me that this passage is correct as I have translated it or if it says the opposite, i.e., "that does *not* surprise me." The original reads "Das sollte mich wundern," which may be a typographical error or a regional form of the expression I know as, "Das sollte mich nicht wundern." The account in the *Allgemeine musikalische Zeitung* 1 (Leipzig, 1799), p. 382, does not clarify the problem. In it Dittersdorf says, "If one has the gift of harmony or accompaniment not to drown out the singer, I do not think it is a fault."

E: What do you think of Haydn?

D: I have never heard his pieces for the theater.

E: You have not missed anything. He does the same thing as Mozart. But what do you think of his chamber [i.e., instrumental] music?

D: It is a sensation in the entire world and rightly so.

E: Is he not a little too playful?

D: He has the gift of being playful without degrading his art.

E: You are right. Some time ago I compared Mozart and Haydn. Will you do the same so I can see if we agree?

D: How does your majesty compare Klopstock and Gellert?

E: Well, they are both great poets. One needs to read Klopstock more than once to catch all his beauties. Gellert can be understood immediately.

D: There is your answer, Your Majesty.

E: Mozart, you mean, is like Klopstock and Haydn like Gellert?

D: That is my opinion . . . May I be so bold as to ask for your majesty's own comparison?

E: I compared Mozart's music to a snuff box made in Paris and Haydn's to one made in London.[21]

To get ahead of the chronological sequence of biographies and autobiographies is justified only to illustrate some of their uses. There are important memoirs by musicians born earlier than Gyrowetz or Dittersdorf which are of value other than the documenting of musical events or anecdotes. There is, for example, the autobiography of Johann Wilhelm Hertel (1727—89). Its modern edition is based on three manuscripts written in 1783—84, conflated and annotated by Erich Schenk.[22] The editor recognizes Hertel's strong feeling for nature as incipient romanticism even though the work still hovers between the old-fashioned moralistic and anecdotal type of autobiography and more modern personal revelation. Even more romantic is Hertel's emphasis on his childhood and *"Bildung."* He criticized other biographers for not paying enough attention to their early years, since, he writes, one cannot understand the young man without having known the boy and the man without having known the

---

21. A slightly more elaborate version appeared in the same place (see note 14). Here the emperor says: "Paris makes them with many tasteful decorations, in London they are simpler but heavily polished."

22. Johann Wilhelm Hertel, "Autobiographie," edited from several manuscripts with commentary by Erich Schenk in, *Wiener musikalische Beiträge*, vol. 3 (Graz: Böhlhaus Nachf, 1957).

youth. Unlike earlier *Berufsbiographien* in which thè apprentice and journeyman-years are told primarily in order to list the author's teachers and travels, his youth takes up half of Hertel's memoirs. (So previously unthinkable a detail as being shown the evils of going to prostitutes by his father takes up nearly an entire page.) Hertel is always kind to his teachers, among them such eminent musicians as the brothers Graun and Franz Benda, less, I think, out of personal warmth than in the spirit of his time in which routine filial piety was elevated to uncritical sentimentality. He described Johann Gottlieb Goldberg as "a student of Sebastian Bach on the keyboard who was then in the service of the Russian ambassador Count Keyserling in Berlin." Nobody was ever better as a sight-reader; he was called a note-eater [*Notenfresser*]. The fragmentary autobiography of the younger Johann Friedrich Reichardt (1752—1814) also described Goldberg.[23]

> My most important musical acquaintance at the time was the sister of the famous great keyboardist, Goldberg, of the school of Johann Sebastian Bach. His name has long been linked with Bach's in adulation. The great artist's facility [*Fertigkeit*] and mastery on the keyboard I heard about from my father who had seen him at Dresden play a difficult new concerto placed before him upside down. He played it through without errors and then contemptuously threw it on the floor. In all his actions he was an extremely peculiar and disagreeable [*störrisch*] man.[24]

Reichardt goes on to describe Goldberg's own compositions, "which, in the manner of Bach, are as difficult for the left hand as for the right, although his melody is often cold and dry and his progressions unclear." Reichardt found it difficult to play Goldberg's compositions and came to the conclusion that Goldberg must have had very special hands, of such size and reach, perhaps, that they were equaled only by those of Joseph Wölfl.[25]

Christian Gottlob Neefe should be of extraordinary interest to us

---

23. Wilhelm Zentner, *Johann Friedrich Reichardt, eine Musikerjugend im 18. Jahrhundert* (Regensburg: Bosse, 1940).
24. Ibid.: 71.
25. Joseph Wölfl (1773—1812), a student of Leopold Mozart and Michael Haydn at Salzburg, was briefly a famous keyboard virtuoso.

in view of his association with the young Beethoven.[26] He disappoints
us, however, since his short autobiography, later supplemented by
his widow, gives us few facts beyond those later incorporated by
Thayer in his *Life of Beethoven*.[27] Franz Benda left us a short
account of his life which, besides revealing his near-illiteracy and his
sardonic sense of humor, also complements the picture of the
times.[28] Short of summarizing them all, one can only list many of the
autobiographies in the hope that their neglect as primary sources will
come to an end.

There is one autobiography that cannot be dealt with so briefly
although it is too long for very detailed analysis here. Its author,
André-Ernest-Modeste Grétry (1741—1813), probably the most
important memoirist of this time, finally gets us out of Germany.[29] In
fact, he gets us out with a vengeance; his book contains only one
short paragraph about German music and refers to only a few
German composers. Among nearly two-hundred names in the index
we find only Handel, Haydn, Johann Caspar Ferdinand Fischer, and,
of course, Gluck. Writing in the same decade as Benjamin de la
Borde, Grétry seems to have been as indifferent as the former to
music not from France or Italy.[30] This is all the more striking
because Grétry's autobiography is not just the story of his life, but
also includes many asides dealing with fundamental musical questions even before he gets to the self-sufficient essays that make up
the second part of his book in the 1797 edition. The Germans, said

---

26. Christian Gottlob Neefe, *Lebenslauf* (1789) edited by Walther
     Engelhardt in Beiträge zur rheinischen Musikgeschichte 21 (Cologne:
     Volk, 1957).
27. Alexander Wheelock Thayer, *Ludwig von Beethoven's Leben*, trans-
     lated (from English) by Hermann Deiters (Berlin: 1866—79). All my
     references are to the edition prepared by Elliot Forbes. entitled
     Thayer's Life of Beethoven (Princeton, N. J.: Princeton University
     Press, 1964).
28. Franz Benda, "Autobiographie," published as an appendix to *Franz
     Benda und seine Nachkommen* by Franz Lorenz under the auspices
     of the Staatliche Institut für Musikforschung, Preussischer Kulturbesitz
     (Berlin: de Gruyter, 1967).
29. André-Ernest-Modeste Grétry, *Mémoires ou essais sur la musique*
     (Pluviôse, 1797). First volume first published in 1789. Reprint of 2nd
     ed., 3 vols. (New York: Da Capo, 1971).
30. Benjamin de la Borde, *Essai sur la musique ancienne et moderne*.

Grétry, had no masters worthy of being imitated although they did invent true instrumental music and had developed a rich and varied harmony (accompaniment), second in importance, he admits, only to precise and delicious declamation.[31] Haydn had to be admired, but Grétry said that he longed for the texts that should be set to his symphonies, texts which Grétry himself mentally supplied.[32]

Grétry's intellectualism is evident from the first paragraph of his memoirs. He too writes much detail about his childhood and, for the first time in all of the autobiographies up to this point, describes the cruelty of one of his early teachers from which he suffered for four or five years without having the courage to tell his father. (The reader of early biographies always has a sense that the upbringing of many musicians was inherently cruel; they were torn from their parents too early and made to work too hard too soon. They never complain, however, and it must have taken some courage to call a spade a spade.)[33] Grétry's voyage on foot to Italy at eighteen brings to mind the German romantic novel; it reminds me of Novalis. Again and again Grétry interrupts his narrative to discuss music, music education, individual composers; in short everything is worthy of comment. Unlike Mozart who seems to have been oblivious to scenery, Grétry was overwhelmed (*fus ravi*) by "the drama offered our eyes when we got to Rome."[34] He is more critical and more skeptical than his German contemporaries when it comes to certain accomplishments. In one of his asides he says, "they tell me that there are many who can play perfectly at sight. I have never encountered this phenomenon unless the music was very easy." Unwittingly he had heard Mozart (unless he unconsciously repressed the name), since he went on to give an example. Once, in Geneva, he had met a child prodigy who supposedly played everything at sight. The child's father dared Grétry to write something brand-new in order to convince himself of the child's ability to play it at sight. "I wrote an allegro in B flat major, difficult though not extremely so. He [the boy] played it and everybody but I cried out at this miracle. True, he did not get stuck even once, but in some places he replaced my modulating passages with different ones."[35]

---

31.   Grétry, *Mémoires*, 1: 418f.
32.   Ibid., 3: 418f.
33.   Grétry was born in Liège, Belgium.
34.   Grétry, *Mémoires*, 1: 70.
35.   Ibid.

Grétry realized that his memoirs were more than just the story of his life. He ended his reminiscences, he says, because ideas about music which used to come so easily when he began, were drying up. However we choose to read it, Grétry's autobiography is a gold mine of musical lore, of aesthetic opinions, musical attitudes, contemporary life, and literary pleasure.

The "Mozart anecdote" Grétry recounts is an unexpected bonus. There cannot be much question that it was Mozart Grétry met, since both he and Mozart were in Geneva in 1766.[36] It seems not to have occurred to Grétry, who was very self-confident, that Mozart might not have liked his "modulating passages" and improved on them. Having no reason to doubt the story — for once not an anecdote told for the glorification of the young genius — it makes a wonderful illustration of the extent to which Mozart's artistic ego was already developed; it even suggests a certain arrogance which probably did not endear the boy to many.

But when it comes to anecdotes, the scholar is equipped to deal only with those for which he can find some factual corroboration or the testimony of direct witnesses. The mere repetition of stories in numerous accounts has little value; they all tend to come from the same source. A psychohistorian may be better able to make sense of anecdotes on the basis of their consistency with the character of a subject. On the other hand, the selectivity with which some modern biographers retell one and suppress the other story, a selectivity to which even psychiatrists are not immune, has more to do with the preconceived image of an artist than with conscious objectivity. It is uncomfortable for us, for example, that most biographies depict Mozart as a one-sided genius with little interest in anything except music. While we are now able to accept his immaturity, his bad management of money, and his scatalogical humor — in the Basel letters as well as in some canons (see KE 382) — his one-sidedness is quite alienating. We can accept it in a chess-genius such as depicted by Nabokov; we could accept it in a mere virtuoso, but that the master who gave us *Don Giovanni* cannot be shown to have been especially wise in other respects or especially interested in people is harder to take.[37] Where could he have learned so much in

---

36.   Otto Erich Deutsch, *Mozart Dokumente*: 57 (letter of Gabriel Kramer).
37.   Vladimir Nabokov, *The Defense*, trans. by Michael Scammell (New York: n.p., 1964).

such a short time? Several of the early biographies go out of their way to defend him against the already prevalent belief in his one-sidedness. Mozart *did* have interests other than music, says Nissen, and *did* take an interest in scenery. In a carriage he used to grow silent looking at the beauties of nature, but he said as little there as he wrote in his letters home.[38] In those it was always music, music, music.

That early biographies of Mozart were largely collections of anecdotes should not surprise us, since even as a child he already fascinated the musical world. His gift did not just *seem* legendary, it really *was* superhuman. When he died, he left a vast body of works at a time when other artists are just reaching their full maturity. Even early audiences heard in his music a depth and complexity that was hard to credit to so young a man. With all the adulation Haydn received, his personality was simpler and his music more readily accessible. The increasing preoccupation with childhood and personal development of this time found a perfect foil in the child-genius. At first this fascination took the form of collecting anecdotes somehow illustrating this or that miraculous trait. Most of these were gathered by Friedrich Rochlitz, then the editor of the *Allgemeine musikalische Zeitung*, who had met Mozart.[39] Rochlitz made it his business to authenticate what he could although his idea of authentication leaves something to be desired by our standards. He used what he found plausible in view of his own impressions of Mozart, and he tested some anecdotes by telling them to people who had known Mozart and who, Rochlitz believed, would either confirm or deny them. Apparently it did not occur to Rochlitz that anecdotes have a way of becoming simplified or "fictionalized" in the telling.

---

38. In a fragment from a projected novel, Carl Maria von Weber describes his hero's reaction to traveling, a curiously relevant passage which might apply to Mozart. "I do not know if other people have the same feelings I have travelling in a carriage. A world opens within me. Incapable of making a sound, I must seem the worst companion to my fellow-travellers. The thousand sights flying by my eyes awaken many conflicting thoughts in me. One theme displaces another. While mentally working out a diabolically complicated fugue, an impertinent rondo-theme jumps into its midst only to be displaced by a funeral march." See Georg Kaiser, *Sämtliche Schriften von Carl Maria von Weber*, ed. Georg Kaiser (Berlin and Leipzig: Schuster und Löffler, 1908).

39   *Allgemeine musikalische Zeitung*, vol. 1 and subsequent volumes.

However authentic it may originally have been, an anecdote eventually becomes a fable. According to Anthony van Hoboken, there is
evidence that Haydn told anecdotes about himself that tended to
vary on different occasions.[40] (Most of us have substituted what we
should have liked to have retorted instead of what we actually said,
and there is no reason why men such as Haydn or Mozart should be
less subject to this petty vice; in fact, one can imagine that the more
famous one becomes, the more important it is to live up to one's
reputation.)

Be that as it may, it appears that later biographers all took their
anecdotes from Rochlitz, especially after they had been collected
into a book and translated into French by Carl Friedrich Cramer.[41]
Some of them had already appeared in Schlichtegroll's obituary, an
account Rochlitz disliked because of its *uncritical* repetition of
anecdotes.[42] Schlichtegroll's obituary appeared in French in the
Magazin encyclopédique in the same year as Cramer's translation,
and together they became the basis for Stendahl's supposedly
plagiarized life of Mozart.[43] While Stendahl's biography of Haydn in
the same book was largely taken from Carpani's *La Haydine*, itself a
fraud, and, if not entirely plagiarized, became even more falsified
by Stendahl, the *Vie de Mozart* adaptation was more orthodox,
especially since Stendahl added his own appreciation to the anecdotes
he took from others. In a sense, the lives of both Haydn and Mozart,
but especially Mozart's, were already common property; they were in
the public domain, so to speak. Several of Stendahl's predecessors
had made use of Rochlitz' collection which to this day is not
acknowledged as the source of sources.[44]

---

40.   Anthony van Hoboken, "Discrepancies in Haydn Biographies," Louis
      Charles Elson Memorial Lecture (Washington D.C.: Library of Con-
      gress, 1962): 15.
41.   Carl Friedrich Cramer, *Anecdotes sur W. G. Mozart* (Paris: Author,
      1801).
42.   Friedrich Schlichtegroll, "Nekrolog auf das Jahr 1791" reprinted in
      Musiker-Nekrologe, ed. by Richard Schaal (Kassel, n.d.). Théophile
      Frédéric Winckler, *Notice biographique sur Jean-Chrysostome-
      Wolfgang-Théophile Mozart* (Paris, 1801). Winckler acknowledged his
      source as the *Magazin encyclopédique* 7 (1798) and 10 (1801).
43.   Giuseppe Carpani, *Le Haydine, ovvero lettere sulla vita e le opere del
      celebre maestro Giuseppe Haydn* (Milan: Boccinelli, 1812); Stendahl,
      Haydn, Mozart and Metastasio.
44.   Otto Jahn was critical of Rochlitz as well as disappointed that
      Rochlitz had never fulfilled his promise to write a biography of

To collect all the anecdotes in a manner similar to that of Rochlitz and group them into related categories would seem to be a matter of common sense in biographical research. Thus, the Grétry anecdote is probably authentic because of the author's seeming ignorance of who the boy was and *because* of his prejudices. Another story that appears to be plausible is the legendary ability of Mozart to write down his works while Constanze read to him. It agrees with the "legend" of Mozart's singular and single-track musical mind as well as the stories that he left his own part in some concertos blank, or the rush in which he wrote the overture to *Don Giovanni*. There could hardly have been such a concept as photographic memory before there was photography, but a photographic mind is what Mozart apparently had, at least when it came to music. It is their consistency which makes all these stories plausible, these as well as his supposed reconstruction of Allegri's *Miserere* or his reading of Bach's motets from parts.

A recent biography by Wolfgang Hildersheimer makes a good case for the fact that Mozart was less affected by those around him than we should like to believe.[45] When one's attention is drawn to the evidence, it is surprising how easily Mozart seems to have accepted the death of his mother and how preoccupied his letters to Nannerl are with the material legacy of his father, not with any emotional impact that the death may have had on him. Add to that the information that the first composition Mozart put down two days after his father died was *Ein musikalischer Spass* (KE 522), and one must suspect that he too was subject to the kind of egocentricity that is common among creative persons.

Mozart. According to Jahn, Constanze had not only supplied him with anecdotes and with some of Mozart's characteristics (supplemented by Nannerl), but had also lent him Mozart's letters. Why Rochlitz did not write a biography remains unexplained. When Jahn pursued the matter, trying to find out if there were materials that had been in Rochlitz' possession, he was dismayed to find not only that Rochlitz, whom he respected highly, had "colored" the stories he told with his own "personal paintbrush," but that many of his supposedly authenticated stories could not be verified. Nevertheless, those anecdotes and those of Schlichtegroll and Niemetschek make up a large part of the biographies of the early nineteenth century. That Jahn exaggerated Rochlitz's irresponsibility is shown by the fact that Rochlitz complained about Schlichtergrolls uncritical repetition of some stories.

45.   Wolfgang Hildesheimer, *Mozart* (Frankfurt a.M.: Suhrkamp, 1977).

Hildesheimer, too, selects from the available material what suits him. "The reception of the opera [*Figaro*] at its Vienna premiere was lukewarm to cool."[46] Hildesheimer has just given us the description of how Mozart looked and acted at rehearsal taken from Michael Kelly's autobiography.[47] But Kelly also reported a few pages later that the audience demanded that every number be encored, applauding and calling for Mozart. Kelly, says Hildesheimer, was the last eyewitness other than da Ponte still alive, then living in New York. Hildesheimer apparently did not look up the memoirs of da Ponte, available in any number of editions. "Meantime," reported da Ponte, "Mozart's opera was shown on the stage. . . . It was a success with the public while the sovereign and other real connoisseurs judged it a thing sublime, not to say divine."[48] One might suppose that Kelly's memoirs were written so long after the event that later successes on the London stage might have influenced his recollections and da Ponte's very large ego was involved as librettist. But why use one story and not the other? Da Ponte was perfectly capable of admitting, as he did several times, that other operas in which he collaborated had failed. One senses in da Ponte's memoirs that he saw his collaborator, Mozart, as his only intellectual equal. Hildesheimer is determined to depict Mozart as a tragic figure, and it is true that the success of *Figaro* in Vienna was not unequivocal. While the opera had relatively few performances, the eyewitness accounts testify that connoisseurs loved the opera. Vienna just did not have enough of them to sustain the success for long.

As has already been suggested, one of the reasons why Mozart anecdotes flourished was that the "bohemian" element in his life struck the early romantic imagination, much as the character of Don Juan had a secret charm for audiences of the time because in spite of all lip-service to conventional behavior and conventional morality one was ready to break out of the mold. Mozart's apparent indifference to anything but his art, his mismanagement of money, his

---

46.   Hildesheimer, *Mozart*, p. 199.
47.   Michael Kelly, *Reminiscences of Michael Kelly* (London, 1826). Reprinted with an introduction by Alexander Hyatt King (New York: Da Capo, 1968).
48.   Lorenzo da Ponte, *Memorie di Lorenzo da Ponte* (New York, 1823), *The Memoirs of Lorenzo da Ponte*, translated by Elizabeth Abbott, edited by Arthur Livingston (New York: Orion Press, 1959): 76.

reputedly casual household, even his early death are elements of what later in the nineteenth century was to become a stereotype. All that was lacking was a turbulent love-life (and here again we should note the apparent placidity with which Mozart bore rejection). In the earliest Mozart biographies there is some attempt to show him as more "normal" than he was; in later biographies both his music and his person are depicted as relatively serene, almost glacially perfect. When Jahn, for example, saw Mozart as the creator of perfect forms rather than emotional depth, he was responding to Mozart's structural conventionality and to his restraint. He was writing at a time in which every succeeding decade brought greater surface emotionalism and a greater widening of structural limitations.[49] Jahn, comparing Mozart's to the music of his day, had to see him as almost godlike in his perfection as well as in his detachment.

The recognition of Mozart's romantic appeal never became overt in his biographies; it is something the reader only senses. In contrast, the autobiography of Christian Friedrich Daniel Schubart (1731–91), who wrote his memoirs in prison, fits the later romantic stereotype of the artist perfectly.[50] Neither a great composer nor a great poet, Schubart lived as if he should have been both.

The adjectives for Schubart that come to mind are flamboyant, overwrought, sentimental, and hyperbolic, all terms for the ingredients of romanticism. But Schubart was too erratic to be anything so disciplined as a genuine romantic artist. Whatever native genius he may have possessed, and one comes to believe that he was probably very gifted, nothing jells into either a writer or a musician of impressive accomplishment. Writing late in life and often seeing the error of his ways, he never understood his basic flaw. Now sober and moralistic, now carried away by one of his outbursts of enthusiasm, insights and platitudes tumble all over each other. His style alternates between sober narrative and dactyllic hexameter; he addresses the reader the way Homer invoked the muse in German translations. Schubart tells us what he read, what he studied, what led him astray, brought him back, how he mistook lust for love, was ill-matched with his wife, how he admired German music ("still the best"), but was

---

49.   Otto Jahn, *W. A. Mozart.*
50.   Christian Friedrich Daniel Schubart, *Schubarts Leben und Gesin-nungen von ihm selbst im Kerker aufgesetzt* (Stuttgart: Gebrüder Mäntler, 1791).

temporarily corrupted by Alberti basses, how good he was at
theatrical sermons and how superficial; the whole is a hodgepodge in
which intelligence, charm, and honesty somehow survive.

Even when Schubart talks about the greatness of German music
one does not quite know what to make of it. He invokes Sebastian
and Emanuel Bach and Mozart, but also a host of lesser names and
lesser talents "Vogler, Ekart, Beeke, especially Mozardt [sic]"[51] while
he condemned Italians equally indiscriminately. "A keyboard player
serves himself badly if he chooses models the likes of Marchands,
Skarlattis [sic] or [Giuseppe] Jozzis. (Clementi is a powerful exception.)"[52]

Schubart recognized the value of anecdotes and complained that
autobiographers as well as biographers were reluctant to tell all of
the truth. "A judgment that does us no honor deems anecdotes petty
and unimportant although we love novels. Some biographies and
especially autobigraphies are written so fearfully that they tend to
suppress the very things that elevate a hero and give him his
individuality [*Selbstheit*]."[53]

Schubart related some Jomelli anecdotes and went on to discuss
Jomelli's accomplishment versus those of Hasse and Gluck. Naturally
a character as flamboyant as Schubart does not inspire trust in his
accounts. It is not that one suspects Schubart of telling falsehoods,
one suspects him of coloring his stories to make them more
dramatic. Thus when he reports that Charles Burney came to see
him, one goes to Burney with baited breath to see what the latter has
to say. Now things become interesting, since the two supplement
each other so well that one wishes all historical research meshed so
smoothly.

Having already had a checkered career as a student, poet, and
minister, Schubart had decided to lay down his ministry and devote
himself entirely to music. By the standards of the other biographies it
was late in life; when Burney visited him, it was 1770 and Schubart
was thirty-one years old. Burney describes him as a great virtuoso on
the organ and harpsichord, a man, furthermore, who realized that

---

51.   Ignaz von Beecke, 1733—1803; Johann Eckhard, 1735—1809, and
      Georg Joseph Vogler, 1749—1814.
52.   Louis Marchand, 1669—1732; Guiseppe Jozzi, c. 1720— ; and
      Domenico Scarlatti, 1685—1757.
53.   Schubart: 120f.

Dr. Burney's mission was of national (i.e., German) concern. Burney confirmed that Schubart was of the Bach school; "*but* [my italics] an enthusiast, an original in genius. Many of his pieces are printed in Holland; they are full of taste and fire. . . . His merit is but little known where he is at present planted: the common people think him mad, and the rest overlook him."[54]

Burney and Schubart communicated in Latin, since Schubart spoke neither French nor Italian, characteristic for one who was a musical and poetic nationalist. His Latin was so fluent, however, that Burney was amazed; "it was literally a living language in his hands." We need not go into the musical scene in Ludwigsburg, since both Burney and Schubart have done so. Instead we should pause over Schubart's report about Burney, since this is another of those forgotten sources to which to draw attention.

> Burney was looking for German music which he could certainly not find in Ludwigsburg. Music there was one of the most beautiful branches of the Italian tree. . . . I helped him get some idea of German dancing, . . . , and national [folk] song. I also played for him chorales and other things I knew had not been coated with an Italian or French veneer. But Burney travelled too quickly and made judgements too boldly and quickly. He is too superficial to teach us much of German, French or Italian music.[55]
>
> "I once said to an Englishman that I was surprised that his great nation had not produced its own great schools of music or art. 'For that we are not disorderly [*liederlich*] enough,' he replied with cold audacity. . . . Genius does tend toward disorderliness."[56]

Under Saxon law, Schubart tells us, musicians had no rights. He cannot blame the public for looking down on musicians who are self-indulgent and vain and devote their lives to whoring, allowing the applause of the public to drown out the voice of their conscience. Fortunately there are the likes of Emanuel Bach and Gluck to whom religion means something. "But you, German *Leiermann* take from

---

54. Charles Burney, *The Present State of Music in Germany, the Netherlands and United Provinces* (London, 1775); published in an edition of Percy Scholes, *An Eighteenth-Century Musical Tour in Central Europe and the Netherlands* (London: Oxford University Press, 1959), 2: 39.
55. Schubart, 1: 135f.
56. Ibid., 1: 136f.

Italians the good, leave them their macaroni and vices!"[57] It became
quite a preoccupation for Schubart who was writing in prison, this
whoring. "*Hominibus piis fornicator est* . . . , quoting from Gregory
of Nyssa in a passage too distasteful for him to translate.[58]

One of the curiosities of this age in which memoirs and biographies are beginning to flourish is the absence of early biographies
of Gluck. It could be that Gluck's life was not colorful enough for the
incipient romanticism with which succeeding generations viewed the
lives of great artists. As widely admired as Gluck was and as
prestigious as his position at court must have been, he lacked the
personal color for the subtly dramatic biography full of anecdotes,
picturesque encounters, and tragic misunderstanding. Like Haydn,
Gluck fought his way to success over considerable obstacles. Once
there, however, it was a steady climb to recognition and wealth, with
the drama strictly limited to the Parisian controversy over his type of
opera and the Italian, a drama in which Gluck himself seems to have
maintained an Olympian detachment. The first book about him,
Leblond's *Mémoires pour servir à l'histoire de la révolution opérée*, is
characteristically a collection of letters and articles published in the
Parisian press pro and con opera reform. When it was translated into
German in 1822 a perfunctory two-page biography was added, but
for a time Gluck's life continued to be ignored.[59]

Anthony van Hoboken puts it very succinctly when he says,
"anyone who reads a Haydn biography of some scope will soon
notice that the greater part of the book is not about Haydn himself.
. . . The recounting of Haydn's life is the smallest portion of these
biographies — and these portions turn out to be seventy five percent
anecdotal."[60]

The first biographies of Haydn are contradictory and incomplete
with anecdotes variously embroidered to make an essentially straightforward life more colorful. (Whatever factual problems Mozart

---

57.   Ibid., 1: 155.
58.   Ibid., 1: 154ff.
59.   Gaspar-Michel Leblond, *Mémoires pour servir à l'histoire de la
      révolution opérée dans la musique par M. le Chévalier Gluck* (Naples
      and Paris, 1781); an unacknowleged German translation by a J. G.
      Siegmeister is entitled, *Ueber den Ritter Gluck und seine Werke* (Berlin:
      Voss'sche Buchhandlung, 1822); the second edition, the only one I
      have seen, has the "Berufsbiographie." It appeared in 1837.
60.   Van Hoboken, "Discrepancies": 1.

biographers left us, the story of his life was treated with a fair degree of consistency.) Not that Haydn's music was unappreciated; he was without question the most esteemed composer in northern Europe in the period that embraced the last thirty years of his life. It was his personality that did not impress his contemporaries as superhuman. It is difficult for us to realize that not only Vienna, but also the rest of continental Europe was teeming with musicians, virtuosos who wrote their own works, opera directors who made their own operas, and *Kapellmeister* who were composers, even gifted amateurs who sometimes were very good or fancied themselves as good as anybody else. There never has been a period with as much musical activity as that from the last decade of the eighteenth century until toward the end of the nineteenth. Haydn was recognized as the best, the greatest among the living musicians of part of that period but, when all is said and done, he was just the first among many.

Nothing gives us a better picture of that situation than the memoirs of Ludwig or Louis Spohr, a virtuoso, a good composer, and a man so rational and objective that his diaries are the most graphic and comprehensive record of his era that exists.[61] One can hardly say that his memoirs, unlike his music, have been neglected (the several editions and translations that have been published over the years testify to that), but neither has his thick book been fully appreciated in all of its implications. Perhaps we are put off by Spohr's lack of appreciation for the works of Beethoven after 1815. We want our sources to share our tastes, but a Spohr must be accepted on his own terms; he has a lot to teach us.

What Spohr reported about Beethoven is very interesting even if, because of his own conservatism, he could not understand the middle and late works at all. Spohr thought that Beethoven's loss of hearing combined with his determination to be original made his later works virtually incomprehensible, though his opinion, he admitted, was not shared by all. Spohr loved the early works and had introduced the Quartets, op. 18, in several places where his "accompanists" were not always able to read them at sight and where the works were not always well received.

---

61.   Louis Spohr, *Lebenserinnerungen*, originally published as *Selbstbiographie* (Kassel and Göttingen, 1860–61); first unabridged edition based on autograph sources edited by Folker Göthel (Tutzing: Schneider, 1968).

With all his lack of sympathy for Beethoven's idiosyncracies, however, his criticism is that of a knowledgeable musician. He found, for example, the first theme of the *Symphony No. 5* not dignified enough for a symphony although it lent itself well to development. "The Adagio [sic] is very beautiful in part but the same passages and modulations are repeated too often and become tiresome in spite of their ever richer figuations. The Scherzo is highly original and truly romantič, but the rumbling bass of the Trio is too baroque for my taste." [62]

Spohr's *Lebenserinnerungen* ought perhaps to be dealt with at greater length; he clearly is no longer of the generation of Mozart, Haydn, and Gyrowetz. But he completed the first part of his memoirs in 1839, actually earlier than Gyrowetz, and they constitute what is still essentially a *Berufsbiographie* in the tradition of Quantz and Gyrowetz, i.e., not narrow and unobservant, but nonetheless extrospective rather than inner-directed. Spohr's is the professional biography to end all professional biographies. In his usage "*Kunst*" still meant basically "craft." Musicians had their pride — a good deal of it, in fact — but it was a pride in their competence not their vision or genius. He was right to see Beethoven as someone trying to be original and, of course, he was bound to disapprove.

Until Cherubini came along, Mozart was Spohr's only operatic idol, and he was quite annoyed at the composer Zingarelli in Italy who thought that Mozart might have become a good operatic composer had he lived long enough, just as he was furious that the *Zauberflöte* had become a travesty entitled *Les Mystères d'Isis* in Paris. He was everywhere, saw everything, reported on everything, and in spite of numerous minor errors of date and time, he is reliable because he kept a detailed diary. His memoirs are not the idealized recollections of an aging man. His report on Beethoven's conducting is reliable because Spohr himself was an innovator as a conductor and because he played under Beethoven. His report on Beethoven as a person is probably more accurate than those of some sycophantic early biographers who were after all just cashing in on their association with the master. While he could not grasp Beethoven's later works, Spohr always retained his respect for him.

The editor of Spohr's *Lebenserinnerungen*, who has done a superb job of detailed annotation, strongly rejects the term *Biedermeier* for

---

62.   Ibid.: 203.

Spohr's musical style. But Spohr was a smug member of a middle-class musical world, comfortable with himself, with his surrounding, with the wealthy merchants who sponsored music and the aristocracy, not a battler for causes or a critic of conventions, certainly no Berlioz. While he died only ten years earlier than Berlioz, the two lived worlds apart. When Spohr was in Paris, Berlioz was still a nobody. Later, when Berlioz traveled in Germany in 1841, he passed through Kassel where Spohr was then director of music. It was seven in the morning, "Spohr was still asleep."[63] There was no reason for Berlioz to wait for him to wake up; Spohr was quite irrelevant.

When all is said and done, there remains no question that Baini's biography of Palestrina is the first scholarly biography of the nineteenth century, making it the first scholarly biography ever.[64] This does not mean committing the besetting sin of the historian, that of finding historical landmarks at all costs, but it is safe to assign due credit to Baini without fear either of contradiction or of the future discovery of an earlier landmark. Baini, of course, had no intention of being a reformer. To judge by his preface, he accepted most of the standard biographies that preceded his, mentioning those of Benedetto Marcello, Haydn, Hasse, and Handel as examples with which he was familiar.[65] If he intended to be a pioneer, it was only with respect to Palestrina whom he wanted to bring to the world's attention. In Baini's opinion, Palestrina was the greatest musician of all time. Angeloni's biography of Guido would have been the first to deserve being called scholarly had Angeloni been a less naïve historian. But Baini ignored Guido's in his list of other biographies as well as in his historical summary of early music where he barely mentions him in passing.

There is no way to write about a composer of the distant past

---

63.   Hector Berlioz, *Mémoires de Hector Berlioz* (Paris, 1870), translated and edited by David Cairns, *The Memoirs of Hector Berlioz* (London: Gollanez, 1969): 347.

64.   Baini, *Palestrina.* See note 5.

65.   Giovenale Sacchi, *Vita di Benedetto Marcello* (Venice: Zatta, 1789) a translation from the Latin of Francesco Fontana (Pisa: 1787). Giuseppe Carpani, *Le Haydine.* John Mainwaring, *Memoirs of the Late George Frederick Handel* (London: R. and J. Dodsley, 1760). Franz Sales Kandler, *Cenni storico-critico intorno . . . del celebre compositore Giuseppe Adolfo Hasse* (Venice: Picotti, 1820).

without research. Except for Angeloni who had freely exploited the
archives of Parisian libraries, Baini for the first time in the history of
biography depended exclusively on old musical scores and old
documents. Unlike most other biographers who had written the
stories of living or recently deceased musicians he could not rely on
anecdotes and personal recollections. Even Forkel's *Bach* still depended on the testimony of Bach's sons, and Forkel made no effort
to unearth either documents or the music not already available to
him. Since Baini wanted to show Palestrina in the proper perspective
as the greatest musician among many, he also investigated the music
of other composers, predecessors as well as contemporaries of
Palestrina, with the result that his biography is the first in a long line
placing their subject in a context from which one can deduce their
achievement and their stature. Like Forkel before him and Spitta
later still lauding German music, Baini was also a nationalist
testifying to the glory of Italian music. Given this bias, the limited
accuracy of available facts, and the absence of even one biographical
model, Baini's work is a monument of the kind. Had he had a less
intuitive understanding of the historian's job, the need to document
and to demonstrate assertions, scholarly biography would have
begun later.

The appearance of Baini's *Palestrina* caused no stir, no editorials
calling on scholars to take him as a model, no immediate flood of
other such biographies. That it was in Italian was reason enough,
since the focal point of interest in history still lay in the northern
countries. The German scholar, Carl von Winterfeld, took exception
to some of Baini's assertions and wrote a kind of counter-biography,
while Franz Sales Kandler, who had previously produced only his
unremarkable biography of Hasse, made Baini's *Palestrina* into an
"improved" German version with corrections, additions, and cuts
that turned the "typically Italian effusion" into a book half as long as
the original mainly by keeping to the facts. Kandler died before his
adaptation was published, and so Baini went through another process
of editing at the hands of Kiesewetter who added still more footnotes
and corrections.[66] Baini's original accomplishment notwithstanding,
scholarly hindsight improved his work so considerably that the
German version is one of the best such books in the field of musical

---

66.   Franz Sales Kandler, *Palestrina*. See note 13.

historiography although modern scholars of Palestrina and the late Renaissance seem to use only the Italian original.

What recognition Baini did receive from his contemporaries paid tribute to him as a historian rather than biographer. While German scholars carped at his Italian bias and his errors, the critic and journalist Friedrich Rochlitz, an early popularizer of musical history, acknowledged that he owed Baini as great a debt as he owed Burney, Hawkins, and Forkel.[67] And Fétis praised Baini lavishly for his uncovering of sources, the very sources among which Baini had spent his life.[68]

Baini was not, however, the first digger among these sources. A number of his footnotes cite Pitoni. It was Kandler rather than Baini, however, who gave Pitoni (1657—1743) his due, not only by means of a longer reference, but also by culling from his manuscript the names of numerous musicians for inclusion in future editions of Gerber's *Lexikon*.[69] The not-quite-forgotten Giuseppe Ottavio Pitoni was a composer of many works as well as an amateur researcher who is now being rediscovered.[70] Presumably Pitoni compiled his manuscript, "Notizia de' contrappuntisti e compositori di musica dall'anno 1000 alla 1700," merely as an avocation, since he gave not the slightest hint that he hoped to publish the work. There is no preface, no list of sources, no explanation of methods, none of the usual apparatus which authors generally present to the reader.[71] One can see that in addition to manuscripts and early printed music he also used theoretical works and culled from them such composers and their works as they contained although he never made clear

67.   Friedrich Rochlitz, "Grundlinien zu einer Geschichte der Gesangmusik für Kirche und Kammer in Deutschland und Italien während der letzen drei Jahrhunderte," *Für Freunde der Tonkunst*, 4 vols. (Leipzig: Cnobloch, 1824—32), 3: 1ff.

68.   Francois Joseph Fétis, *Biographie universelle*, articles on Baini and Palestrina.

69.   Specifically for new editions of Ernst Ludwig Gerber's *Neues historischem-biographisches Lexikon*.

70.   See Siegfried Gmeinwieser, *Giuseppe Ottavio Pitoni: thematisches Werkverzeichnis*, Sacri concentus 2, (Wilhelmshaven: 1976). Professor Othmar Wesseley informs me that he plans to publish Pitoni's *Notizia de' contrapuntisti* in the near future.

71.   Giuseppe Ottavio Pitoni, "Notizia de' contrappuntisti e compositori di musica dall'anno 1000 alla 1700" (Ms. Biblioteca Apostolica Vaticana).

what his methods were. At the time he compiled his manuscript, a sort of primitive biobibliographical dictionary, in the decade between 1730 and 1740, there was absolutely no precedent for such a work and probably so little hope of publication that the possibility may never have occurred to Pitoni. He divided his list of composers and their works into periods, the first few hundred years into centuries, later, when names proliferate, into periods of fifty years. Some rough periodization was absolutely necessary, since in many cases Pitoni had no precise dates. Sometimes he listed only a name, more often he knew some works, sometimes many, and in many cases he gave short biographies. Since he was no linguist, he took names and titles as they came, perhaps helpfully, since it enables us to relate his musicians to the sources in which he must have found them. Often it is also amusing. My favorite name is Andrea Ornito Parcho for Ornithoparchus, and the title "Dunch auler amer" is not likely to lead one to "Dungh aultre amer," no matter how one pronounced it.

The first signs of historicism arose late in the eighteenth century and Pitoni was probably too early to be part of the trend. Historicism grew prevalent as social institutions became shaky and finally toppled. It probably arose along with the search for explanations and precedents as well as nostalgia for "simpler" times, as the German romantics made quite clear. The writers who coined the term "romantic" explained that they were looking to the Middle Ages for their material and their models, since modern times were too disturbed to suit them for settings of their novels. Musicians were technically not bound by such considerations, but the general interest in the past and its revival affected them as well. Baini might have done his work in any case, since he was motivated primarily by the love of Palestrina's music. In the next ten years, however, the trend became clear with the appearance of such works as Kiesewetter's *Guido of Arezzo*, Winterfeld's *Johannes Gabrieli und sein Zeitalter*, as well as Rochlitz's popularization.[72] From the biographical perspective, they culminated in François-Joseph Fétis' *Biographie universelle*, the first volume of which appeared in 1835.[73] While Winterfeld's *Gabrieli* is often referred to as a classic of biography, it is not a

---

72.   Raphael Georg Kiesewetter, *Guido von Arezzo sein Leben und Wirken* (Leipzig: Breitkopf und Härtel, 1840); Carl von Winterfeld, *Johannes Gabrieli und sein Zeitalter* (Berlin: Schlesinger, 1834).
73.   See above, note 7.

biography at all. In a highly stylized combination of scholarly research with romantic writing, it is a history of music in Venice from the time of Willaert to the first half of the seventeenth century. True, the work contains a short biography of Gabrieli which is its focal point although Gabrieli is not as central as the title implies. All those who cite it as a "life of Gabrieli" have simply not read it.

First to point this out was Fétis whose article on Gabrieli took von Winterfeld to task for not having stuck to his subject. Fétis is not notable for his consistency. It was he who had reprimanded historians for not giving their readers an overview of history. When someone actually did so and lived up to the title of his book, Fétis complained.

The *Biographie universelle* is not usually considered in the context of musical histories, an oversight against which Fétis already protested in the preface to the second edition of his magnum opus. He disowned the appellation "compiler," insisting that he was no more a compiler than other researchers; he was a true historian whose particular function it was to make the work of other historians that much easier. In fact, in the preface to the second edition of his encyclopedia he had become totally exasperated with historians who, he wrote, mistook musical archaeology — the digging up of artifacts — for history. His exasperation was the result of disappointment. Thirty years before, in the preface to the first edition, he had said that he had gone on with his tedious work, five to six hours daily, year after year for fifteen years, in order to make it possible for other historians not to get bogged down in detail. He wanted them to focus on the larger picture even then. There was also a practical reason for his disgruntlement. When he sent the manuscript of *Biographie universelle* to the appropriate agency in the government hoping to obtain a subsidy in the form of printing at government expense, he had received compliments, even homage, but no help. The committee recognized his achievement but felt his work was not a proper history and therefore not eligible for assistance. Fétis was as deeply offended by this official rebuff as Berlioz on different grounds, especially since he was also at work on a narrative history. (We who sympathize with Berlioz and his trouble with officaldom might give a few seconds of silent commiseration to a mere historian.)

Between the first and second editions of his *Biographie universelle*, Fétis developed a theory of history that was relatively sophisticated. He rejected the idea of absolute progress in the arts even though he thought that progress was real enough in the sciences and technology.

Music had progressed merely in its materials, not in content, in fact, what some considered progress was really decadence. In his own day, for example, the "mania for development" produced only boredom and distaste; somehow composers had lost their perspective. Music had begun among the people until eventually their creativity weakened and dried up. It was at that point that individual genius asserted itself and took command. So far this appears to be a progressive view. But it must have been clear to Fétis that a progressive view could not be reconciled with his distaste for much contemporary music. However innovation might extend the means of composition and performance, in the long run it was the expression of feeling that mattered. In its essentials music never becomes dated. Those who claimed that they could no longer listen to anything but Rossini would never understand the beauty of all genres of all times. The basic aim of music was, after all, to touch the emotions and to move the soul.[74]

Fétis arrived not at some sort of cultural relativism, he formulated a biological theory. Styles grow, reach maturity, and then decline and die. Modulation, for example, had reached perfection in the music of Mozart, while the use of excessively distant keys as well as the frequent and abrupt shifts of tonality in recent music was getting further and further away from the perfection of the past. If music continued in this way, in fact, tonality would die.

We think we know some of the composers at whom he was pointing a finger although one has to read both editions of his dictionary to find confirmation. His article on Berlioz in the first edition which appeared in 1835 is a veritable blast at the young man. "Des effets, toujours des effets!" His melodies lack meter and rhythm and his harmony, "assemblage bizarre de son," does not always deserve to be called harmony. He went on to say that his opinion was shared by many although by no means all musicians; he did not wish to give his opinion more authority than was warranted. Some, especially young people, liked the very things that offended him. Most of Berlioz' admirers, wrote Fétis, were painters and writers, however, generally people who did not know much about music.

In the second edition this strong language was softened except for a statement that the *Damnation of Faust* was a "bizarre" departure from Goethe's intentions and failed when it was presented to an

---

74.   Fétis, Preface to the first edition of *Biographie universelle*, p. xxxiv.

audience of common people rather than intellectuals. By then, either because Berlioz had gained in status or, less plausibly, because Fétis himself had come to like his work, did the latter treat him more discretely. Some disdain still reared its head in his calling Berlioz a brilliant propagandist for his own cause.

In the article on Wagner in the second edition, that composer was treated with kid-gloves as well. Again one senses in what is not said that Fétis disapproved; the article gives far more space to Wagner's ideas than to his music. *Tristan* is listed among the works but nothing is said about it. Perhaps Fétis had not seen a score but in any case he chose not to cope with this extreme of modulatory music. What he really thought can be found in his article on Liszt in which he reported Liszt's very practical support of Wagner. In reporting performances of *Tannhäuser* and *Lohengrin* sponsored by Liszt, he called these operas bizarre also; bizarre was apparently one of his favorite adjectives.

In the first edition, Fétis called Schumann an original composer and distinguished critic whose approximately forty works were marked by great originality which however sometimes sank to the level of mere *bizarrerie*. In the second edition Schumann had dropped in Fétis' esteem as a journalist and esthetician as well as composer. His works for piano were dismissed as charming, the first orchestral works showed a lack of training while the later ones were redolent of the composer's incipient madness. If Schumann had still been alive he might have taken comfort in what Fétis said about late Beethoven whom he had earlier revered as a "force of nature." In the last works, however, Fétis wrote that Beethoven made up for his lack of creativity with complexity. At that point Fétis was no longer an admirer.

Schubert proved himself a genius in his "ballades et chansons." As a composer of *Lieder* he had many imitators but no rivals. (This in 1840!) Each of his little compositions is a complete drama. Yet his other works, especially the quartets, have not quite the same "cachet."

When one reads such criticism, one can only wonder if Fétis really had as much knowledge of the music he talked about as he implied. To say that all of Schubert's songs were little dramas seems to be based solely on "Erlkönig" or perhaps "Gretchen am Spinnrad"; it cannot be said of all of the songs. That Fétis was always so ready with a generalization makes one wary in retrospect.

The suspicion that there was a certain degree of charlatanism in

Fétis' character, that learned though he was, he had to pretend to
even greater learning, was first raised by August Wilhelm Ambros in
his obituary of the great scholar.[75] Ambros claimed that Fétis was
not a reactionary despite his disapproval of Mendelssohn, Schumann,
and Berlioz. The futurists of the fifties, Ambros wrote, may have
hated Fétis but in France his name carried such authority that Fétis
finally began to think of himself as a "musical Dalai-Lama." In the
contest sponsored by the Koninglijk-Nederlandsche Institut van
Wetenschappen, Letterkunde en Schoone Kunsten for an essay
about the contributions of the Netherlanders to the development of
music, Fétis had been beaten by Kiesewetter who won first prize.
Fétis never lived down his resentment of Kiesewetter and the two
became involved in numerous bitter controversies, but Ambros, who
should know, says that the two were the only musical scholars in
Europe who could even qualify to compete, the possible third having
been Baini had he not been so preoccupied with the glory of
Palestrina and only Palestrina. Ambros pointed out that Fétis was
willing to invent citations from sources in order to win an argument
and that although no single scholar could personally examine every
document there was, Fétis pretended that he had. With all these
foibles, however, Ambros, still respected Fétis' accomplishments
almost as much as Fétis had been respected in France.

   It was certainly not orthodox for a compiler of a dictionary even
in early times to have critical opinions on nearly everyone. The usual
policy to which modern dictionaries still adhere is guided by the
implication that having been included is value-judgment enough. The
customary way to deal with strong opinions is to use adjectives such
as great, important, or major, for positive reinforcement and just to
give the facts if an artist must be included even though the compiler
may not like him. Naïve as they may have been, Fétis' predecessors
had understood this. Such compilations as Mattheson's *Ehrenpforte*
carried the approbation of the title which covered even the least
among his subjects.[76] The same is true for *Le Parnasse françois*.[77]
Walther had observed the unwritten rule as did Gerber.[78] As a

---

75.   August Wilhelm Ambros, "Fétis," *Bunte Blätter* (Leipzig: Leuchart,
      1872): 141ff.
76.   Johann Matthesohn, *Musikalische Ehrenpforte*.
77.   Titon du Tillet, *Le Parnasse françois*. Johann Gottfried Walther,
      Musikalisches Lexikon.
78.   In both editions of his *Historisch-biographisches Lexikon*.

result, such biographical dictionaries are usually rather bland. Fétis may have been something of a charlatan and much too opinionated to be a true lexicographer, but he was certainly never bland. "Usually," he wrote, "biographers follow Voltaire's maxim that we owe the living respect, the dead only the truth." As far as he, Fétis, was concerned, we owed everyone the truth, the truth in any case, as Fétis saw it.

The second edition of *Biographie universelle* is still on the reference shelves of every self-respecting scholarly library along with Eitner.[79] We use both primarily to retrace the fate of forgotten composers or missing sources. Since Eitner incorporated so much of Fétis, putting it through the sieve of his German sobriety in the process, most scholars resort to Fétis only when Eitner fails them. One should like to see this trend reversed, or if not reversed, Fétis should at least be consulted for his own sake. Not only was Fétis a true pioneer of modern collective biography, but his entries have a sense of immediacy that Eitner can no longer recapture. The events leading to the recovery of Guillaume de Machaut, for example, represent a part of history in which Fétis had a share. Reading his account under the entries for Machaut as well as Machaut's forgotten rediscoverer, François-Louis Perne, gives us the feeling of being participants. True, Eitner was more accurate and less inclined to make snap-judgments, but his subtle disdain for the flamboyant Belgian is sufficiently apparent to have prejudiced several generations of scholars against the latter.

Anyone interested in the history of biographical lexicography naturally turns to Eitner's and Fétis' prefaces, assuming that both would begin with a survey of the biographical literature of the past. Surprisingly, neither does although it is encouraging that there is a catalogue of the books Fétis' heirs sold to the Royal Library at Brussels.[80] But while this catalogue is comprehensive enough, it lacks the highlighting and evaluation of a critical bibliography. The preface to the less readily available first edition of *Biographie universelle*

79. Robert Eitner, *Biographisch-biblioqraphisches Quellenlexikon der Musiker und Musikgelehrten der christlichen Zeitrechnung bis zur Mitte des 19. Jahrhunderts*, 10 vols. (Leipzig: Breitkopf und Härtel, 1899—1904).
80. *Catalogue de la bibliothèque de F. J. Fétis* (Brussels: C. Muquardt, 1877).

does discuss all the standard sources as well as many obscure ones. Fétis' evaluations generally agree with those of this writer, even if this writer's point of view is a culturographical one rather than lexicographical. While this raises one's confidence in Fétis' good sense, it is even more interesting to find him listing sources that are no longer widely known. Several of them are manuscripts which survive in the Bibliothêque Royal Albert Ier. along with the other works from Fétis' collection.[81] Two seemingly extraordinary compilations were burnt in the fire that destroyed the Bibliothêque de la Ville of Paris in 1871, although much of their contents survives in the *Biographie universelle*, itself a document we cannot continue to treat cavalierly. The original preface inexplicably dropped in the second edition in favor of a long discussion of Guido of Arezzo should somehow be restored to the literature about biography and history.

---

81.   One of them by an unknown author is "Histoire complète de l'académie royale de Musique . . . depuis son établissement en l'année 1669 jusques et compris l'année 1758." Another is entitled "Mémoires pour servir à l'histoire de l'Académie Royale de Musique." These manuscripts are now in the Bibliothèque Royale Albert Ier. at Brussels.

CHAPTER VII
THE COMPOSER AS ROMANTIC HERO

When Hermann Abert spoke of a golden age of biography, presumably the last third of the nineteenth century, he must have had in mind more than the great achievements of Otto Jahn, Philipp Spitta, and Friedrich Chrysander. He probably included the general interest in biography that had come to dominate popular as well as scholarly writing about music. As a trend it was the logical outcome of a new attitude toward artists who had become the agents of progress. Once this view was in the air, it was only logical that the educated public should seize on it as the preferred way to humanize musical history; it was a way to make interesting otherwise dry chronological narratives in which composers were more or less incidental. In general, curiosity about personality had begun to flourish ever since the appearance of the first romantic novels at the end of the eighteenth century. The novel had changed from the picaresque to an emphasis on inner development. Where once heroes had established their heroism by great deeds in literal confrontations between good and evil, daring and renunciation became internalized in the new *Bildungsroman* which led the protagonist by way of moral dilemma from callow youth to full personhood. In fiction and reality the artistic genius was a ready-made protagonist who had to choose between integrity and wealth, great achievement on his own terms, or sacrifice and renunciation. While there were not very many novels that had composers as their hero in the early nineteenth century, real composers, living as well as dead, could be substituted for the idealized personas in romantic biographies.

A new reality had a great deal to do with this new image, since real artists once securely in the employ of church or aristocracy now had to establish themselves in a competitive world. But even the employed artist of earlier times came to be seen as put upon by those to whom he had to appeal, be they the Archbishop Colloredo of Salzburg or the church-fathers of Leipzig.

The position of the composer between about 1730 and 1820 had already begun to be less certain depending on the place in which he functioned. Such early free-lance composers as Handel, Haydn, Mozart, and even Beethoven occupied dubious social spheres. While Mozart probably considered himself unemployed rather than free, and was constantly seeking stable positions (in which he probably could not have functioned), Beethoven had the best of both worlds, a stipend as well as popular success for the most part. For a long time after him most composers had to function as performers to support themselves either as virtuosos or conductors of operas and orchestras. It was rare that publishing music and getting it performed paid sufficiently well to support anyone even in a modest middle-class style.

This despite the fact that the market for music was increasing rapidly. At the same time the new public was becoming divided into high- and middle-brow consumers. Up to about 1830 the musical audience appears to have been relatively homogeneous. The aristocratic and middle-class public *of the era* must have had its share of Philistines, but it knew what it *ought* to like. The effects of the Revolution and the rising industrialization of Europe broadened musical literacy. Such a broadening, however, did not produce a high-minded public exclusively. Instead a large part of the public preferred what is now called *Unterhaltungsmusik*. This music, not technically distinguishable from high-minded compositions, made up a large part of the new repertoire, especially for amateurs, a large part of the new mass of consumers.[1] Where once the middle classes

---

1.   See the essays in *Studien zur Trivialmusik des 19. Jahrhunderts*, edited by Carl Dahlhaus, Studien zur Musikgeschichte des 19. Jahrhunderts, 8 (Regensburg: Bosse, 1967), especially the contribution of Monika Lichtenfeld, "Triviale und anspruchsvolle Musik in den Konzerten um 1850." A term that is better than either our "popular music" or the "*Trivialmusik*" of the title is another German noun, "*Unterhaltungsmusik*." It connotes neither any derogation as does *trivial*, nor the separate category of the English "popular music." Irmgard Keldany-Mohr, "*Unterhaltungsmusik*" *als soziokulturelles Phänomen des 19. Jahrhunderts*. Studien zur Musikgeschichte des 19. Jahrhunderts 47 (Regensburg: Bosse, 1977).

had imitated the aristocracy, the public now assumed that its taste was as good as anyone's. Certainly a great deal of snobbery must still have prevailed, but more and more people put their money where their preference lay. This becomes obvious in the musical life of Paris in the eighteen hundreds. The artist, on his part, faced a new tyranny, that of a public at least as capricious as even the most coldhearted patron. The very trend that had elevated the artist as individual made it possible to question authority; in fact the opposition to authority grew to be an essential part of the heroic personality.

To what an extent the change in the public's view of him quickly became part of the artist's self-image is fascinating to trace. Quite likely, most composers of earlier times accepted their lot, took it for granted, and only when economic opportunity made rebellion possible do we find rebellious personalities becoming more common. Collectively speaking, biographers tended to gloss over such benevolent patrons as the Princes Esterhazy, and to some extent they still do. Mozart's appointment at court is still seen rather negatively even though his salary of eight hundred guilders was approximately the same as that of Salieri, and Mozart's duties were virtually non-existent.[2]

The fact is that a fixed income must have been comfortable even if it forced the recipient to cater to the whims or prejudices of his employer. The aging Haydn had the ideal position when he retired with a pension; he could risk free-lancing as much as he wanted. The facts that his popularity was assured in any case and that he was not a rebellious man are relevant only because the nineteenth century tended to dismiss artists like Haydn as not quite serious.

But if the artist was now a public hero in the abstract, i.e., as a historical or fictitious person depicted as talented, original, willing to risk poverty and disapproval in order to follow his destiny, it was an image not necessarily reconcilable with practice. When such a figure appeared in its midst, the same public, so sentimental over its heroes, was as likely as not to condemn him as arrogant, indifferent to their good taste, and incomprehensible. The benefits of the new stereotype did not really become apparent until in our century the public reached a point where it could be shamed into at least tolerating the

---

2.   Mary Sue Morrow, Concert Life in Vienna, 1780—1810, Ph.D. dissertation, Indiana University, 1984.

avant-garde. Having been told over and over for more than a hundred years that great art is always misunderstood at first, the individual member of the disdainful public found himself resembling a historical caricature.

The artist as iconoclast, supposedly not caring one whit about approval, is now typical. He is eccentric, wild, poor, rebellious, a figure, however theoretical, bathed in an aura that places him above conventional standards even of morality. He is given a name, he is a "bohemian," a term once meaning "gipsy" that came into new usage in about 1848, according to the *Oxford English Dictionary*. An English literary critic described both the era and the individual artist as follows:

> [these were] times of angry enthusiasm and of wild revolt; [with] ecstatic emphasis laid upon the freedom, the spontaneity, and the originality of the creative genius. The attribution to that genius of miraculous and daemonic powers, invested the cult of genius and the worship of originality with an exaggerated and mystical importance. ... The new conception of the artist as genius, as a creature of passion and fire, above the law, and the popular deification of this ideal tended to produce the beings thus imagined and adored.[3]

In the biographies and biographical dictionaries of the eighteenth century the term genius never occurs. That word along with various adjectives appears with any regularity only in Gerber's *Lexikon* of the 1790s. Early journals reviewing new music did recognize the superiority of such composers as Haydn and Mozart, but they clearly regarded their works as the products of excellent craftsmen rather than of men of original genius.

It is now difficult for us to accept the fact that music was once a commodity provided at several levels of craftsmanship, but early reviewers treated it as such, catering to the growing number of amateurs who needed to know what was worth buying and what was not, as well as how difficult it was. Throughout the early nineteenth century publishers were still inclined to accept or reject music on the basis of its marketability even if they respected the genius of its creator. The firm of Schott made quite clear in its correspondence with Schubert in 1828 that it likened him to Beethoven in esteem,

---

3. Logan Pearsall Smith, *Four Words, Romantic, Originality, Creative, Genius*, Society for Pure English, Tract 17 (Oxford, 1924): 36.

but it did not let that esteem affect the belief that for the moment his Piano Trio in B flat (D. 898) was unacceptable. There were already too many trios in their catalogue.[4]

Nor had early composers themselves assumed that it was their mission to subjugate the prevailing musical idiom and make it into a personal language although they could not always help but be original. In most music before the end of the eighteenth century, current taste dictated the product. Innovation was not so much the result of pioneering by outstanding individuals as it was, say, of new systems of notation, national cross-pollination, or the development of new instruments. If we take as our example the most drastic change of style of all — until our century, that is — the *stile nuovo* of circa 1600, we can see that it was singularly devoid of an overpowering agitator or a conspiracy. The paradoxical result of a desire to revive a glorious past, that revolution was brought about by reasonable men with very practical ideas. That expressiveness was one of their goals does not alter the picture, since their desire to be expressive is quite different from that of the nineteenth century. It was an extroverted, a theatrical expressiveness that was sought, not the yearning of creative artists to convey their own inmost feelings. Until the nineteenth century it there remained part of the composer's craft to be able to convey emotion via music, not a matter of individuality. That their music is distinguishable from that of others did not result from *wanting* to be different; it was inherent in one's abilities. It might even be concluded from, say, the literally thousands of symphonies and concertos following well-established formulas in the eighteenth century, that artists took pride in their mastery of formulas, the mastering of sameness.

The first composer who was conscious of creating works the meaning of which went beyond music seems to have been Beethoven. His listeners also heard his powerful personality and accepted him as a new kind of artist, at least until his idiosyncracies went beyond their ability to follow. Then, for a while, they felt that originality had gone too far.

In the second quarter of the nineteenth century the subjectivism of the late works of Beethoven came to be the ideal and originality the inevitable criterion distinguishing one artist from another. It was then

---

4.   See Otto Erich Deutsch, *Schubert, A Documentary Biography*, trans. by Eric Blom (London: J. M. Dent, 1947): 736f and 817f.

that originality became the means by which musical art progressed. Toward the middle of the century the idea of progress had become so entrenched that a theorist such as Adolph Bernard Marx only questions the direction progress ought to take.[5]

As the century drew to a close, one revolution followed another as each artist found his own language, while critics and theorists debated the historical merit of every new development and audiences often squirmed in their seats. It was taken for granted that art must always renew itself by new means, a view based at least in part on ignorance of those non-Western societies in which new work is always possible in very old traditions, where art is a sort of divine game the rules of which never change.

While the subjectivism of early-nineteenth-century artists may briefly have remained below the conscious surface, it soon emerged as an ideal and subsequently spread very rapidly. As early as 1835 Liszt wrote to George Sand that the artist was a tragic figure, isolated from society and destined to pursue his own course without regard to fashion.[6] In the 1870s the professional biographer la Mara wrote of the consequences in her biography of Brahms,

> Since modern subjectivism came to music and individualism demanded recognition in art, relativity has replaced the absolute in beauty. Universal ideals· have been pushed aside by personal ones. The modern artist demands to be understood for himself.

Inevitably art was now controversial.

> The more individualistic and special a work of art, the narrower the circle of those who can empathize with its content of feeling and the more multifarious its opposition.[7]

---

5.   Adolph Bernhard Marx, *Die Musik des 19. Jahrhunderts und ihre Pflege* (Leipzig, 1855), published in English as *The Music of the Nineteenth Century* (London: Cocks & Co., 1855).
6.   The letter was published under the title, "Reisebriefe eines Baccalaureus der Tonkunst," in Franz Liszt, *Gesammelte Schriften*, vol. 4, ed. by Julius Kapp (Leipzig: Brietkopf und Härtel, 1910): 13ff. The letter appeared originally in the *Revue et gazette musicale* in 1835.
7.   La Mara's biographies appeared separately in so many editions that it is difficult to give valid citations for them. Collectively they appeared as *Musikalische Studienköpfe*, 5 vols., between 1868 and 1882 with a second edition (Leipzig: Breitkopf und Härtel, 1883).

La Mara is of special interest to the historian of biography and the student of trends, because she knew personally or corresponded with those whose lives she described. But even more valuable for *Rezeptionsgeschichte* is the fact that she wrote for the educated middle-class, the same class that accepted or rejected the composers who were her subjects. Her popularizations made no concession except in being non-technical although her own musical training as well as that of her audience should have allowed her to be at least somewhat analytical. La Mara's elegant clear prose only occasionally lapsed into the sentimental hyperbole not uncommon to her age.

However widely read La Mara's popular biographies may have been, such works did not sit well with the scholarly community. In the *Vierteljahrschrift* of 1888, Hermann Deiters takes even the respectable W. J. von Wasielewski to task for venturing into the field of popular Beethoven biography. He writes that the scholarly work Wasielewski had done had managed to displace dilettantism by "the sensible" assumption of tasks such as he had mastered.[8] Still, said Deiters, popular biography perseveres in its dubious preoccupation, "work we shall not reproach as long as it transmits scholarly findings to a wide circle of readers." The scholar had better things to do. It therefore troubled Deiters to encounter Wasielewski on the broad path of popular biography. He goes on to criticize Wasielewski at great length for the various errors and misinterpretations he perpetuated in spite of his otherwise sound scholarship.

Early encyclopedias reflect a changing attitude. In Pietro Liechtenthal's *Dizionario* of 1826 a genius is still seen as one possessed of great facility. Liechtenthal's only example is a familiar old anecdote according to which Telemann reported that he could write a composition with eight real parts as easily as other people write letters.[9] By 1840 genius was being defined in a new way

---

8.   Hermann Deiters, "W. J. von Wasielewski, *Ludwig van Beethoven.*" Review in *Vierteljahrschrift für Musikwissenschaft* 5 (1888): 496ff. Whatever La Mara's merit as a writer, her biographies of early composers contained many of those oversimplifications we now consider clichés. There is Mozart's clarity, formal grace, and sensibility soaring above sorrow. Bach was unqualifiedly austere and Handel an extrovert. Haydn is characterized as possessing harmless gayety, lovable innocence, and naïveté, etc. etc. Even though such descriptions were not yet clichés, we find it difficult to excuse them.

9.   Pietro Lichenthal, *Dizionario e bibliografie della musica*, 4 vols. (Milan: A. Fontana, 1826): 289f.

by August Gathy whose examples were Homer, Napoleon, and Beethoven.[10] In music to be a genius meant to be able to "create new and excellent ideas, to develop them and to give them form." Genius, he wrote, was a driving power, a divine instinct guided by godlike thoughtfulness (*Besonnenheit*). But creative genius required listeners of receptive genius, persons able to understand and accept superior work even if they were not creative themselves. (At about the same time Schumann wrote that only genius could recognize genius.) An article by the esthetician William Wolf in Mendel's *Lexicon* of the 1870 places the heaviest stress on originality and observes that it is understandable that originality cannot be evaluated immediately, since in itself it can be either good or bad.[11] The public, he writes, should reserve its approbation; only time could tell what was good. Since genius was indefinable, the only criterion by which one could judge an artist was the universal appeal his works would have several generations later. It had taken three generations for Beethoven's late works to find universal acclaim. Mendelssohn, Schumann, and Wagner were still controversial because they were not yet distant enough for the weeding process of posterity to have taken place. The unstated but no less clear implication was that no great artist could expect immediate recognition. (After Mendel's *Lexikon*, musical reference books no longer have entries under "genius.")

La Mara was ambivalent toward the already prevalent idea that all great artists must encounter misunderstanding. As a professional biographer she had a unique problem of course. She could not take sides in the controversies between various schools of composition such as the one between the Brahmsians and the Wagnerites.if her biographies were to appeal to their respective followers. Brahms she depicted as content to carry on the tradition of absolute music, preoccupied not with form, however, but with expression. Over all of his music hovered the sorrow (*Schmerz*) of Beethoven's late quartets. True, Wagner had been the most embattled of all composers, meeting with greater hostility and ridicule than any predecessor, yet he triumphed in life as well as in death. It was possible, La Mara

---

10. August Gathy, *Encyclopädie der gesammten Musik-Wissenschaft* (2nd ed., Hamburg: G. W. Niemeyer, 1840): 163.
11. Hermann Mendel and August Reissmann, *Musikalisches Conversations-Lexikon*, 11 vols. (2nd ed., Leipzig: List & Franke, 1880—83), 4: 185ff.

implied, to be an artist without being a martyr, to be a great composer like Mendelssohn and yet not a battler for causes. But heroes are not made in daylight. ("Ein Heldencharakter wird freilich nicht im Sonnenlicht gezeichnet.")

At mid-century most writers and critics still accepted Mendelssohn's stature in spite of his easy life and early success. Later in the century when the notion of the rejected genius had become practically axiomatic, it was also inverted. If great artists are always misunderstood, then it now followed that easy acceptance and an easy life disqualify an artist from the category of genius. While this implication is at first tacit, it is finally stated by Anton Rubinstein.[12] Mendelssohn, he writes, could not be taken seriously, since his wealth and success prevented his work from having any depth; he was a minor figure. Now early composers too had to be made into tragic figures, a revisionism not difficult to rationalize in such cases as Beethoven, Schubert, and Mozart. Since it was impossible to make a tragic hero of Haydn, he was patronized.

I know only one direct witness to this sort of revisionism. The obscure Bach biographer, C. L. Hilgenfeld, objected to Bach's classification as an unappreciated genius, mainly because it would derogate his era. In spite of much that was "stiff, pedantic and baroque" in the eighteenth century, it was possible to transcend the ordinary and still receive recognition. "In recent years," writes Hilgenfeld, "a strange tendency has risen to the surface. Heroes of art [Kunstheroen] immediately issue their plaintive cries at the least slight and complain about how this or that great artist was [also] unrecognized in his time."[13] (Although Hilgenfeld was a poor biographer, there is no reason to disqualify him as a witness to the contemporary scene.)

The bathos of romantic biography did not immediately make its appearance. True, Forkel's biography romanticized Bach, but he did not make him into a martyr. If we can call him the first romantic biographer — as we did in the previous chapter — it is for other reasons.

La Mara's life of Berlioz demonstrates her ambivalence toward

---

12. Anton Rubinstein, *La Musique et ses représentents*, trans. from the Russian by Michel Delines (Paris: Heugel, 1892).

13. C. F. Hilgenfeld, *Johann Sebastian Bach's Leben, Wirken und Werke* (Leipzig: 1850, reprinted by Fritz Knuf, Hilversum: 1965), pp. 163–65.

the idea of unappreciated genius. Her book opens with the dramatic statement that Berlioz died of grief over his lack of recognition. But already her next sentence contradicts that sentiment by suggesting that it was in the nature of the man to consider himself a martyr. Her protest against this self-imposed martyrdom is emphatic.[14] She quotes at length from a letter of Liszt to Richard Pohl.

> He [Berlioz] could not accept the idea that genius cannot go unscathed and that no innovator can demand recognition from those who are old-fashioned. His anger at the Parisians, by the way, those "*gredins et crétins*" was unjust; he could have found their like anywhere. In spite of his exaggerated regard [*courtoisie*] for foreign places, it was a fact that until now no composer had received such honors at home as Berlioz. . . . His many concerts in Paris were always well attended. If their proceeds were not great, it was because of the cost of personnel and copying.[15]

Liszt, not unfamiliar with vituperation himself, is an ideal commentator on the martyr syndrome. He also equated genius with innovation and took for granted that novelty would meet with at least some dissent, but he did not equate controversy with lack of appreciation. The recipient of his letter, Pohl, chose to ignore Liszt, however, and laid on the bathos with a trowel, depicting Berlioz' as the fate of all great men.

> Again and again the cruel play of artistic fame and human fortune is repeated before our eyes. Again and again it saddens us but the play never changes. There are only a few tragic heroes but a multitude of those who misunderstand them and aggravate them to death.[16]

Pohl knew very well that Berlioz' German tours had been successes but instead he chose to dwell on the adverse opinions Berlioz had encountered. At the same time Pohl was realistic enough to point out that only those who had heard Berlioz' music performed by

---

14.   I am referring to the 11th edition of her biography, *Hector Berlioz* (Leipzig, 1923; Breitkopf und Härtel, 1911).
15.   The letter La Mara quotes was originally published in the *Allgemeine deutsche Musikzeitung* of October 24, 1884. A very inaccurate translation can be found in *The Letters of Franz Liszt*, ed. by La Mara and trans. by Constance Bache (London: H. Grevel, 1894): 454.
16.   Richard Pohl, *Hector Berlioz. Studien und Erinnerungen* (Leipzig: B. Schlicke, 1884).

orchestras rather than in piano-arrangements were in any position to appreciate it.

As one reads about Berlioz in the writings of persons who knew him, it becomes quite clear that Liszt's and La Mara's assumption of his self-imposed martyrdom was shared by others. A letter of the composer, Stephen Heller, a close friend of Berlioz, to Eduard Hanslick delicately suggests that Berlioz liked the rôle of rejected revolutionary with his string of disciples.

> In 1838 when I first arrived at Paris, Berlioz already stood out above all other artists there. Even then nobody could deny him the reputation of the daring artist striving for great things. His work, his talk, his entire bearing gave him the air of a revolutionary against the musical establishment, a regime Berlioz liked to consider obsolete. . . . I saw in only the first few months of my acquaintance with him that he had begun to figure as head of all the misunderstood geniuses of Paris. He was misunderstood, that is true, but as one who must be misunderstood. Berlioz raised the misunderstanding of talent to a dignified level; the recognition, even the admiration of a large circle allowed his being misunderstood to stand out so glaringly and unlovely that it won him new friends every day . . . Meanwhile many more or less gifted artistic disciples and apprentices, themselves, more or less misunderstood, lined up behind their chief. . . . Add to these a small number of good and true musicians capable of recognizing the daring and grandiose, the often miraculous originality and the magical orchestration, and you will have to admit that Berlioz was not as alone as he liked to pretend. Beginning in 1838, later even more often, some of his compositions found general, even brilliant acceptance.[17]

Another composer, Ferdinand Hiller, one who was close to Berlioz in his youth says, "Berlioz had no harder battle than any other 'tone-poet,' just a noisier one."[18] Hiller subsequently elaborates. His life was complicated by the fact that he wrote works requiring extraordinary forces. He was neither a performer nor a teacher nor *a popular* (my italics) composer, talents which made it possible for even the greatest to earn their daily bread. Had he lived in Germany

---

17. The letter is quoted by Hanslick to whom it was addressed, in his autobiography, *Aus meinem Leben*, 2 vols. (Berlin: Allgemeiner Verein für deutsche Literatur, 1894), 2: 147ff.
18. Ferdinand Hiller, *Künstlerleben* (Cologne: Mont-Schaubergsche Buchandlung, 1880): 63ff.

he might have been a conductor in one of the many cities that had orchestras, since conducting was his forte. In France he had to live in Paris and could have been a conductor only at the opera. But he would have been an impossible conductor anywhere, since he loathed so much of the repertoire he would have been obliged to present.

It appears to be Berlioz who is the first major composer to clothe himself in the new image. That he saw himself as the new type of artist is evident from his libretto of *Benvenuto Cellini* in which there is far less ado over Cellini's work than over the rebellious response to those Cellini saw as his oppressors. That Berlioz was a likely candidate cannot be denied; few of his innovations met with universal acclaim, several with none. But it has to be said that in some respects Berlioz was a "misfit," not a performer and not willing to support himself as a conductor of many other people's music. It is true that since the turn of the century a number of composers were unable or unwilling to concertize. To name Schubert or Schumann as two candidates for the distinction does not explain why neither seems to have seen himself as unappreciated. Schubert was just a few years away from genuine success when he died while Schumann had a private income, several years as a conductor (albeit unsuccessful), and the help of Clara. He seems to have managed. Chopin whose income from publishing was quite good, although not good enough for his standard of living, could have concertized much more frequently had he chosen to. Whenever he performed, his fees were quite high. The truly successful artists were virtuosos and opera composers, Rossini, Meyerbeer, and numerous others. Those occupations brought in the funds as well as acclaim. While Berlioz and after him Wagner were entirely right to see themselves as unjustly underrewarded, that is not the point. The point here is that they wore the new image, an image that was to become the standard defense-mechanism of the avant-garde artist, talented or not.

It was not necessarily an attitude limited to the financially pressed. Liszt can hardly be said to have been among the latter. When he speaks of the artist's loneliness there must be more to it than meets the eye. And indeed, financial and critical success might come. But once art had to be constantly reinvented and once it became the vehicle for the artist's deepest feelings, an artist could accept acclaim only if it was totally on his own terms. More often than not, composers thought of their works as pearls before swine, sometimes gobbled up only because swine will eat anything. One can find this attitude often enough in Berlioz' writings. After the tremendous success of *L'Enfance de Christ*, for example, he wrote to Liszt, "so be it — I have become a good little boy, human, clear, melodic; I am at last writing music like everybody else."[19]

If this smacks of contempt for the audience the reason lies in the new division of the public into those who have taste and those who do not. Once a composer saw himself as a hero, a martyr to his unassailable integrity, he could not afford success, since it meant that he must have compromised his ideals.

As Hiller put it:

> [The public] buys its artistic pleasures in department stores [*Warenlagern*]. There they can find good taste and bad, fashion or charlatanism, valid and invalid reputations.[20]

Or Berlioz in his own kind of musical weather-report.

> [There was now] a rain of albums, an avalanche of romances, a torrent of airs with variations, a spurt of cavatinas, dramatic scenes, comic duos, soporific adagios, diabolic evocations, classic sonatas and rondos romantic, fantastic, frenetic and fluoric,

which made up the bulk of musical publication.[21]

Both Hiller and Berlioz are of course absolutely correct in their description of the musical situation in Paris. But it is not only that one suspects oneself of being a purveyor of inferior goods whenever the public stops at one's display to buy something, it is also a matter of an endangered self-image probably as strong as any in the psychiatric literature. It is an attitude that still prevails.

An aspect of the artistic personality that has not been investigated, because it is difficult to examine, is the *ability* to write inferior music. A composer such as Chopin could probably not produce the kind of music that made up most of the standard salon pieces being purchased in extraordinary amounts. (The fact that his honoraria were better than those of many composers of easier or more popular

---

19.   Quoted by Jacques Barzun, *Berlioz and the Romantic Century*, 2 vols. (New York: 3rd ed., Columbia University Press, 1969), 2: 86f.
20.   Hiller, *Künstlerleben*, p. 97.
21.   Berlioz as quoted by Arthur Loesser in *Men, Women and Pianos* (New York: Simon and Schuster, 1954): 392.

works is not relevant in this context.) It is easy to accept that, in an era in which the musician had been a craftsman producing more or less standard works, the degree of his ability was accepted as a kind of divine game of roulette. A few composers left us inspired masterpieces because they could not help it, not because they made a conscious choice to be different or superior. This does not mean that the superior artist did not realize that he was superior, but one wonders how many times one or another of these inspired men might have wished to be more ordinary. It is not likely to be acceptable to promulgate such a view in retrospect. Could a Berlioz or a Wagner secretly have wished that they were more like Meyerbeer or Rossini, i.e., not inferior but more conventional? If not, it was probably the new view of the artist as hero that helped them to accept their "inability" to produce more popular music.

That Berlioz may have been the first composer to see himself as an unappreciated genius is historically unimportant. What is important is the fact that this self-image has become standard and is partly responsible for whatever avant-gardism has dominated the history of our art ever since. Even more important to objective history is the retrospective application of this image to eras in which it does not apply, since it keeps us from looking at various impersonal aspects of that history. When Hermann Abert spoke of the need to rewrite biographies every fifty years because we are so conditioned by our own time that we can never be objective, he might have used the idea of the unappreciated genius as an example had he not been so conditioned by his time that he probably could not see it.

The history of music publishing, for example, is still largely *terra incognita*. While we have long come to know most of the technical aspects of printing, the commercial side and the dissemination of music as an aspect of *Rezeptionsgeschichte* have been dominated by biographers who usually dwell on the neglect of great composers on the part of publishers. As a consequence there is no comprehensive history of publishing in terms of the dissemination of music. Even more disturbing is the reluctance on the part of the oldest publishing houses to allow scholars to examine their archives. Publishers are afraid that their past business-practices will reinforce their reputation as the composer's traditional enemy.

Chapter III demonstrated that the number of works published by Sebastian Bach, however small, represented a relatively large number for a *German* composer of his generation. In the case of Mozart, Alec Hyatt King enumerated a mere 144 works out of more than

600 that were published while he lived.[22] While this is difficult to understand for a Mozart-adoring public in the twentieth century, it represents a number that was then among the highest. In the catalogue of Artaria, one of Vienna's leading publishers, Mozart has forty-nine entries up to 1791 while Haydn is represented by seventy-six and Ignaz Pleyel by eighty-four.[23] This is only a partial picture and does not explain why there should have been more works of Pleyel's in the catalogue than even of Haydn's (whom nobody would care to consider an unappreciated genius), but it does not suffice to rely on the inevitability of martyrdom for the greatest as explanation. Such an approach keeps us from analyzing and perhaps discovering the roots of taste and success in the various periods of history.

A similar problem exists in the case of Schubert whom the publisher Schott sought out in 1827. As I said above, Schott seems to have considered Schubert Beethoven's logical successor. The composer eagerly supplied Schott with a list of available compositions. But Schott refused several of the works be had submitted on various grounds.[24] Nevertheless, when Schubert died at the age of thirty-one years, i.e., after about seventeen or eighteen years of creativity, he had published approximately one hundred opus numbers which actually represent three-hundred individual compositions. Shortly before he died he was approached by another publisher, Heinrich Probst of Leipzig, who wrote that he was sure it would be possible to spread Schubert's reputation "to all of Germany and the North."[25] In any case, Probst was willing to take on the piano-trio in E-flat even though trios were not good sellers, the probable reason why Schott had turned it down. In 1846 Jules Janin was able to say that "*Schubert, expiré . . . au moment où la gloire allait lui venir.*"[26] In France demand for his songs had been growing since about 1830.

---

22. Alec Hyatt King, *Mozart in Retrospect* (London: 3rd ed., Oxford University Press, 1970): 8.
23. Alexander Weinmann, *Vollständiges Verlagsverzeichniss Artaria und Co.* Beiträge zur Geschichte des alt-wiener Musikverlages, Reihe 2, Folge 2 (Vienna: L. Krenn, 1952).
24. See note 4. Hans Lenneberg, *Breitkopf und Härtel in Paris. The Letters of their Agent Heinrich Probst, 1833—1840,* in preparation.
25. Deutsch, *Schubert:* 735.
26. As quoted in Joseph-Marc Bailbé, *Le Roman et la musique en France sous la monarchie de juillet* (Paris: Lettres Modernes Minard, 1969): 130.

What makes the study of biography so interesting and so much more valuable than Guido Adler ever suspected is, in fact, a shuttling back and forth between earlier views and modern interpretations of them. Yet not even the most cynical reader of biographies wants his icons disturbed, even while realizing that the sentimentality of past views is a handicap to historical realism. One can trace in many cases an awareness on the part of a historian that the facts we know do not match the image we are preserving. Yet, even when that historian suggests that the image is not appropriate, the suggestion is likely to be ignored.

One can see the process at work in the case of Sebastian Bach as viewed by Friedrich Blume. Unease is evident in his *Johann Sebastian Bach im Spiegel der Geschichte*. While the romantic view ultimately prevails in this book, Blume makes an attempt to deal with earlier signs of recognition.[27] For Bach's reputation Blume uses the metaphor of a river which swells from its first trickle before 1750 into a powerful stream. Fed mainly by underground rivulets, the river gradually widens until it reaches its full, albeit muddy, width with the revival of the *St. Matthew Passion* in 1829. Blume believes that Bach had virtually no reputation as a composer while he lived; he was not forgotten because there was nothing to forget. This is true only by later standards. On a continent that thought it had few rivers of any size, even a small stream would have been impressive. In a time and place in which musicians were still essentially craftsmen, Bach was one whose craftsmanship was widely known and admired, even if his religious works were not part of what was known about

---

Bailbé has many illustrations for various aspects of this chapter, among them the term *la grande bohème* in George Sand's *La dernière Aldini* of 1838, references to indifference to appearance, and this quote about the artist's indifference to fame and fortune in a novel of Philippe Busoni:

Il travaille à un grand ouvrage sur la philosophie de la musique. Il prétend en faire la base d'une langue universelle, commune à tous les peuples [. . .] avec son nom allemand et sa tête jeune et inspirée, sa réputation eût été grande. *Mais réputation et fortune, tout lui répugne.*

27. Friedrich Blume, *Johann Sebastian Bach im Spiegel der Geschichte.*

him. While his obituary in Mizler's *Musikalische Bibliothek* stood side by side with those of lesser men such as Stölzel and Bümler, only Bach was referred to as "world-famous" — a world-famous organist, to be sure, but how many other German composers deserved the adjective?[28] In the "Preface" to the first publication of the *Art of Fugue* in 1752, it was possible for Marpurg to state, "The name of the composer is sufficient recommendation for a work of this nature."[29] Somewhat later, in Emanuel's "Preface" to the first edition of his father's chorale-settings (in 1765), he could say, "The late author is not in need of my recommendation. One was accustomed to seeing nothing but masterpieces come from him."[30] That the *Art of Fugue* sold only thirty copies is a tragedy that has little to do with the reputation of its creator, its severity and the supposed absence of instrumentation, or its untimeliness.

When, as early as 1750, Padre Martini could write to another musician that "the singular merit of Bach was too well known and admired, not only in Germany but in all of Italy," there cannot be much doubt that Bach's reputation as a composer, not just as an organist, was established far more widely than we had assumed. His letter was a response to one Giovanni Battista Pauli who had sent Martini one of his works while including several of Bach's. (According to Eitner, the *Kyrie* Pauli sent to Martini is the only one of his works that survives.)[31]

Even the rebuke of Bach published in *Critischer Musikus* in 1737 by its editor, Johann Adolph Scheibe, disguised as an anonymous correspondent, was a backhanded compliment.[32] "This great man would be the admiration of whole nations . . . ," wrote Scheibe, "if he did not take away the natural element in his pieces by giving them a turgid and confused style and if he did not darken their beauty by an excess of art. . . . Every ornament, every little grace, and everything

---

28. Lorenz Mizler, *Neu-eröffnete musikalische Bibliothek* 4 vols. in 3 (Leipzig: 1739—54; reprinted F. Knuf, 1966): 158ff.
29. See the translation in Hans T. David and Arthur Mendel, *The Bach Reader* (rev. ed., New York: Norton, 1966): 266ff.
30. Ibid.: 270f.
31. Anne Schnoebelen, *Padre Martini's Collection of Letters in the Civico Museo Bibliografico Musicale in Bologna* (New York: Pendragon, 1979). The quote is from her English summary of letter 3996.
32. *Bach Reader*: 237ff.

that one thinks of as belonging to the method of playing, he expresses completely in notes." It was not yet common for a composer to be publicly discussed in the German press, and all the other references Scheibe makes to Bach are highly laudatory.

Of the several assessments of German musicians that survive in books and periodicals from before 1750, Bach, Handel, and Telemann are virtually always on the list of the best. Other names vary, depending on the author's preferences; often they include themselves. We are not really certain how Bach achieved his eminence. We know that his playing, i.e., his instant composition, was heard by many musicians; we do not quite know how his reputation as a composer spread as widely as it did. We have no idea, for example, how many copies of the few works he published in his lifetime were sold, though that seems to be a minor point, since Johann Gottfried Walther tells us that publishing was not really worthwhile. For every engraved copy sold, ten handwritten copies were made.[33] There is considerable evidence that the *Well-tempered Clavier* began to circulate early in secondary copies made from the ones Bach's students took away with them. By the time the work was finally printed in 1801, an enormous number of corrupt copies must have been in circulation.[34]

The far greater success Handel enjoyed in England where public performances and profitable publication were facts of life, took place in an environment in which free-lance composing existed side by side with patronage. In Germany, the public performance that was not limited to opera and *collegia* took place in churches; publishing was a negligible factor and the publication of Lutheran church-music virtually non-existent. While this phenomenon has been reported before, as well as being evident in early autobiographies, it is still sufficiently mysterious to defy final explanation.[35]

---

33.   Werner Neumann and Hans-Joachim Schulze, eds., *Bach-Dokumente II: Fremdschriftliche und gedruckte Dokumente zur Lebensgeschichte Johann Sebastian Bachs 1685—1750* (Kassel: Bärenreiter, 1969), No. 381: 268.

34.   Hans-Joachim Schulze, ed., *Bach-Dokumente III: Dokumente zum Nachwirken Johann Sebastian Bach* (Kassel: Bärenreiter, 1972), No. 955: 486f.

35.   Friedhelm Krummacher, *Die Ueberlieferung der Choralbearbeitungen in der frühen evangelischen Kantata*, Berliner Studien zur Musikwissenschaft (Berlin: Merseburger, 1965): 45ff.

Krummacher's belief that the decline in German music-publishing in the eighteenth century was due to the effects of the Thirty Years War cannot be supported by evidence, since publishing flourished during that war. While he thinks that a social history of the period is still needed, he proposes several theories. One of these hinges on the existence of small *Kantoreien*, "cantorships," which had different forces of varying capabilities at their disposal and needed their own music. It was the cantor's duty to supply this music, not only in accordance with his ability to get it performed, but also according to the ideals of worship held in his community. At the end of the seventeenth century, the quality of these cantorships seems to have deteriorated. Henrich Schütz, in the preface to his *Christmas Oratorio*, had already pointed out that he was publishing only the Evangelist's part, since inadequate musical organizations were likely to make a botch of the unfamiliar [Italian] style of the more complicated sections.[36] Schütz implies that publishing was much more usual in his day. Still he did not think highly of the sophistication of local cantors. One can easily imagine that Bach's music could not have been performed in many *Kantoreien*, certainly not in enough to warrant the expense of publication.

By any, but especially by German standards, Handel's success was spectacular. It must have been incomprehensible in Germany, the reason, perhaps, why the German echo of the noise he made in England was relatively weak. Comparing the entries in Walther for Bach and Handel in 1732, we find Handel getting even less space than Bach.[37] Eight years later, Handel's supposed friend, Mattheson, devoted nine pages to him, not as many as to Printz, Keiser, Telemann, or for that matter, himself.[38] In his *Lebensbeschreibungen* Hiller had a clearer perspective in 1784, although his book, supposedly devoted to the biographies of famous composers, lumps together Bach and Handel with composers who even then were not in the same class — men such as Georg Gebel the Elder, Georg Bümler, and Felice Salimbeni.[39] Hiller, taking his information where he found it, gave Handel more space than he gave Bach. He had

---

36.   Henrich Schütz, *Historia der freuden und gnadenreichen Geburth Gottes* (Dresden, 1664); in *Neue Ausgabe sämtlicher Werke*, vol. 1, ed. by Friedrich Schöneich (Kassel: Bärenreiter, 1955).
37.   Johann Gottfried Walther, *Musikalisches Lexikon*: 64 and 309f.
38.   Johann Mattheson, *Grundlage einer Ehrenpforte*.
39.   Johann Adam Hiller, *Lebensbeschreibungen*.

Mainwaring as a source for the former but only the *Nekrolog* for Bach.[40]

The question of Bach's reputation while he was alive as well as posthumously is just one example among many of the story of the artist as martyr and hero. It must suffice here to limit ourselves to such samples and to emphasize that the image has become fixed.[41]

That artists must suffer for art and must make sacrifices also accounts for Freud's idea that creativity is compensation.

> As we have long known, art offers *substitute gratifications* [italics mine] for the oldest cultural renunciations, still the ones most deeply felt, and for that reason it serves as nothing else to reconcile men to the sacrifices made on behalf of culture.[42]

This seems to be Freud's cautious and restrained way of admitting his inability to fathom the psychological sources of art.

In fiction we have Adrian Leverkühn, the composer-protagonist of Thomas Mann's *Doktor Faustus*, who sells his soul to the devil in order to realize his artistic aims. Thomas Mann, who was an appreciated genius as soon as he was published, does not attribute Leverkühn's bargain to the desire for enthusiastic large audiences or money. Neither popularity nor money enters into Leverkühn's reckoning. Instead his deed is that of a self-absorbed artistic personality, the kind that has come to dominate our image of the artist. However idealistic the image may seem, it perpetuates the disregard of audiences that we already found in Berlioz. It is an image elaborated in that amusing book, Nicolas Slonimsky's *Lexicon of Musical Invective*, or in the stories of fiasco at the premiere of Stravinsky's *Sacre du printemps*. Slonimsky in effect gives a rule of thumb for the time it takes for "a modernistic monstrosity" to be accepted: twenty years to turn it into a curiosity, twenty more to achieve the status of masterpiece. Is it possible to change this

---

40. John Mainwaring, *Memoirs of the Life of the Late George Frederick Handel* (London: R. and J. Dodsley, 1760). For the *Nekrolog*, see above, note 28.
41. See further, Hans Lenneberg, "The Myth of the Unappreciated (Musical) Genius," *The Musical Quarterly* 66 (1980): 219f., as well as Chapter VIII of this volume.
42. Sigmund Freud, *Gesammelte Werke*, 16: 335, as quoted by Ernest Jones, *The Life and Works of Sigmund Freud*, 3 vols. (New York: Basic Books, 1953—57), 3: 414.

mythology which, although it has only existed for slightly more than 170 years, is dear to the public's heart?

The wish to make artists into figures of suffering is not limited to real or supposed lack of success. There is a powerful tendency to make Beethoven's deafness into a part of his greatness or to see in Schumann's madness the inevitable destiny of genius. Beethoven's triumph over his inability to hear may have some bearing on his more radical late compositions, but neither Hugo Wolf nor Schumann functioned as composers when they lost touch with reality, and even the fictitious Adrian Leverkühn no longer produced intelligible music at that stage of his disintegration. It is interesting to follow recent tendencies to ascribe homosexuality to various composers, since we cannot possibly tell from music what the sexual orientation of its author was. When we discuss contemporary artists, we hardly trouble ourselves over such matters, and yet the desire to ascribe to the masters of past times some sort of suffering seems to exceed biographical curiosity. It is natural to want to understand great persons; it is fascinating to see, as we do so often, the disparity between the person and his work. But as long as we subject ourselves to our preconceived idea that great art must come from suffering, we are not likely to arrive at true insight into the creative personality.

CHAPTER VIII

AROUND WASIELEWSKI AND HIS SCHUMANN BIOGRAPHY

In recent years Wilhelm Joseph von Wasielewski has been receiving some attention at last.[1] He was Robert Schumann's first biographer, and he himself is a source of documentation for both Schumanns since he knew them quite well for a period of approximately six years.[2] While his biography is still occasionally the subject of mild debate, it is as a gatherer of factual data that he has never received the scrutiny he deserves.[3] Considering that some of his contemporary critics were distinctly hostile to his book, their disagreements, especially those of Franz Brendel who had known Schumann nearly as well, must be taken into account.[4] Wasielewski also happens to be

---

1. His name also appears as Joseph Wilhelm von Wasielewski.
2. *Robert Schumann, eine Biographie.* An article on Wasielewski's biography by Renate Federhofer-Königs, "Wasielewski als Düsseldorfer Konzertmeister und Biograph," in *Robert Schumann — ein romantisches Erbe in neuer Forschung.* (Robert-Schumann-Gesellschaf:, Düsseldorf. Mainz: Schott, 1984): 67—85, lists the sequence of revised editions and explains their revisions. The first edition appeared in 1858, the others respectively in 1869, 1880 and 1906. The last, the one referred to in this essay, was edited by Waldemar von Wasielewski.
3. Renate Federhofer-Königs, *Wilhelm Joseph von Wasielewski im Spiegel seiner Korrespondenz.* Mainzer Studien zur Musikwissenschaft 7 (Tutzing: Hans Schneider, 1974) makes a valuable contribution to this aspect of Wasielewski.
4. Franz Brendel, "R. Schumann's Biographie von J. W. von Wasielewski. Zweite Besprechung. *Neue Zeitschrift für Musik*, vol. 48 (1858), nos. 11 to 18. (Hereafter *NZfM* 1858.)

of some, importance to the history of biography, since his work stands out above others depicting then recent composers. One of Wasielewski's reviewers acknowledges this in an otherwise lukewarm article. Compared to the idle chatter of Schindler's Beethoven, writes Richard Pohl, the dilettantism of Ulybichev's Mozart, and the narrow scope of Anton Schmid's Gluck, Wasielewski had considerable merit.[5] Even the seeming oxymoron of the Wasielewski article in *The New Grove*, that his was "the first definitive biography" of Schumann, represents a valid estimate.[6] Until Boetticher's far more ambitious and of course far more modern study appeared and until the diaries and account books began to be published, Wasielewski had no rival either as Schumann's biographer or as a source of documentary biography.[7] (Unlike most biographers, Boetticher does not review the merits of his predecessor.)

Some of the more influential hostile critics of Wasielewski, of whom those writing in the *Neue Zeitschrift für Musik* must have been the most hurtful, virtually dismissed his biography, calling it cold and unsympathetic, musically naïve or worse, and generally disappointing. Something of the sort was also the opinion of Johannes Brahms who wrote in a letter to Clara, "A biography can in my opinion only be written by a good friend and admirer. Impartiality is a good thing

---

5. Hoplit (Richard Pohl) "Robert Schumann. Eine Biographie von Joseph W. von Wasielewski. Erste Besprechung." In ibid. nos. 6 to 8. Anton Felix Schindler, *Biographie von Ludwig van Beethoven*. 1st ed. (Münster, Aschendorff, 1840). Alexandr Dmitrievïch Ulybichev, *Mozarts Leben, nebst einer Übersicht der allgemeinen Geschichte der Musik und einer Analyse der Hauptwerke Mozarts*. 3 vols. (Stuttgart: A Becker, 1847). Anton Schmid, *Christoph Willibald Ritter von Gluck* (Leipzig: F. Fleischer, 1854). For some reason, Pohl did not mention the fine biography, the first that can be called scholarly, Giuseppe Baini's *Memorie storico-critiche della vita e delle opere di Giovanni Pierluigi da Palęstrina*, nor its German adaptation by Franz Sales Kandler published by Breitkopf und Härtel in 1834. Perhaps Pohl felt that the biography of a sixteenth-century composer was not pertinent in this context.
6. David Charlton and George Grove, "Wasielewski," *The New Grove Dictionary of Music and Musicians*, 20: 227.
7. Wolfgang Boetticher, Robert Schumann, *Einführung in Persönlichkeit und Werk; Beiträge zur Erkenntniskritik der Musikgeschichte und Studien am Ausdrucksproblem des neunzehnten Jahrhunderts* (Berlin: Hahnefeld, 1941).

(and difficult as well) but it must not be cold."[8] That Brahms did not refute the biography in print was due only to the fact that such things were "not my métier."

The critics were not so naïve as to expect Wasielewski to have the last word. Nor would they have denied him the right to be critical. Brendel may have thought that he had earned the right to be the first biographer, since he had already produced a series of articles about Mendelssohn and Schumann in 1845.[9] Everyone knew that a definitive biography was not in Wasielewski's power, since he had not been able to get complete documentation. He solicited what letters he could and, according to his memoirs, had considerable success.[10] (Brendel, who owned numerous letters of Schumann, admitted that he could not at the moment lay his hands on some of them, a rather startling admission for one who deemed Schumann one of the most important composers of his time.) Clara, the source of sources, having earlier encouraged Wasielewski in his plan to write a biography and promised him access to her memorabilia, suddenly changed her mind. At about the same time her letters to Wasielewski, once warm, even affectionate, turn decidedly cooler.

The modern reader, knowing Brahms' integrity, is more inclined to accept his evaluation rather than those of other critics. But neither Brahms nor Clara probably understood Wasielewski's effort to be objective, a subject Wasielewski tells us about in his memoirs. Panegyrics, he says in effect, are easy. It is not possible however, to create a lifelike portrait without shadows. Prejudices, inclinations, and special predilections are what the biographer must rid himself of. Wasielewski found detachment very difficult to attain because he had known Schumann.[11] For us his efforts not to let his fondness for

---

8.   Excerpt from a Brahms letter of January 19, 1859, as quoted by Renata Federhofer-Königs in *Wilhelm Joseph von Wasielewski*: 55.

9.   Franz Brendel, "Robert Schumann mit Rücksicht auf Mendelssohn-Bartholdy und die Entwicklung der modernen Tonkunst überhaupt." *NZfM* 22 (1845): 63, 81, 89, 113, 121, 145. (Hereafter referred to as *NZfM* 1845.) A recent article by Jurgen Thym, "Schumann in Brendel's *Neue Zeitschrift für Musik from 1845 to 1856*," in a symposium, *Mendelssohn and Schumann*, ed. by John Finson and R. Larry Todd (Durham, N.C.: Duke University Press, 1984): 22ff., also discusses this article. Professor Thym and I read it somewhat differently.

10. Wilhelm Joseph von Wasielewski, *Aus siebzig Jahren* (Stuttgart and Leipzig: Deutsche Verlags-Anstalt, 1897).

11. Ibid.: 161.

Schumann cloud his judgment are almost palpable. What Wasielewski produced is in fact a good narrative, blending Schumann's life with his letters, personal recollections, and secondhand information into a smooth account. He does not confine himself to following a strict chronological story. Instead he manages to pursue topics according to their inner logic and then return to chronology without any loss of continuity. Wasielewski's style is good and reflects a solid education. (According to his memoirs, he had attended a *Realschule*, a type of Gymnasium which did not emphasize only classical education. In school he had studied Latin, French, and English as well as physics and chemistry.) But for those others who had also known Schumann he may have been too objective; perhaps they were simply too warm, too romantic.

As an example of seeming coldness one might select Wasielewski's report on the death of Robert's sister in-law, Rosalie, which is rather matter-of-fact in tone and consists of just a few sentences.

> Rosalie, one of Schumann's three sisters-in-law, died and the news produced a state of mind which especially during the night, he [Schumann] calls it "the terrible night of October 17," rose to morbid exaltation alternating with the most painful anxiety.[12] His "terrible depression," as the notebook has it, only gradually retreated and for a time it produced complete apathy in Schumann.[13]

Wasielewski was inclined to attribute Schumann's state at least in part to his late nights and to his drinking, something almost calculated to anger Schumann's admirers.

When it comes to Wasielewski's musical criticism the modern reader may occasionally be irritated by his disparaging attitude toward the early works in which Wasielewski appears to be rather formalistic. The imaginative freedom of *Papillons* could be admired but the work was not really classifiable. Wasielewski finds its lack of *Durcharbeitung* regrettable. Even Schumann's rather free variation-forms could only be liked for their inventiveness. Wasielewski has a tendency throughout his book to deprecate the primacy of fantasy over intellectual control. "The perfect command of form and tight organization in the highest artistic sense remained difficult for Schumann, the consequence of having begun his studies too

---

12.   *Biographie*: 110.
13.   Ibid.

late. This was to remain the Achilles' heel in a number.of his compositions." [14]

On his part Brendel, in his long critical survey of Schumann's
work published in 1845, had concluded that the spontaneity of
Schumann's free imagination, characteristic of the early work, is
what made him modern because it represented an extension of
Beethoven's subjectivism. While Schumann gradually had to learn
form, writes Brendel, which he had to develop out of his own efforts
to broaden his scope, Mendelssohn had the opposite task. He had to
learn to inject his individuality into the forms passed on from Haydn
and Mozart.

Wasielewski never quite freed himself from his classicistic tendencies which are often hinted at in other evaluations of music in his
biography. Many of his descriptive and critical evaluations are quite
laudatory, especially when they deal with works that achieve a high
level of form as well as invention such as the two chamber works
with piano, the Quintet, op. 44 and the Quartet, op. 47. Wasielewski
praises these works warmly but does not go into detail. More
extensive comment is reserved for the really *important*, i.e., something like the Symphony in B flat, the first. He does this work
full justice although he compares its developmental technique to
Schubert rather than Beethoven, i.e.: if he was tempted to disparage
what he calls the shifting of passages to different tonalities rather
than true *thematische Durchführung*, he avoids doing so by means of
this comparison. His criticism is confined to comments about the
treatment of instrumentation (not orchestration) which he finds too
often based on idiomatic piano figurations and, sometimes, to
occasional flaws of orchestration. Wasielewski anonymously has
earned a niche in history with this biography by way of such criticism
which one finds repeated over and over, often in the same phrasing,
in the literature ranging from Philipp Spitta's short biography to the
program notes for a recording of *Das Paradies und die Peri*.[15]
Wasielewski, however, adds that these minor miscalculations in no
way detract from the work and that they are quite understandable in
a first effort to write for orchestra.

---

14.   Ibid.: 96.
15.   Philipp Spitta, "Ein Lebensbild Robert Schumanns," in Paul Graf
      Waldersee, *Sammlung musikalischer Vorträge*, series 4 (Leipzig:
      Breitkopf und Härtel, 1882): 1ff.

Brendel, whose most frequent complaints are about Wasielewski's musical criticism, admitted that he himself occasionally disapproved of a composition by Schumann. It was, he felt, the painful duty of a critic who must ignore his personal friendship with the composer in such a case. Wasielewski, he goes on, always carped, however, and seemed intent on finding fault. Even when he was not carping he had only lukewarm praise. To us there is nothing lukewarm in Wasielewski's comments about Schumann as a composer of *Lieder* or as a symphonist even when he criticizes some aspect of an individual work. Brendel, on the other hand, is quite willing to find negative elements in the songs which he reviews in somewhat greater detail. They are among Schumann's most successful works, yet Brendel finds that they occasionally lack melodic line, that in some the voice has little more than a declamatory part while the emphasis lies too strongly in the psychologizing piano accompaniment. What distinguishes Wasielewski's judicious voice from others was that it was too judicious. We come to know him as rather stiff and a bit pedantic.

In *Schumanniana*, a kind of late supplement to the biography, Wasielewski takes up the relationship between Mendelssohn and Schumann ostensibly to squelch gossip about its one-sidedness on Schumann's part.[16] Mendelssohn, he writes, reciprocated whole-heartedly and any suspicion that he considered Schumann a rival is unfounded. Perhaps he was forced to admit to himself that he could not achieve Schumann's depth of musical expression although in regard to form and technical devices he knew himself to be superior. (One can observe here the already prevalent notion that Mendelssohn lacked depth.) In regard to form, Wasielewski continues, Mendelssohn was somewhat "touchy," and it is not impossible that this aspect of Schumann's music gave him some pause. In fact, Mendelssohn did not share Schumann's great admiration for most of Schubert for this reason. Nor was Mendelssohn very pleased with Schumann's critical work, since he did not believe it was a composer's business to write about music.

Since in his earlier book Wasielewski had expressed some doubts

---

16.   Wilhelm Joseph von Wasielewski, *Schumanniana* (Bonn: Emil Strauss, 1883). According to the *National Union Catalog*, there are only two copies of this book in the United States. A third was found in the Newberry Library, however.

about Schumann's ability to build formal structures, this seems
something of a reversal. Of course by 1883, Wasielewski had
acquired a vested interest in Schumann and may gradually have
overcome his reservations. That the rumor of Mendelssohn's disdain
persisted can be seen in the little biography of Schumann by Philipp
Spitta who admits, however, that there is nothing in Mendelssohn's
writing to confirm what was so often said.

> In Mendelssohn's published letters one can find no judgements about
> Schumann's music. The fact is that in Schumann's early works for
> piano he [Mendelssohn] found lacking the power or the need to
> construct larger forms. Occasionally he said something to this effect.
> Soon, however, he had the chance to change his opinion and he often
> referred to his warm sympathy for the compositions of his friend.
> Whether he ever embraced Schumann's musical peculiarities is prob-
> ably doubtful. Their respective natures were too dissimilar.[17]

Spitta's biography is an implied compliment to Wasielewski, since
it is largely based on the latter's book albeit without very much
acknowledgment. In fact, for the great biographer of Bach this
monograph is not an outstanding accomplishment. However well
summarized a life Spitta wrote, it is totally lacking in documentation.
(Spitta's short biography was the basis for the Schumann articles in
the first three editions of *Grove* where the interested reader can
peruse it in English.)

In his memoirs Wasielewski points out that he had never intended
to write detailed musical analyses. But his critics had a point. His
somewhat jaundiced attitude toward Schumann's supposed lack of
formal skill and discipline is never far below the surface. Of course,
Wasielewski writes, Brendel was so preoccupied with *Zukunftsmusik*
as to be incapable of responding objectively. Brendel was determined, he says, to see Schumann as a progressive at all costs.
Perhaps Wasielewski was putting it too strongly, but it has all the
more validity because elsewhere Brendel had developed his own
critical reservations. In his earlier article on Mendelssohn and
Schumann, Brendel identified Schumann as the representative of
a new German style, the true romantic, taking the lead from
Beethoven's late works and making music more subjective and
representational.

---

17.   "Lebensbild": 28.

Juxtaposition, the breaking down of compositions into opposing elements [of mood] . . . was the principle that already in Beethoven's music had gained considerable predominance . . . It should be considered ideal for the instrumental music of the present. Schumann is the one among younger composers battling hardest to seize this element and formalize it, especially in his earlier period.[18]

Brendel admits that not all the works succeed but the overall aim and the overall effect justify the whole. Schumann, writes Brendel, represents a new ideal; he represents the demands of history.[19]

Wasielewski had no such Hegelian preconceptions either tacitly or overtly. A work achieves its aims on its own terms and history does not enter into it. Curiously, Brendel's critiques and Wasielewski's are frequently not very different, and any number of Brendel's comments open with phrases admitting this, phrases such as, "this is very apt," or "while this is essentially correct," before they go on to a "but" or its equivalent.

Considering that Brendel's views and Wasielewski's are never far apart one must wonder what it was that produced Brendel's sharp review. Most likely Brendel felt he should have written the book, not because Wasielewski had preempted the field entirely, but rather because Brendel could only have written a very similar biography, at least when it came to commenting on the music. Brendel might have taken a wider view; he would have assigned Schumann a place in history. It is amusing in a way that the far better critic, Brendel, a writer with a vision as it were, and the narrower mind, Wasielewski, agree in their judgments in all but detail. The early article of Brendel cited above is a remarkable essay on the historical situation of German music since Bach, criticism that takes social and political aspects into account without oversimplifying. In the controversy, largely one-sided on Brendel's part, there is no villain. What Wasielewski had in place of the historical perspective was access to sources and a clear sense of how and when to use them.

This brings us back to Clara and her broken promise to help Wasielewski with material in her possession. It is not at all clear what caused her disenchantment. In a letter to Eduard Hanslick she complained that Wasielewski had misrepresented Robert's problems in

---

18.   *NZfM* 1845: 90.
19.   Ibid.: 93.

Düsseldorf, that Schumann had never been dismissed, as Wasielewski reported.[20] On the contrary, the orchestra committee in Düsseldorf continued to pay his salary while he was in the hospital. But, she went on, how could a Wasielewski ever do justice to her beloved husband? How could so untalented and insensitive a man have understood the wonderful character and creative powers (*herrliches Gemüth und schöpferische Kraft*) of a Robert Schumann? While she claimed never to have read·the biography, she was puzzled by Hanslick's good review. Hanslick, conceding that Wasielewski was not perfect, stuck to his guns, and with all due respect to Clara, maintained that it was essentially a good biography.

In the same article in which Hanslick reprints Clara's letter and repeats his good opinion of Wasielewski's biography, he also writes about the latter's memoirs which he finds rather disappointing and, on the whole, of interest only to members of Wasielewski's family. The book's only contribution, he writes, lay in Wasielewski's reports about music and musicians.

We are equally disappointed, especially because Wasielewski makes no attempt to explain what had happened between him and Clara to cause their rift. At the point at which their friendship comes to an end, Clara is no longer mentioned except as a performer. Before that the portrait of both Schumanns is warm and affectionate; in fact Wasielewski is a good source for some of Clara's traits, a source that none of her recent biographers have noticed. Thus, Wasielewski tells several anecdotes about Clara all of which add up to a person of extreme sensitivity who was close to tears whether Robert disagreed with her tempos (of his work), the kind of wine she served at dinner, or an innocent joke Wasielewski made that Clara took to be an implied criticism.[21] One would guess that the strict fathering Friedrich Wieck had exercised left its mark on his daughter who needed approval in all things.

If one hopes that Wasielewski has more to say about their rift in *Schumanniana*, one is bound to be disappointed there as well. When *Schumanniana* appeared, Clara was still alive and whatever she may have thought of him, Wasielewski was a gentleman, a gentleman,

---

20.   Published in Eduard Hanslick, "W. J. von Wasielewski," *Aus neuer und neuester Zeit*, 2nd ed. (Berlin: Allgemeiner Verein für Deutsche Literatur, 1900).
21.   *Aus siebenzig Jahren*: 120f.

furthermore with strong loyalties. It is quite clear from his memoirs that he did not lose his admiration for Clara whatever she may have felt for him. Similarly, Wasielewski could not bring himself to be unkind to Friedrich Wieck's memory, since Wieck had been his source of much information about Robert. In *Schumanniana* he describes Wieck as highly intelligent, an excellent pedagogue, and very practical, a man who in spite of his pronounced egotism was always ready to help those who interested him. He also had a quick and loud temper as well as a sharp tongue and "grotesquely coarse" ways of expressing himself.[22] His love of money grew out of his poverty as a child. His family had often had to beg for credit. He was both spiritual and intelligent as well as a philistine. "In the heated battle with Schumann he bore a great part of the responsibility."[23]

The chapter in *Schumanniana* dealing with Schumann's associates, particularly those involved with the *Neue Zeitschrift für Musik*, is the most interesting part of the little book. This is especially so because Wasielewski's treatment of Schumann's activities as a critic and editor also aroused Brendel's ire.

Again we find Brendel praising with faint damns. He quotes Wasielewski as recognizing that the "mostly metaphorical dress in which Schumann clothed his critical ideas was often just right and often characterized [a work] with exactitude." You see, says Brendel, Wasielewski recognizes his gift but almost immediately withdraws his recognition again.[24] What Wasielewski had not granted Schumann was objectivity. It is true, says Brendel, that objective penetration in the strict sense was not Schumann's forte. It was wrong, however, to expect it of him. It was artistic intuition that predominated in Schumann's reviews. Given that presupposition, his reviews were quite penetrating. Schumann, says Brendel, had undertaken his work as critic and editor because German musical criticism was in a sad state. Only Adolph Bernard Marx stood out as superior and for a while so had Ludwig Rellstab. Brendel found that Schumann's writing came out of an inner necessity; that he was rarely able to provide balanced judgments because he was responding to his own inner convictions.[25]

---

22.   *Schumanniana*: 53.
23.   Ibid.: 55.
24.   *NZfM* 1858: 157.
25.   Ibid.: 158.

What turns out to be a surprise is that, according to Brendel, Schumann did not consider his editing job a burden most of the time. He was a meticulous editor who pasted all of his own reviews and articles into a scrapbook so that when he decided to publish his *Gesammelte Schriften* they were all at hand. His accounts and correspondence were also in very good order. When he was composing, especially later when the scale of his works grew to larger proportions, he would neglect *NZfM*, and eventually he came to realize that he could not continue to devote himself to both activities. But, says Brendel, shortly after he turned the journal over to him, Schumann was like a pensioner who did not quite know what to do with himself. This too, he adds, was something Wasielewski could not understand, since he thought that editing the journal was nothing more than an onerous duty Schumann had imposed on himself. Wasielewski, according to Brendel, seemed to assume that reviewing was Schumann's means to clear a path for his music. In actuality, he continues, it had the opposite effect, since *NZfM* could hardly take up its editor's cudgels. By involving himself in journalism, Schumann actually kept his music from receiving earlier recognition.

In the history of music there have occasionally been amanuenses who, when their master died, took themselves to be their official representatives on earth, *à la* Schindler. Wasielewski was not one of these and, in any case, as long as Clara was there to protect Schumann's posthumous reputation, there was no need for any other representative. In many ways she was the ideal protrectress, Robert's intellectual equal as well as endowed with all the maternal qualifications, and the performer of his music but not *merely*, his music. Rumor has always had it that she destroyed some of Robert's late works and, even if she had advice from Brahms, this is regrettable. But who was there in those days, who would have done otherwise? If one asks oneself that question, the most likely candidate would be Wasielewski, not because he was wiser than the others, but rather because he was a natural historian. Instead of persevering in the quest to vindicate himself vis-à-vis Brendel, Pohl, and Herman Deiters, he went on to other matters, to write what was for a long time the standard history of violin-playing and violin music and, following this, the history of the cello.[26] It was as a historian as well

---

26. Wasielewski's main historical studies are the following: *Die Violine und ihre Meister* (Leipzig: Breitkopf und Härtel, 1869); *Die Violine*

as an admirer of Schumann that he began his work on the biography while Schumann was still alive. He recognized it as a mission and, while he was not the first biographer of a living composer, he was the first whose work still deserves our serious attention. Would the book have been published had Schumann not died? Would Schumann perhaps even have approved of it?

---

im XVII. Jahrhundert und die Anfänge der Instrumental-Composition (Bonn: M. Cohen and Sohn, 1874); *Geschichte der Instrumentalmusik* (Berlin: Guttentag, 1878); *Das Violoncell und seine Geschichte* (Leipzig: Breitkopf und Härtel, 1889).

CHAPTER IX

THE MEMOIRS OF EDUARD HANSLICK

The memoirs of critics are not nearly as compelling as those of creative artists unless, like Hanslick, they themselves become controversial historical personages and especially when their memoirs include descriptions of many famous contemporaries. Hanslick's are primary source material for a variety of reasons, but in this context they are included because his life paralleled the careers of several generations of composers. His many journeys took him nearly everywhere and despite the shift of focus from Vienna to Leipzig, Munich, Paris, or Milan, Vienna was still mecca for every touring virtuoso or traveling composer. It seems the Viennese remained relatively receptive to novelty and could not be avoided. For a long time the city retained the cachet of being a musical center. Before Hanslick came to Vienna he had lived in Prague which many people, including Berlioz, wrongly thought to be provincial. At Prague, Hanslick had studied with Tomášek who, although no longer a leading composer, dominated the musical education of the place. He taught Hanslick harmony, counterpoint, and piano but had no patience for either history or aesthetics.[1] Those were subjects in which Hanslick was consequently self-taught. He also relied on

---

Note: Unless otherwise indicated, all translations in this chapter are my own.

1. Jan Vaclov Tamášek's autobiography survives in a journal, *Libussa*, published in Prague between 1845 and 1850. Excerpts, translated by Abram Loft, may be found in *The Musical Quarterly*, 32 (1946): 244ff.

himself to keep up with the newest music which, he said, could be rented almost as soon as it appeared. He made the acquaintance of Berlioz who had been persuaded not to avoid Prague on his tour in 1846. Hanslick claims to have served as Berlioz's guide and translator, although Berlioz in his memoirs remembers the future musical historian August Wilhelm Ambros in that rôle and does not even mention Hanslick.[2] Hanslick assumes that some unfavorable reviews he had written in later years had lost him the friendship, but he never stopped admiring either the genius or the originality of the Frenchman. Berlioz, whom Hanslick describes as having the leonine head and eagle eyes familiar to us in the portrait by Delacroix, was traveling with his mistress, Marie-Geneviève Recio. (He tried to pass her off as his wife but, because everyone had heard of the Irish actress, Harriet Smithson, then his wife, this was awkward. Berlioz introduced Miss Recio as his wife and when people were taken aback, he pretended his first wife was dead and she was his second wife.)[3] Miss Recio dominated Berlioz who fetched and carried for her in the rôle of the henpecked lover, a part ridiculously at odds with the composer's arrogance — nor did it suit those eyes and that head.

To the man who had been depicted as Beckmesser it may have been flattering to be called "the Bismarck of music criticism" by so august a person as the aged Verdi, although it seems that the phrase must have contained at least some sarcasm.[4] Hanslick could not have guessed that he would be identified forever with Beckmesser, that the character could hardly be mentioned without explaining whom he was supposed to represent.[5] Would Hanslick have been remembered by posterity at all if it were not for Wagner? Hanslick and George Bernard Shaw are among the very few critics of the past still

---

2. Hector Berlioz, *The Memoirs of Hector Berlioz*, translated and edited by David Cairns (London: Gollanz, 1969).
3. Eduard Hanslick, *Aus meinem Leben* (Berlin: 1894; 2nd ed., Berlin: Allgemeiner Verein für deutsche Literatur, 1911), 2 vols., 1: 57.
4. Hanslick, *Leben*, 1:284.
5. A small selection of Hanslick's criticisms published in a recent monograph by Norbert Tschulik, *Also sprach Beckmesser* (Vienna: Bergland, 1965), patronizes Hanslick in the preface. According to the compiler, Hanslick was wrong about Wagner and Bruckner but his work still holds "some" interest.

being read today. As clever and witty as he is, would Shaw still be read were it not for his literary status?

At the time Hanslick wrote his memoirs he was close to seventy. Perhaps the years had mellowed him enough to take Wagner in stride if he had ever been truly angered by him. Even late in his life he was still being taunted by the composer Hugo Wolf who as critic never missed a chance to condemn those of whom Hanslick approved, rarely without a more or less open reference to him.[6] By comparison to Wagner Hugo Wolf was of course a gentleman. Wagner had even stooped to call Hanslick a Jew. Hanslick claims he did not mind, although it would be difficult to find even a trace of Jewish blood among his ancestors who had for generations been of German stock.[7] That the Wagnerites considered him a pedant, he thought, was ridiculous. "The scribe, Beckmesser," he writes, "is the type of pedant who clutches at petty detail and secondary matters, a philistine without either a sense of beauty or intellect. . . . He marks every deviation from the rules as a crime against art."[8] Hanslick claimed that he had never attacked Wagner over details or violations of rules. "My reviews written over forty years prove conclusively that I never cared about such things." On the other hand there was Wagnerian Beckmesserism. "Its practitioners write sixty pages about one phrase in *Parsifal,* identify ninety *Leitmotive* in the *Ring* and explicate every consonant of every couplet in every work."[9]

Those who may not care any longer about that old controversy and do not therefore read Hanslick the critic should know him as a historian. His two-volume book about concert life in Vienna is an unexpectedly thorough and vivid history, still of considerable value not only as history, but also as an early example of a documentary approach to history.[10] Vienna was spectacularly interesting, of course, as the city that had been the center of European musical

---

6.   See Henry Pleasants, *The Music Criticism of Hugo Wolf* (New York: Holmes and Meyer, 1979).
7.   Hanslick briefly refers to it in *Leben,* 2: 10. In his article, "Eduard Hanslick. The Perfect Anti-Wagnerite" (*The Musical Times;* 116 [1975]: 867f.), Eric Sams states that Hanslick's mother was Jewish without giving any sources. I have not been able to verify his statement.
8.   Hanslick, *Leben,* 2: 227.
9.   Ibid.
10. Eduard Hanslick, *Geschichte des Concertwesens in Wien,* 2 vols. (Vienna: Braumüller, 1869).

history for about one hundred years. Our modern sophistication might lead us to expect little of such a book, especially since we know that Hanslick was an amateur, but then so were they all at the time, Baini, Ambros, and Kiesewetter. There had never been the kind of training in research we now take for granted.

Those were difficult times for a critic of integrity who could not possibly favor everything taking place on the musical scene. We tend to forget that it was a turbulent century. Berlioz, Schumann, Chopin, Mendelssohn, Liszt, Wagner, and Verdi were all born within ten years of each other. Meyerbeer, the subject of Wagner's special animus, was actually older than Schubert, and Bruckner, now rarely mentioned except in tandem with Mahler, was born before Brahms. In the 1860s a new generation of composers was born. Although Strauss, Mahler, Wolf, and Debussy did not make their musical debuts until the 1880s, they must have made Hanslick's last years difficult as well as stimulating. One should also remember the so-called lesser composers, many of whom were more than merely competent and had to be reckoned with by the practicing critic. Hanslick's influence must have been considerable, yet he appears to have remained fundamentally modest. The focus of his writing is only occasionally on himself a far greater portion of his book is taken up with vignettes of contemporaries.

When Hanslick began his career as a critic it was not yet possible to earn one's living by criticism and *belles lettres*, at least on the Continent. Practically every writer on music he knew who was not actually a composer or dramatist, men such as Kiesewetter and Ambros, had government posts and still managed to write and to do research in quantities that make individual modern scholarship pale by comparison. Although it is true that these writers had little to study by way of secondary sources, they needed to gain access to original documents, translate and edit them, and understand the early theorists to find paths in a wilderness that few explorers had seen. Apparently government officials in Austria worked only in the morning, had long and frequent leaves, and functioned more or less by rote. One wonders if it was an advantage or disadvantage for a critic to hold amateur status. It would not be easy today to accept the musical reviews of a writer so intimately involved with his subjects, so warm a friend of some, so hot an enemy of others. To judge by the periodicals of the late eighteenth and early nineteenth centuries, there were different reviewers for printed music. The latter were mostly practicing musicians or theorists while concerts were reviewed by musical *literati*. It is not clear how well the reviewers of published music in the professional journals were paid. There is a good deal of writing about musical criticism in terms of its ideas, but the history of musical criticism as a profession has so far been neglected. It must certainly have become difficult for the professional musician to retain his objectivity in an environment that became more and more competitive and was more and more inclined to divide itself into schools. (Hugo Wolf was hardly objective when he wrote a diatribe against Brahms' choice of E minor for a symphony merely on the grounds that it was supposedly unprecedented.[11] He never explained what was wrong with that choice of key.)

A critic like Hanslick who was not a practicing musician had other problems. It was obviously difficult for him to be truly critical of Brahms whom he regarded as the champion of his time. Even when he disapproved of a work such as the *Double Concerto for Violin and Violoncello*, op. 102) — his boredom and dismay is almost palpable — he goes no farther than to call it less important than other compositions.[12] The English journalist Henry Fothergill Chorley expressed concern with the rising influence of critics who now had musicians at their mercy. Whereas, not so long ago, musicians had made their living by pleasing a court or a congregation, they now depended on the approval of a paying public who often, in turn, depended on critics for help in deciding to approve or disapprove.[13] Chorley found this a heavy responsibility although he believed that ultimately the musician's independence from patronage was to be preferred. Hanslick had other doubts about the function of the critic. When at the end of his memoirs he discusses criticism with Theodor Billroth,[14] the famous surgeon and extraordinarily gifted amateur, and perhaps Brahms' closest friend, he says that the public frequently overruled critics by its attendance or nonattendance. In the long run, Hanslick thought, the public was usually right. (What Hanslick had to say about criticism takes up only a short section of his memoirs. Billroth, who had apparently seen part of the manu-

---

11.   Pleasants, *Music Criticism of Hugo Wolf*: 185.
12.   Eduard Hanslick, *Aus dem Tagebuche eines Musikers* (Berlin: Allgemeiner Verein für deutsche Literatur, 1892): 264ff.
13.   Henry Fothergill Choreley, *Modern German Music* (London: 1854), reprint edited by the author, New York: Da Capo, 1973), 2: 66ff.
14.   Hanslick, *Leben*, 2: 308.

script, had complained that Hanslick said nothing at all about it and joked that he, Billroth, would take responsibility for a chapter on the subject. As a result, Hanslick framed this section of his memoirs in the form of a dialogue with Billroth.)

Although he was sorry that it was necessary to review so many performers who came to Wienna chiefly to obtain the good reviews needed for engagements in more provincial places, Hanslick found daily reviewing a stimulant for which he never acquired a tolerance. If he regretted anything, it was his lack of enthusiasm for old music and literature. To be honest, he writes, he would give all of Sophocles for one *Faust*, rather see all of Schütz' music consumed by fire than one *German Requiem*. The same went for Bach; Hanslick vastly preferred the quartets of Brahms and Schumann. He had loved Schumann's music from his very youth, having belonged to an unofficial branch of the *Davidsbündler* in his student days in Prague. Later he never ended a day without playing one of Schumann's piano pieces before retiring. Musical history might go back centuries but the music close to his heart started with Mozart. "Why do I not include Wagner among the giants of modern music? Because I cannot rouse myself to enthusiasm for him. I recognize his brilliance and his uniquely great talent in creating a new blend of poetry, art and music and see it as a powerful new brew of opera. But his music leaves me cold."[15]

The Bismarck of nineteenth-century Viennese music criticism was only human after all. We may be shocked to realize that one of the most notorious controversies in the history of music ultimately comes down to the megalomania of Wagner who could bear no criticism at all, and the personal taste of his most famous adversary. Should we be equally shocked by Hanslick's indifference to Schütz and Bach? Brahms certainly did not share his friend's limitations in that respect. Not only did he have recourse to old forms and devices in his own music, but he was also an advocate as well as an editor of reissues of old music.

The section in which Hanslick speaks of his own preferences is the only confessional part of his memoirs. In an earlier chapter on the nature of autobiography also addressed to Billroth, Hanslick reported that he had destroyed his diaries of some twenty-five years in a fit of depression. He had not wanted to leave them to posterity.

---

15.   Ibid., 1: 336.

His private joys and sorrows, the secrets of his inmost heart, should remain private. His published memoirs are thus almost entirely external; they are the memoirs of a journalist concerned with events. In spite of his one work of musical history and his book on aesthetics, Hanslick was basically a very superior journalist. However knowledgeable, however competent he may have been, we cannot burden him with literary or philosophical ambitions he never claimed for himself. Hanslick realized that he had shortcomings in this respect. *Vom Musikalisch-Schönen*, he writes, was only a beginning. "That it was only a preliminary sketch or skeleton [of an aesthetic theory] was clear to me, just as it was clear to me that its negative and polemical style overwhelmed what was positive and systematic in it. To write a truly systematic aesthetics of music would have required unlimited time and perfect concentration."[16] It also required a great deal of reading. Philosophy tired him. Instead it was the history of music that began to fascinate him and he began to think that an aesthetics of music could be written only with a thorough knowledge of history. "What is beautiful in music? Different times, different peoples and different schools have given quite different answers to these questions. The more deeply I delved into musical history, the vaguer and airier became aesthetics."[17] That he should come to this conclusion was almost inevitable. Even if he had not read all that history, the ever-changing musical situation was such that an absolute theory of what made for beauty in music would have been virtually untenable; there was so much revolution in the air. The need for some stability must have been stronger for Brahms who, in the face of controversy about his rôle in the development and progress of music, probably took comfort in the older masters he studied and edited. One senses that his passacaglias and other old musical forms reflect a conviction that there was still life in the old body.

Hanslick may have been indifferent to early music, but this preoccupation with history served to prepare him for the post of lecturer in the subject at the University of Vienna, the first lecturer in music the university ever employed. For the first time, too, the auditorium in which he lectured was furnished with a piano. Women, who were then not admitted to the university, wanted to share in his

16.   Ibid., 1: 242—43.
17.   Ibid.

erudition and he thus initiated private lectures. On one occasion Brahms served as assistant, playing the *Diabelli Variations* to illustrate Hanslick's talk.

Soon Hanslick was named *ausserordentlicher Professor* of music, extraordinary because one did not then "major" in music. His classes were attended primarily by students in other disciplines. According to Guido Adler who studied at the University of Vienna, one could not learn there the systematic kind of musical history that interested him. Still, Hanslick encouraged him. When he read Adler's thesis, *Die historischen Grundklassen der christlich-abendländischen Musik bis 1600*, Hanslick immediately recognized it as a new approach to the subject. In fact, Adler writes, Hanslick embarrassed him by declaring it good enough to serve as his *Habilitationsschrift*.[18] Berlioz' supposed guide, the historian August Wilhelm Ambros, lived a life very similar to Hanslick's. He was almost nine years older than Hanslick and far more learned, had also written a book on aesthetics, a response to Hanslick's *Vom Musikalisch-Schönen*, worked as a journalist, and eventually accepted a professorship at the University of Prague which made it possible for him to give up his career as a public prosecutor. While he is deservedly remembered as a historian, his reviews are no longer read. His opinions seem not to have had the impact of Hanslick's. "How is it," wrote the latter, "that Ambros who understands music ten times better than any other Viennese critic has so little influence on public opinion? People find his reviews entertaining but are not swayed by them. He makes so many jokes, quotes so excessively and wastes so many ideas that the main line of his articles disappears among an abundant and not always tasteful embroidery. . . . He speaks as he writes, without regard to form, a wittily erudite polyhistor as well as wee as an improviser in the same person. . . . He finds it difficult to write an article about Gounod without going back to sixteenth-century Venice or the Verona of Monteverdi."[19] Those remarks about Ambros' lack of form and his prolixity are confirmed by our own reading of his essays which do indeed vacillate between great erudition, perceptive insights, and an occasional obscurantism that borders on the absurd. With the historian's proclivity for generalization, for example, Ambros divided German "classicism" into three stylistic periods: Bach's, "the

18.   Guido Adler, *Wollen und Wirken* (Vienna: Universal, 1935): 18.
19.   Hanslick, *Leben*, 1: 366ff.

period of strict style"; Mozart's, "the era of beauty"; and Beethoven's, "the period of richness."[20] What we so casually call romanticism was also then still in flux; the contemporary historian saw distinctions that are still of interest.

Hanslick was always clear and to the point, the probable reason for his greater influence òn a lay public. It was in 1861, when he was only thirty-six, that he became a professor. At about the same time he was more and more frequently called upon to represent Austria at world's fairs where instruments and competitions of performers were judged. As a result of his travels he came to know almost every musician in Europe and his vignettes are invaluable.

Whether Hanslick was part Jewish or not, it is a fact that anti-Semitism is a recurrent subject in his memoirs. He is hardly fierce in his condemnation; rather, his tone is one of distaste. Toward the end of the second volume he describes his meeting with the writer Berthold Auerbach whose very German collection of stories from the Black Forest, entitled *Schwarzwälder Dorfgeschichten*, had made him one of the "darlings of the German people."[21] This did not prevent Auerbach, however, from being rejected during the surge of anti-Semitism in the last third of the century, the same anti-Semitism in which Wagner wallowed. A liberal German novelist and journalist, Gustav Freytag, responded to Wagner's essay against Jews in music by writing that all of the traits of which Wagner accused Jewish artists were Wagner's own.[22] Wagner himself was guilty of "the preoccupation with coldly calculated effect, was himself incapable of giving expression its full melodic and harmonic due, was himself neurasthenic [*nervös*], and also tried to make up for his lack of invention by means of witty ideas and purely external devìces."[23] It is a measure of Hanslick's tacit rancor that he endorsed Freytag's not very insightful musical criticism, a kind of criticism he would never have written. Hanslick also believed that with friends like Wagner's, one did not need enemies. He deemed the biography of Wagner by Ferdinand Praeger, a supposed admirer, the most unflattering

20. August-Wilhelm Ambros, "Die neu-romantische Musik," *Culturhistorische Bilder aus dem Musikleben der Gegenwart* (Leipzig: H. Mattes, 1860): 51.
21. Hanslick, *Leben*, 2: 206.
22. The article, originally published in 1869, may be found in Gustav Freytag, *Gesammelte Aufsätze* (Leipzig: Herzel, 1888), 2: 321ff.
23. Ibid.

portrait of all. The book, *Wagner as I Knew Him*, now generally unavailable, was, Hanslick thought, a realistic depiction of the composer.

Like most of his contemporaries, Hanslick was himself tainted by subtle anti-Semitism, an anti-Semitism that was practically endemic and of which the practitioners were probably not even aware. Hanslick criticizes the dramatist Hermann von Mosenthal as a seeker after cheap effects, one of Wagner's complaints about Jewish artists. If this is not in itself indicative of anti-Semitic criticism, it becomes so when Hanslick links Mosenthal with Auerbach whom he also finds guilty. None of this prevented Hanslick from being friends with either man, nor did it prevent him from praising Mosenthal's libretto for Otto Nicolai's *The Merry Wives of Windsor*.

When Hanslick met Meyerbeer, he could not get the composer to talk about Wagner except to acknowledge Wagner's success. It must have taken some daring to compare Offenbach to German composers of more serious music. "I think if one gave ten German composers the text, 'Ah, que j'aime la militaire,' nine of them would set it to stanzas of four trochaes."[24] While Offenbach's arias seldom ventured beyond tonic and dominant harmony, his melodic invention was superior to most composers of opera and nobody could rival his sense of piquant, lively rhythms. As a theatrical inventor only Wagner could be compared to him except that in his later works Wagner had lost all sense of proportion.

In introducing him as the Bismark of musical criticism, Verdi demonstrated that Hanslick's reputation had reached beyond the borders of German-speaking countries and that he was considered powerful. It also suggests that Verdi thought him something of a despot. Perhaps it was only the natural animosity of the artist toward a critic, but in any case Hanslick quotes the phrase proudly.[25] For a critic of Hanslick's usual perceptiveness his lack of understanding for Verdi's *Falstaff* was obtuse. He saw the work as the weak effort of

---

24. Hanslick, *Leben*, 2: 83.
25. Reading Hanslick's reviews of various operas of Verdi leads to the conclusion that whatever praise he could muster was never unequivocal. While he recognized Verdi's genius, he usually found him tasteless. This accusation is most often based on Verdi's choice of librettos, but Hanslick often pointed out that Verdi could not rise above the text. See also Massimo Milo, "Verdi e Hanslick," *La Rassegna musicale*, Vol. 21 (1951): 212ff.

an old man to indulge a lifelong desire to write a comic opera. The absence of arias, he writes, was a matter of default. Verdi was no longer capable of inventing melodies. He was compensating for the loss of youthful vigor by experience and pure technique, producing something called "dialogue music" ("*Konversations-Musik*"), fine and lively and neither crude nor "effeminate." But all in all, he thought, *The Merry Wives of Windsor* was better.

Although Hanslick is traditionally blamed for his lack of sympathy for Wagner, Bruckner, and Strauss, or for his intolerance of program music, this faint praise of *Falstaff* is perhaps a truer failure, not only because he did not recognize it for the masterpiece it was, but also because he was unaware that intentionally or not the work was inherently anti-Wagner. What Verdi achieved was truly a dialogue-opera, a genuine *Musikdrama* with means that had been available in the finale of the *opera buffa* ever since the eighteenth century. Could it be that with all the liberalism Hanslick showed toward such a composer as Offenbach, he could not manage to take *Falstaff* quite seriously? It was, after all, just another comic opera by an Italian composer. His rejection of Wagner was based on more serious philosophical grounds even if it was primarily the result of intense dislike. Perhaps acceptance would have been easier if Verdi had matched the pomp and circumstance of Wagner's aesthetics with theories of his own.

CHAPTER X
DOES DOCUMENTARY BIOGRAPHY HAVE A FUTURE?

The most recent composer for whom Otto Erich Deutsch compiled a documentary biography was Franz Schubert.[1] Apparently Deutsch hoped to do the same for Beethoven but realized that he could probably never finish such a work. For major composers after about 1830 the kind of sources that go into such compilations proliferate so rapidly that the task becomes virtually impossible. Beethoven was already an institution, internationally known and discussed years before he died even though he never left Austria once he settled there. Schubert's short life had also been spent exclusively in Vienna and environs but he had not yet become famous. Had Beethoven continued concertizing widely, he would have left an even broader trail. Eva Badura-Skoda, to whom Deutsch proposed documenting Beethoven, was overawed by the project, especially since there was not yet a complete edition of Beethoven's letters or of his notebooks, materials not in themselves part of a documentary biography, but rather the basis on which a documentary book might have to be built.[2] Dating Beethoven's own materials is exceedingly difficult, since he was casual about dates and his handwriting is often indeci-

1. Otto Erich Deutsch, *Schubert, a Documentary Biography*. Trans. by Eric Blom. (Revised edition, London: Dent, 1947).
2. Eva Badura-Skoda, "Probleme einer Dokumentar-Biographie Beethovens," in Gesellschaft für Musikforschung, *Berlicht über den Internationalen Musikwissenschaftlichen Kongress Bonn 1970*, ed. by Hans Heinrich Eggebrecht (Kassel: Bärenteiter): 331ff.

pherable. In view of the stream of visitors who seem to have called on Beethoven, the notes, letters, and conversation-book are essential in order to retrace the testimony of all who met him.

Had Schubert lived even one decade longer, it is likely that material about him would have accumulated at a similar pace. When in the 1830s his songs were gaining popularity in Paris he would have become a celebrity, especially since he looked like the sensitive hero of many French novels.[3] If nothing else, he would have had to protect his works from piracy and published them simultaneously in Germany, France, and England, in itself a source of correspondence that might take up volumes. There would have been reviews, articles, travelers' reports, and diaries, all reflecting the hunger of the public for heroes.

To imagine the consequences of popularity one needs only to contemplate the lives of Franz Liszt or Giacomo Meyerbeer. In the case of Liszt, first a prodigy, subsequently a romantic hero, the task would be awesome. (Since he wrote a great deal, there is even some question about which of the writings attributed to him are genuine.) The voluminous correspondence of Meyerbeer is now being collected.[4] Our interest in him is not primarily romantic or even musical. It lies in the correspondence of a practical man of the theater rather than that of an intellectual. But if we cannot see him as the prototype of the romantic composer, all of his letters not written to members of his family take us into the world of the theater and the business of music. We gain considerable insight into his dealings with publishers, agents, librettists, and impresarios, an insight no historian can hope to duplicate. (The fact that the editors of his correspondence have carefully annotated it brings the volumes close to documentary biography probably not otherwise feasible in the thorough fashion Deutsch considered essential.) A similar attempt to document the image of Wagner in contemporary literature will probably reach seven volumes even if limited to German-language journals and newspapers. The journals so far consist of only those specializing in music, theater, and belles-lettres and will presumably

---

3.   Joseph-Marc Bailbé, *Le Roman et la musique en France sous la Monarchie de Juillet.* (Paris: Lettres Modernes de Minard, 1969).
4.   Giacomo Meyerbeer, *Briefwechsel und Tagebücher*, ed. by Heinz and Gudrun Becker, 4 vols. (Berlin: de Gruyter, 1975—).

omit periodicals of a more general nature or those political in character.[5]

The central figure in documentary biographies is always a major composer, of course. Who else would deserve so tedious and probably ungrateful an untertaking? (Like that of bibliographers, the lot of documentary biographers is probably one of rather grudging admiration, since their work supposedly does not constitute "original" contributions.) Documentary collections traditionally required a central figure, but the realization that some other subject could be the focal point around which to collect contemporary sources is becoming evident. One still reasonable type of documentation is represented by *La Musique à Paris en 1830—1831,* highly selective but still practical.[6] Another far more comprehensive one is the collection entitled *Situationsgeschichte der Musikkritik und des musikalischen Pressewesens in Deutschland.*[7] When it is ultimately completed (assuming it ever can be), it will have required many volumes and will serve primarily as a source in which by means of various indexes one can find particular topics. One must suspect that, when the collector's net is cast too widely, such collections result in comparatively small returns. It is probably more practical to select a single topic or a single person, be it a critic, a publisher, or a period. Eduard Hanslick comes immediately to mind as a candidate. He is a man who is in many ways a typical center for documentation. Because for decades Hanslick has been held in such low esteem due to his posthumous Beckmesserian reputation, he has not been read widely, except perhaps as an esthetician. Only those of us who share his skepticism about Wagner (admittedly a dwindling group) have rediscovered him as an extraordinary critic. In the process of reading his many collections of essays and his autobiography, we discovered furthermore that he left many miniature portraits of contemporaries. These were all grounds for the kind of vindication we tried for in the previous chapter.

---

5. Helmuth Kirchmeyer, *Situationsgeschichte der Musikkritik und des musikalischen Pressewesens in Deutschland; dargestellt vom Ausgang des 18. bis zum Beginn des 20. Jahrhunderts.* Subseries, *Das zeitgenössische Wagnerbild.* Studien zur Musikgeschichte des 19. Jahrhunderts, 7. (Regensburg: Bosse, 196—).

6. François Lesure *et al., La Musique à Paris en 1830—1831* (Paris: Bibliothèque Nationale, 1983).

7. See note 5.

We shall not try further to rehabilitate Hanslick except to establish his reliability as a witness. We are naturally inclined to regard him as biased when it comes to Wagner and his disciples, although he always admitted that he could not bear the man.[8] Even so he was able to admit to grudging admiration for Wagner's genius and his concepts.

In one of his essays the supposed archphilistine Hanslick discusses a little book by Ferdinand Praeger, published in England as *Wagner as I Knew Him* and subsequently in Germany as *Wagner wie ich ihn kannte.*[9] The German version roused some of Wagner's more unsavory followers to such rage that they managed to persuade Breitkopf und Härtel to destroy all the copies the publisher could retrieve. Hanslick wrote not only that the Praeger book seemed plausible to him, but also, almost prophetically, that the way to attack a book was not by means of physical destruction but with the words that ought to demolish it.[10] The issue is relevant here, since the truly impossible task of documenting the life of Wagner and his environment is not helped by eliminating anything controversial. Political considerations begin to enter at this point, because the proto-Nazis who destroyed the book were unwilling to see Wagner depicted as a revolutionary, while the journals of Wagner's "associate," the anarchist Bakunin, survive only in literature issued by the Soviet press.

What makes Hanslick so valuable in this context is that among his intimates were many of the best-known musicians of Europe. Reading Hanslick is not only revealing about them directly, but also, one vignette often leads to another. His kind of *feuilleton* becomes a link in a chain of potential documentation. The prócess has so many implications for the documentalist that it might actually frighten him away. Thus, for example, when Hanslick toward the end of his life sometimes ventures into printing letters from musicians — always with their permission — it becomes a problem to pursue their

---

8.   Eduard Hanslick, *Aus meinem Leben*, 2 vols. (2nd ed., Berlin: Allgemeiner Verein für deutsche Literatur, 1911), 1: 336.
9.   Ferdinand Praeger, *Wagner as I knew him* (New York: Longmans, Green, 1892), in German, *Wagner wie ich ihn kannte* (Leipzig: Breitkopf und Härtel, 1892).
10.   See Eduard Hanslick, "Richard Wagner und Wendelin Weissheimer," *Aus neuer und neuerster Zeit* (Berlin: Allgemeiner Verein für deutsche Literatur, 1900).

implication and verify the facts as they are mentioned. Surprisingly many letters are often still otherwise unknown. Even more surprising is it to find that Professor Badura-Skoda's complaint about the lack of complete collections of Beethoven's letters and of his notebooks frequently also applies to other major and minor composers. While this is easy to understand in the case of the less celebrated, their papers are just as valuable, sometimes even more so, since many *Kleinmeister* are less egocentric than the great and are consequently better observers. The fact is that the sort of documentary biography for which we admire Otto Erich Deutsch may have at least as much value for an insight into the general environment of a composer as for the composer himself.

A general historian interested in documenting the ramifications of some types of information by perusing various kinds of documents stumbles on this sort of biographical material and is likely to become so enamored of it that he loses sight of the original goal. In the case of the present writer, the history of publishing was his original preoccupation. Since the archives of many old publishing houses are not accessible for one reason or another, the author began to read the letters of musicians to their publishers, current journals, information about honoraria and copyright, contemporary criticism, etc., all the same materials that represent grist for the mill of the biographical documentalist. The letters of their Paris agent Heinrich Probst to Breitkopf und Härtel, for example, contain so much that might be considered gossip that in some respects their biographical value is as great as what he writes about the business of publishing.[11] For a short period Probst was rather closely involved with Robert Schumann and it is only logical that one should pursue this relationship in order to verify what Schumann thought of him and so to understand how central Probst is to issues of publishing. The name Probst comes up numerous times in the early years of Schumann's diary as a prominent Leipzig publisher with whom Schumann played four-hand music.[12] Probst may have introduced the composer to

---

11. Wilhelm Hitzig, "'Pariser Briefe.' Ein Beitragzur Arbeit des deutschen Musikverlags aus der Jahren 1833—1840," *Der Bär*, 1929/30 (Leipzig: Breitkopf und Härtel, 1930): 27—73. Hans Lenneberg, *Breitkopf und Härtel in Paris. The Letters of Their Agent Heinrich Probst, 1833—1840.* In preparation (Pendragon).

12. Robert Schumann, *Tagebücher*, ed. by Georg Eismann (Leipzig: Deutscher Verlag, 1975).

some of Schubert's music. Apparently Schumann liked the man although later, in some of Clara's letters to Robert, she says that she does not trust Probst and she absolutely refused to allow a daughter of Probst to be her "chaperone" in Paris.[13] Some of the ramifications of this acquaintance can serve to illustrate the pleasures and torments of the documentalist. The pleasures are those of a historian finding that various fragments of information all fit together; the torments are caused by the realization that once one gets beyond the eighteenth century, there is no end. No matter how many one finds, there are always other sources, often so voluminous that time does not allow their pursuit. Working with the Breitkopf archives in the Staatsarchiv Leipzig, for example, the writer found volume upon volume of *copialettere* which, while they turned up little about Probst, await exploitation in a variety of other contexts.

In the course of the pursuit Clara Wieck briefly becomes a focal point primarily because Probst writes to Raymund Härtel about her Parisian tour, information that needs to be verified.[14] The problem of documentary biography finds here an ideal illustration, especially since the latest biographers of Clara Wieck-Schumann have not encountered all of the same material and their subsequent conclusions differ somewhat from those of this writer.[15] No blame attaches to them; rather their omissions reflect an almost hopeless situation.

Part of the Clara Wieck story demonstrates the proliferation of documents, their problems, and the complex process of verification. Even in her early years when Clara was not yet the institution she was to become later one can see how quickly documentation proliferates in the early nineteenth century. Worse, one must begin to choose among contradictory materials, and every omission on the part of the collector can result in a different interpretation. One of her recent biographers, for example has had access to the diary Clara kept jointly with her father, new letters from and to Robert Schumann, the Schumanns' household books, and other such materials, but somehow neglected an interesting book, namely,

---

13. Robert und Clara Schumann, *Briefwechsel*. Kritische Gesamtausgabe ed. by Eva Weissweiler (Frankfurt a/M: Stroemfeld/Roter Stern, 1984), 1: 236.
14. See Hitzig, letter 57 (p. 63).
15. Joan Chissell, *Clara Schumann, a Dedicated Spirit* (New York: Taplinger, 1983). Nancy B. Reich, *Clara Schumann, the Artist and the Woman* (New York: Cornell University Press, 1985).

Wasielewski's *Schumanniana*.[16] Wasielewski's first biography of Schumann, clearly a labor of love, omitted many personal recollections, some of which he published in *Schumanniana*. Eventually Wasielewski wrote his own memoirs. This is a rather dull book containing the kind of detail only his family could have found interesting. Still, as Hanslick already pointed out in his review, there are a great many fascinating details in it, especially about Clara as well as about Mendelssohn as teacher and conductor, and for the documentor it is one of many hidden essential sources[17]

Here again, as if to illustrate the need for them, letters are the point of departure. There are, for example, the letters Friedrich Wieck wrote home from his several tours with his daughter Clara between 1830 and 1838. A number of these have survived and have been published.[18] We do not know whether Wieck undertook the tours primarily to show off the musical gifts of his daughter or whether he set out to make money and to advertise his teaching. Whatever motivated him, however, the letters tell us much more than such crude intentions might lead one to expect.

On their first journey Clara was just eleven and one must wonder who decided what music she would play. Wieck's seeming vulgarity makes one doubt that he would have requested the many serious pieces her programs contained, many more than was customary among the traveling virtuosos of her time. In publishing a list of Clara's recital pieces, Pamela Susskind Pettler demonstrates how much more serious her programs became after 1835 than before, but even her earlier programs already consist of more than half of the kind of music we still regard highly, if we count works played more than ten times.[19] Reading Wieck's letters one has the impression of a blunt crudeness that is not altogether pleasant. But it fits the descrip-

---

16. Joseph Wilhelm von Wasielewski, *Schumanniana* (Bonn: Strauss, 1883).
17. Joseph Wilhelm von Wasielewski, *Aus siebzig jahren* (Stuttgart and Leipzig: Deutsche Verlagsanstalt, 1897). See also Eduard Hanslick, "W. J. von Wasielewski und Clara Schumann," *Aus neuer und neuester Zeit*: 313ff.
18. Käthe Walch-Schumann, *Friedrich Weick Briefe aus den Jahren 1830—1838*. Beiträge zur rheinischen Musikgeschichte, 74 (Cologne: Volk, 1968).
19. Pamela Susskind Pettler, "Clara Schumann's Recitals, 1832—50," *19th Century Music*, 4 (1981): 70ff.

tion given by Wasielewski who characterized Wieck as volatile and vehement, occasionally noisy and uncouth, but with a deeply spiritual and a witty side.[20] If Clara selected her own recital programs, it is quite likely that her father must have approved.

That Clara was an extraordinary child is beyond doubt. Not that performing prodigies were so rare in her day as to make her stand out for that fact alone. It is her early composition of relatively high caliber that lends her talent a special dimension. Even her contemporaries recognized the superiority of these pieces of hers, perhaps written mainly to show off her technique. In Dresden in 1830, when she was just eleven years old, the composer Karl Gottlieb Reissiger put her through her paces, asking her to improvise on a theme he gave her. He was amazed at her musicianship. Wieck writes that all the pianists of Dresden (he refers to them all in the feminine gender), were green with envy and he was afraid they would try to stop Clara from giving a public concert.[21] Wieck says that once her musical genius was recognized, Dresden society could not believe that she accepted her divided world, part of her a prodigy, part a child, without making greater demands. Judging from Wieck's letters she was either very docile or very self-assured. She ate too many sweets once and took great pleasure in her new braids, but he had no complaints that she was a difficult travel companion. The public self-confidence — as opposed to her private insecurity — her letters to Robert Schumann of some years later convey was probably developed quite early. Clara, writes Wieck, "one of us two monkeys from the Leipzig menagerie," plays with self-assurance as never before, but is otherwise totally the same girl as in Leipzig where nobody pays too much attention to her.[22]

In 1838, at nineteen, she went to Vienna where her concerts were triumphs and where a critic points out how superior her programs were. They were even superior to those of Liszt whose series of eight concerts followed hers almost immediately. Liszt arrived in Vienna while the Wiecks were still there. Clara played him some of her own transcriptions of Schubert songs, as well as Schumann's *Carnaval* which, she writes to Robert, made a deep impression on Liszt.[23]

---

20.   *Schumanmana*: 55.
21.   Wieck: 22—23.
22.   Ibid.: 27.
23.   Berthold Litzmann, *Clara Schumann, an Artist's Life*, translated and

She could have played every night, her father said, but she was not a horse. When she finally left Vienna she had received the title of Imperial Court Pianist and an honorary membership in the Gesellschaft der Musikfreunde. But, says the critic, Heinrich Adami, it was fortunate that she played before Liszt came. Once the latter appeared, everyone including Clara was totally eclipsed.[24]

What makes a group of letters such as Wieck's so trustworthy is partly his casual style. One could say anything in letters home. It becomes clear that he tends to exaggerate but the basic truth of his observations can be verified in such a source as Vienna's *Allgemeine Theaterzeitung* (*AT*), in Clara's own observations written to Robert, and in the accounts of contemporaries. *AT* had already been published for thirty years in 1838 and one can see why it was so successful. The periodical which appeared five times a week was entirely devoted to culture. *AT* published serialized novels, short stories, theater, music and book reviews, news of the arts, and various oddities. It was highly literate and very amusing, an early *New Yorker* without the advertising. To whet the public's interest in Clara, *AT* reprinted a review from a Berlin paper before she played, a report calling her reputation entirely justified. "She is not merely a technician," writes the Berlin critic, "her playing is of such musicality [*genialität*] that we are inclined to forget the facility with which she overcomes the greatest technical difficulties. . . . In its externals her playing reminds one of Felix Mendelssohn's spiritual, humorous, bold, sharply accented approach, although Mendelssohn plays with more detachment than his rival who allows herself to be carried along by her enthusiasm, without ever exceeding the boundaries of feminine grace."[25] The review goes on to compare her with another "rival," Theodor Döhler (1814—56), whose performance is said to have many feminine characteristics, while Clara's was permeated with masculine power and imagination. His letter home, reporting

---

abridged by Grace E. Hadow, 2 vols. (London: Macmillan, 1913), 1: 150. The accuracy of Clara's report is confirmed by Liszt's letter to Schumann using almost the same phrases (in French) as hers. See *Briefe und Gedichte aus dem Album Robert und Clara Schumanns*, edited by Wolfgang Bötticher (Leipzig: Deutscher Verlag, 1979): 109.

24.   *Allgemeine Theaterzeitung und Originalblatt für Kunst, Literatur, Musik, Mode und Geselliges leben*, 31 (1838): 355. All references will be to the same volume and will be abbreviated as *AT.*

25.   *AT*: 8.

the event, is typical of the way Wieck blunts and exaggerates. "The public is really taken with Döhler, but in the cafés it is being said that Clara is the man, Döhler the woman."[26]

Wherever one looks, one is confronted by the treatment of virtuosos as rivals who seem to have been in a contest equaled today only in sports or perhaps touring orchestras. An anonymous report from Vienna quoted from the *Neue Zeitschrift für Musik* compares some leading pianists in a long list of characteristics from which we cite just a few.

"Cleanness of playing: Thalberg, Wieck, Henselt, Liszt.

> Improvisation: Liszt.
> Profound artistry: Liszt, Wieck.
> Affected behaviour: Henselt."

The critic, Eduard von Lannoy, took vehement exception to this sort of invidious comparison in an article to which *AT* devoted a front page.[27]

Since Clara played many private concerts, which were not reviewed, not everything Wieck writes can be verified. His letter of January 2 reports, for example, that Clara played *Carnaval* as well as Robert's Sonata in F sharp minor, op. 11. "His *Carnaval* created quite a furor. . . . The sonata was not understood equally well. The Baroness (known for twenty years as the greatest Beethoven interpreter), as well as Cibbini declared loudly on the spot that the sonata had never been performed in Vienna quite so profoundly and so brilliantly. We are told that that performance raised Clara's reputation in Vienna to its highest level.[28]

Apparently Clara played *Carnaval* several more times but even though Wieck said that it made Robert's reputation in Vienna, reviews do not mention it.

Not all her public concerts were reviewed in *AT* either. The Viennese whom Mozart had already called fickle were apparently unwilling to read about the same personality again and again. When Holy Week began on April 9 in 1838, Wieck wrote home that they

---

26. Wieck: 64.
27. *AT*: 417.
28. Wieck: 79. The baroness was probably Dorothea von Ertmann (1781 to 1849), a pianist who had been a friend of Beethoven. Cibbini was Antonia, née Kozeluch.

ought to leave at the end of the week or else Clara would have to play a benefit for the citizens of Pest who had just suffered a devastating flood. The Wiecks at that time had been in Vienna for about three months, but in the last few weeks there were no more reviews. On the fourteenth of April *AT* reports simply that Clara is about to leave for Paris. Wieck writes they will be leaving on the twentieth. They went on to Graz, but Paris had to wait till next year.

On the twenty-first Liszt's concert of three days before is reviewed, and Heinrich Adami who had consistently raved about Clara writes more cooly.

> Liszt is so special and surprising a phenomenon that I find it difficult to describe his playing or to find the right words for the impression he made on me. One thing is certain, the enthusiasm aroused by Clara Wieck will not suffice. It is odd that just when one has thought to have seen near perfection in art and believes it cannot be surpassed, something appears that makes all previous statements about perfection a lie. . . . Talent collects what there is and builds on it, genius conquers and widens the limits of art . . . genius discards the old and makes new rules. . . .
>
> We have now heard Liszt for ourselves. Against him only Thalberg can maintain his own weight. . . . Which of the two is better is a question not easy to answer. In the end, one can only say, "each in his own way." [29]

Wieck himself had been equally impressed and according to him, Clara was too. What probably really hurt was not that Liszt was considered a greater artist than Clara but the comparison with Thalberg, a virtuoso Wieck thought Clara had vanquished. In his letter somehow mistakenly dated March 5, 1832, Wieck reports.

> Yesterday we heard Liszt. It must be an unforgettable experience for a pianist. Even if the public understood only half of his Fantasy on *I Puritani* [*Réminiscences des Puritains*], only a quarter of his *Teufelswalzer*, and even less of his *Étude*, the *Conzertstück* of Weber was played perfectly. Perhaps it was a little too fast, but it had extraordinary intelligence, originality and creativity.
>
> The seriousness of the concert, Liszt's charisma and his incredible technical command elicited the stormiest applause. Who could describe his appearance as a concert-artist? After he destroyed Thalberg's Erard piano in the first piece, he played the fantasy on a

---

29.   AT: 355.

Graf, broke two copper-strings, fetched another, a walnut Graf, from a corner himself, and played his etude, breaking two more strings. Before that he told the audience that he was not satisfied with his playing of the etude and played it again.[30]

Last night Clara played Schumann's *Carnaval* for him and some of her own transcriptions of Schubert songs. Today she will play him her concerto.[31]

Clara was deeply impressed. In the diary she and her father kept jointly, however, Wieck has some reservations. "His [Liszt's] passion knows no bounds; not infrequently he jars one's sense of beauty by tearing melodies to pieces. He uses the pedal too much, thus making works incomprehensible, if not to professionals, at least to amateurs."[32] Clara herself was depressed. In a letter to Robert from Graz she writes, "my playing seems to me so dull now and I do not know why, but I have lost the desire to travel further. Since I have heard and seen Liszt's bravura, I feel like a student."[33]

For those of us who assumed that Beethoven's piano music was always a permanent part of the concert repertoire, it must come as a surprise that the critic Adami felt it necessary to defend Clara's inclusion of Beethoven in her program.

Her programs consist of nothing but excellent works and she excludes all that useless stuff such as bravura variations, rondos, so-called fantasies, caprices, etc., with which other virtuosos ply us.... But only a talent such as hers is able to allow an audience which has rarely or never heard [the 'classics'] to understand them. ... It happens that a less gifted performer finally deciding to play one of the classics makes them into something indifferent, even boring. It is then assumed to be the composer's fault, that the music is old and passé and that modern times have broken new ground. ... But if the old things are not grateful, as they say, how is it that when a significant talent . . . returns to the good old days . . . these works blossom once more into fresh and youthful creations.[34]

Adami is not defending music as old as Bach or Haydn, he is

30.   Wieck: 94. According to the review, what Liszt played was the [*Grande*] *Valse de bravura* of 1836.
31.   Wieck: 94.
32.   Ibid.
33.   Litzmann, 1: 149.
34.   *AT*: 28.

referring to Clara's Beethoven, specifically the Sonata, op. 57. If Clara played serious works, it is plain that she did so because she could make them convincing. When she had played a Bach fugue in Berlin the year before, the applause had been "*furchtbar.*" She had subsequently received anonymous letters asking her to play more Bach.[35] She played the same fugue again in Vienna. Apparently it was then the only Bach in her repertoire. But her concerts in Vienna do not reflect the high proportion of serious works found on Ms. Pettler's list. While she clearly played more good music than other virtuosos, she also played a considerable amount of lighter stuff. The repertoire of most performers reflects Hiller's statement that traveling virtuosos played largely their own pieces; it was up to dilettantes to play the old works.[36] Considering the vast number of virtuosos traveling around Europe few of whom are remembered as composers, his statement is at first difficult to understand. What Hiller meant was that all the virtuosos *wrote* their own showy pieces even if they had no talent at all. Again Wieck's report falls into place. "Hummel and Herz are played to death here. The great [female] pianists — there are hundreds of them, "secretly" play Beethoven and Chopin, etc., but they do not appear in public. Clara comes with something that is nearly a piano-revolution. The public shows up and is beside itself with gratitude [*ist ausser sich*] because she is giving pianism a wholly new direction."[37] (We have already encountered Wieck's exaggeration, but "hundreds," "great," "beside itself," a "piano-revolution"!) In any case, the situation had apparently changed somewhat since 1827 when Hiller reported that dilettantes were serious competition for the professional musicians of Vienna. They had even charged admission. The only professional performers he heard during six weeks in Vienna were Schuppanzigh and his colleagues playing chamber-music.[38] Many of those ladies obviously used to play in public.

Apparently even the most highly acclaimed virtuoso did not expect to sustain a solo-recital as we understand it. Liszt as well as Clara frequently included chamber music, orchestral overtures, had singers come to sing Lieder, or presented melodramas. In addition to

---

35. Wieck: 62ff.
36. Ferdinand Hiller, *Künstlerleben* (Cologne: Du Mont-Schauberg, 1880): 44f.
37. Wieck: 84.
38. Hiller, *Künstlerleben*: 44f.

such variety, Liszt included his arrangement for piano of two movements from the *Symphonie fantastique*, the "Ballroom" movement, and the "March to the Scaffold." At another concert six instrumentalists joined him in Johann Nepomuk Hummel's Septet, a work that was then quite popular. Clara managed to get Joseph Mayseder and Joseph Merk to play a movement of the *Archduke Trio* with her, perhaps out of piety for the memory of Beethoven or in exchange for playing some of Mayseder's music.

Sampling reviews of other concerts given in the months Clara was in Vienna, one finds that orchestral concerts almost invariably included works by the classic masters, solo-recitals, rarely. Even Liszt played only two Beethoven sonatas in his eight concerts. In the solo parts of a concert, the performer's own pieces were generally the featured works. Ensembles usually played works by currently fashionable names. The ones which recur most frequently in Vienna that season are the names of Hummel, Henselt, Thalberg, Pacini, and Mayseder. Sometimes pianists who engaged larger ensembles played a Beethoven concerto, but one looks in vain for the repertoire that we thought was never neglected. Clara's concerts included quite a few works of Chopin, but what she played most often on her tours were the *Variations on "la ci darem la mano,"* op. 2. (They are mentioned so often that Wieck refers to them as "the Lacidarem," in one word.) In Vienna Clara's one Bach fugue was received with wild enthusiasm and had to be repeated.

Wieck's letters from Vienna end abruptly with that of April 3, 1838. On her tour to Paris in 1839, Clara was alone and the lack of a proper chaperone seems to have raised some eyebrows. But self-confident and courageous as she was in spite of some doubts ("I shall not be treated with proper respect if I have not an old lady to go into society with me"), she managed quite well despite her unconventional behavior. In her first letter to Robert from Paris she says that Probst and Fechner were trying to persuade her to go home. "Father would give something to have me back again, but I will not go."[39]

Heinrich Probst, who had founded a publishing firm in Leipzig only to sell it to Karl Friedrich Kistner thirteen years later, was living in Paris in 1839, and acting as Breitkopf's agent there. His letters to the firm are a veritable gold mine of detail about musical life in Paris

---

39.   Litzmann, 1: 200.

between 1833 and 1840.[40] He reported everything of relevance to the publisher who employed him, recommending works for publication, suggesting the composers' fees, telling of the successes and failures of concerts and artists; in short, his letters are of extraordinary interest. One could only wish he had written many more over a much longer period.

Probst reports to Breitkopf on Clara's first concert. "Wieck will probably vanish from Paris without leaving a trace; she is too tactless for this world."[41] Two weeks later he writes, "Clara Wieck is not causing a great stir and is not likely to make romantic playing the vogue here. Thursday she played five pieces!! at a Schlesinger concert of the *Gazette* and received very moderate applause. One found her playing too rough and her scales, in fact, lack the Clementi smoothness, the way Herz and Kalkbrenner demand them. This is between us; don't let old Wieck find out."[42]

Clara's playing too rough? We have been hearing about her technique and Probst's report does not ring true. Then we find the explanation. She was playing on an Erard piano which, with its double-escapement mechanism probably had a deeper action, making it somewhat harder to play than the pianos to which she was accustomed. "I have an Erard in my room that is dreadfully stiff. I had lost all heart, but yesterday I played on a Pleyel and they are a little more manageable. I must study for another three weeks before I can play a note in public. I could have three grand pianos in my room already; everyone wants me to take his. If only I knew how to begin playing on a Pleyel without offending Erard."[43]

She was not quite ready for her first concert. On March 21 she writes, "I should also get more used to the pianos; these are so stiff that it is dreadful. And yet I played well yesterday."[44]

A review in the *Revue et gazette musicale* of March 22 says nothing about inferior playing although it is not as enthusiastic as the reviews were in Vienna. "Mlle. Clara Wieck who is the musical lion of the moment, the female Thalberg of the piano, was heard for the first time. Her talent is intelligent, pure, elegant and conscientious

---

40.   Wilhelm Hitzig.
41.   Ibid.: 65.
42.   Ibid.: 66.
43.   Litzmann, 1: 194.
44.   Ibid.: 212.

and she does not seek after effect."[45] Of course this particular reviewer, Henri Blanchart, was writing for the journal that had sponsored her concert, the publisher Schlesinger's house-organ. Clara's letter to Robert is very enthusiastic. "I played at Schlesinger's matinée and in the evening at Zimmermann's and created a great sensation, especially in the evening when there were many connoisseurs present. They called me the second Liszt, etc."[46] Her program would not create great enthusiasm on our part. She played Henselt, her own transcription of Schubert's *Serenade*, her *Hexentanz*, and some Thalberg.

Probst may have been right. She was not quite ready to meet Paris standards, standards set by Chopin, Liszt, Thalberg, etc., all of them accustomed to French pianos. But even Probst finally came around. "Clara Wieck gave a good concert and earned much applause as well as 2,000 francs."[47] Clara writes, "I created a genuine sensation such as no artist has produced for many a day. . . . It was extremely full, but expenses are such in Paris that there cannot be anything left over." The *Revue et gazette* reports that she played her own scherzo ravishingly and that she was a pianist of the first rank with a great poetic gift.

Whether she meant that her living expenses were such in Paris that she would have little left over, or whether it was a problem of renting halls and paying other participants is not clear. It is estimated that one could live in Paris, modestly that is, for 1,500 francs per year, but a young lady in her position living by herself probably had to maintain a certain style. In their effort to persuade Friedrich Wieck to let them marry, Robert stated that she had saved 4,000 thaler; apparently she did usually tour at some profit.[48]

When it came to going to London, her courage did not sustain

---

45. *Revue et gazette musicale*, 6 (1839): 93f.
46. Litzmann, 1: 211.
47. Hitzig: 67.
48. Litzmann, 1: 225. Robert estimated that their combined income would be 1,340 thaler yer year. Mendelssohn, in one of his letters to Ignaz Moscheles, tells the pianist how much it cost to live comfortably in Leipzig in 1846. A large sunny apartment was about 350 thaler per year, three servants, 150, wood, 350. Taxes were negligible. He goes on to say that Clara Schumann had only two students at 2 thaler per lesson and that Moscheles might have many if he charged 1.50 thaler, perhaps even 2.00. Moscheles' income at the conservatory was to be 1,500 thaler per year.

her. "I cannot go to London without a man to protect me. One important point is that one goes to London after having been in Paris, and I am still too little known in Paris and it is already too late."[49]

Robert was hurt that she was not playing his music in Paris. Clara's judgment, however, indicated to her that Paris audiences would not like it. She wrote back that she played it only for connoisseurs, that she could not bear it if even a few of the listeners disapproved. Her judgment was probably sound. Probst's letters repeatedly tell Breitkopf that Paris was not a market for someone like Mendelssohn, that the French did not take to him. He finally managed to sell one of the works, most likely Book III of *Songs without Words*, for 200 francs to Schlesinger after much haggling.[50] Chopin was generally getting ten times as much for an equivalent number of pieces. Mendelssohn, writes Probst, is not terribly popular here but highly respected. (At the same time Troupenas offered Meyerbeer as much as 40,000 francs for one opera.)[51]

Having seen that Clara Wieck was a courageous woman, we now see her as sensible as well. Even a short selection from her letters, those of her father, and Probst's outlines her portrait quite clearly — a portrait against a background that is entirely realistic.

Probst's letters complement the picture of music in Vienna in the 1830s with an even more detailed landscape of Paris. Their author is an entirely different species, "an old hand in publishing," he calls himself in one letter. His letters are stenographic in style, entirely preoccupied with business, musical gossip, and occasionally his questionable ethics. Because of their preoccupation with the commercial side of publishing, they are probably the best single source about publishing from that period that is currently accessible. Although his judgments are sometimes dubious in the long-range view, he was not dogmatic. Thus, while he reports at one point that Berlioz will probably soon seem ridiculous, or that the premiere of *Benvenuto Cellini* was a disaster, he is able to write some months later that Breitkopf ought to buy the opera which they can have virtually for nothing, that it has marvelous things in it but that

---

49.   Ibid.: 212.
50.   Hitzig: 71.
51.   Ibid.: 63.

Berlioz is inclined to kill fleas with a cannon.[52] "Chopin's *Nocturnes*, op. 15," he writes, "are heavenly and that lovable man gains wider acceptance every day."[53] Or, "don't speak to me of Ferdinand Hiller. When it comes to a work like *Deborah* the young man has over-reached himself."[54] "You tell me that I should buy Pacini at any price and you are surprised that I would not think of it."[55]

Clara played Henselt very frequently but Probst writes, "nobody is going to buy Henselt's etudes here sight unseen and Mendelssohn's concerto is out of the question."[56] As for Clara's rivals, Döhler and Kalkbrenner, he reports, "Döhler had a *succès fou* here and is off to London. His compositions are truly miserable. But Thalberg drags him along in his wake, and he is a handsome chap . . . driving women to ecstasy."[57] A little later, however, Döhler had a concert that was a total flop even though the ladies were still wild about him. As for Kalkbrenner, who was successful nearly everywhere, he had just come back from Vienna at the end of May 1838. Vienna had frightened him, writes Probst.[58]

Probst received 4,500 francs a year from Breitkopf and was worth every centime of it, although, when he asked to become a partner, he was turned down. Here is a different example of his acumen. "Mendelssohn symphonies are not for local tastes but I'll get some of them performed at the Conservatoire soon."[59] As for Probst's ethics, they are questionable. Thus, while he was working for Pleyel, he was sending drawings of their pedal mechanism to Breitkopf. It was Probst who presided at the demise of Pleyel's publishing venture when Pleyel decided to sell only pianos. They were in such demand, according to Probst, that 600 a year could not satisfy the demand and even 1,200 might not.[60]

---

52.   Ibid.: 33 and 65.
53.   Ibid.: 33.
54.   Ibid.: 40.
55.   Ibid.: 49f.
56.   Ibid.
57.   Ibid.: 53.
58.   Ibid.: 54. Apparently Kalkbrenner was afraid to play so soon after Liszt. According to *AT* of May 26, 1838 (468) Kalkbrenner was going straight home to Paris from Munich instead of coming to Vienna first. Supposedly, family problems called him home.
59.   Hitzig: 54.
60.   Ibid.: 34.

One example of Probst as gossip should suffice. Reporting on his negotiations for the *Preludes*, op. 28, he says that Chopin is quite ill. "He has gone to Spain with his mistress ... presumably to bury himself in sand."[61]

Wieck, of course, was equally preoccupied with money. Whatever "spirituality" he may have possessed, when he traveled with Clara he was her manager and as such full of talk of fees, expenses, plots, and self-congratulation. One cannot use his business data quite so easily as Probst's, since the context has not yet been established clearly enough. In that respect, Probst should be helpful in setting some pattern, since he often also reports on concert fees. In the light of William Weber's efforts to associate class with taste, one must be taken aback by the following: "How many poor people from the suburbs here [Vienna] have paid their hard-earned 20 groschen [to hear Clara] but it cannot be helped, we cannot lower admissions."[62] Statistics of the various social classes and their musical tastes are not giving us the whole picture, it appears, since we can assume that concerts as popular as Clara's attracted music-lovers of all classes. Nor, as we can see, are public concerts the whole story, neither in Vienna nor in Paris, since Clara played in public as well as in private for fees. As we utilize more and more of the material in letters, diaries, periodicals, and business records, our picture of the nineteenth century will become much more realistic than it is now. On the other hand, the excerpts from a putative documentary biography illustrate the extent of the information and the huge problem of verification. *AT* is only one of the journals reporting on the state of music in Vienna. Wieck must be read with skepticism, thanks to his tendency to exaggerate, and even Clara herself may be giving a false impression. Thus, when it comes to the self-confidence exhibited in letters to Robert from her tour, this is in direct conflict with some of Wasielewski's descriptions.

According to Wasielewski's *Schumannia* Clara was likely to break into tears when Schumann made any unfavorable comments about her playing of a particular work or even criticized the potatoes at dinner. While one of her latest biographies characterizes her as a somewhat impatient housewife, a rather typically egocentric per-

61. Ibid.: 56.
62. William Weber, *Music and the Middle Class* (New York: Holmes & Meyer, 1975), and Wieck: 87.

former, she appears to have been far more complicated than that. Even as a child, years before Schumann had any romantic interest in her, he wrote, "what a creature Clara is. . . . Her heart is hardly three feet above the ground, yet it has reached a development that frightens me."[63]

The digression into Clara's life illustrates the vast problem of collecting such materials and of using them. In fact, the issue is not just the difficulty — one could always gather such collections by committee. The problem is one of diminishing returns. Too bulky a documentary collection may not serve us all that well.

On the other hand, the brief excursion with Clara on her early tours leads, as we have hoped to have shown, to all sorts of interesting sidelights. Perhaps that is the most rewarding part of nineteenth-century documentary biography.

In our time, Igor Stravinsky, even while he was still alive, became the subject of debate over some of the early biographies and his conversation-books. His published correspondence so far issued is not usable as documentation because it has been edited. Add to this the wide coverage by the press, film, television programs and recordings, the reviews, and the liner-notes on records and in program-notes and his documentary biography will become a veritable industry. The twentieth century has carried the idea of the hero-artist to such an extreme that works matter less than personality. One would think that recordings had settled the problem of correct performance and eyewitness accounts of a composer performing would have been made redundant. But even here we find doubts. Is the composer truly the best performer of his works? Were his recordings truly conducted by him or was the orchestra prepared by someone else and patches — one of the new ways to make inauthentic what should be reliable — in a recording supplied by someone other than the composer? One of the first books dealing with the composer as recording artist is about Sir Edward Elgar.[64] It quickly makes clear that matters are more complex than they seem. The reception of new works has been made controversial in part by the tendency of biographers to make the composer into a martyr or by other complicating factors. Even there, one of the first books to

---

63. Robert Schumann, *Tagebücher*: 345.
64. Jerold Northrop Moore, *Elgar on Record. The Composer and the Gramophone* (London: Oxford University Press, 1974).

deal with such a subject, *Igor Stravinsky, Le Sacre du printemps*, has confined its compilation to readily available journals and newspapers.[65] But would wider coverage have served any purpose? To what extent will documentalists of the future have to confine themselves to representative samples? In view of the historian's justified distrust of editorial selectivity, even the most carefully chosen samplings will not do if one is interested in absolute documentation. The bulk of compilations about any of the heroes of the twentieth century is likely to be so huge that for most purposes documentary biographies would be ridiculously large. Landon's biography of Haydn, not even an attempt to be absolutely comprehensive, already consists of five volumes. Since Haydn reached a wide public, the materials about him, his environments, the chronology of his works, the music that influenced him, have all become so extensive that they constitute too much material for the standard biography.

Even for some eighteenth-century musicians compromise is already in the air. Anne Schnoebelen's edition of Padre Martini's letters consists of summaries of each letter.[66] It is an exemplary solution in most respects, since anyone interested in pursuing the complete letter touching on some matter of interest can use her summaries and indexes to send for photographs of the complete document. The disadvantage of abstracts, on the other hand, is the subjectivity of any summary. Does the abstractor really see what an individual scholar would consider interesting or revealing?

A good example of how an issue in documentation has changed is the question of Haydn and *Sturm und Drang*. Did the movement influence him? How did it touch this relatively uneducated man who seems not to have been highly interested in literature? A similar question hardly arises in the twentieth century when composers tend to be intellectuals in a period in which the latest trends are quickly communicated. How much of an interest composers such as Stravinsky might have taken in Expressionism or *Neue Sachlichkeit* is not a matter of whether they knew of these trends, but rather the extent of such influences as it can be found in their works. Artists

---

65. François Lesure, *Igor Stravinsky, Le Sacre du printemps. Dossier de presse* (Geneva: Minkoff, 1980).
66. Anne Schnoebelen, *Padre Martini's Collection of Letters in the Civico Museo Bibliographico Musicale in Bologna* (New York: Pendragon, 1979).

such as Picasso or Stravinsky were quite conscious of their position in old as well as current history and even used parody-techniques in their works in order to absorb older ways of creating new art. Here the best method is probably musical analysis rather than documentation.

If it is an overstatement to assert that documentary biography is no longer possible, it is certainly clear that the type of documentation that is relevant will have to be somewhat different. While the kind of gathering of materials for which Deutsch set the example is still necessary and useful for musicians before the nineteenth century, especially when it comes to Renaissance masters about whom we have little direct biographical material, it is probably still feasible only for more obscure composers of the nineteenth and twentieth century.

CHAPTER XI
AUTOBIOGRAPHY, CREATIVITY, AND MUSICAL MEANING

The context of real biography should probably not include fiction. But when we consider that one of the most interesting questions, one of the reasons we are so fascinated by artistic lives, is creativity, we should be allowed to include novels. Presumably the novelist has not only the imagination to approach the subject, but he can also project his own experiences into his protagonist and thus perhaps illuminate what a composer cannot put into words and what the historian-biographer has to omit because he must base his story exclusively on hard fact.

It happens that there are not many fictitious composers by authors of any stature. Hoffmann's Kreisler (1820) is of great interest perhaps mainly because its creator was also a composer and because in its time the novel's wild romanticism was central to all the arts.[1] At the other end of the era at the beginning of the twentieth century came *Jean Christophe*, written by a musical historian who knew a great deal about his subject.[2] The book was already anachronistic when it appeared, but however composers themselves were changing, the public continued to identify with the hero who in this book is tormented by the jealousy of lesser rivals and by misunderstanding. *Jean Christophe* fired the imagination of at least two generations of adolescents before it began to fade from the scene.

The most ambitious novel to have a musician as its central figure

---

1. Ernst Theodor Amadeus Hoffmann, *Die Lebensansichten des Kater Murr*, 2 vols. (originally published Berlin: Reimer?, 1820—22).
2. Romain Rolland, *Jean Christophe*, 4 vols. (Paris: Ollendorf, 1905—6).

as well as the only great such work is *Doctor Faustus*.[3] In it, Thomas
Mann's seemingly extraordinary musical sophistication comes from
outsiders although the setting represents the author's direct experience. Mann had technical help from Theodor Adorno and the fact
that he used Schoenberg's ideas, attributing them to his protagonist,
Adrian Leverkühn, angered Schoenberg. There is in actuality not
very much that Schoenberg and Leverkühn have musically in common; the theories remain largely theoretical. The description, for
example, of one of Leverkühn's mature works, "Apocalipsis cum
figuris," so convincing that it ought to exist, depicts an eclectic work
that is like one of Alban Berg's rather than Schoenberg's. (One is
also reminded of Berg's *Violin-Concerto* by the concerto Leverkühn
is induced to write for a friend, a travesty of the conventional
romantic concerto that still dominates the virtuoso repertoire.)
Leverkühn himself is a composite figure, a conflation of Nietzsche
and such composers as Hugo Wolf and Schumann. Leverkühn's
hatred of sentimentality seems to come from Stravinsky, not
Schoenberg.

   Doctor Faustus is of course much more than an imaginary
biography. To deal with it here in this dimension only and as cultural
history means that the actual biographies of twentieth-century
composers are not nearly so revealing. In their autobiographies the
composers of our time are rarely introspective; they seem to be
afraid of being either boring or too romantic. Leverkühn's life and
work described by his scholarly friend, on the other hand, represents
a kind of apotheosis of romanticism in its hero's total absorption in
his art. It is closer to autobiography than biography because the
narrator is as omniscient as a novelist and much of what he tells us
comes from the composer himself. The imaginary author's rather
one-sided intimacy with Leverkühn is unlike any real biography, on
the other hand, although his pedantry often intrudes on the narrative.

   The idea that insight and achievement are gained at a price has
always been a factor in Mann's work. In *Doctor Faustus* it becomes
part of the plot, so to speak, when the composer-hero deliberately
trades his soul for a limited period of heightened creativity. Leverkühn
has been predisposed to such a trade from early childhood, but to
call him cold because of his detachment from others is an oversimplification. What could be more passionate than a willingness to

---

3.   Thomas Mann, *Doctor Faustus* (Stockholm: Fischer, 1947).

trade one's soul for art? And while in his younger years Leverkühn rejects the "stable-warmth" of romanticism, his mature works become so intense that one of them strikes the narrator, Serenus Zeitblom, as having gone too far, perhaps like Schoenberg's *Survivor from Warsaw*. As his payment the devil exacts the absence of warmth and love in the composer's life, but it is the awesome realization of what he has sold that makes Leverkühn into a composer of great intensity.

Like all novels *Doctor Faustus* is of course autobiography in a way, since it incorporates Mann's own experiences and views. It also stands as a metaphor for the fate of all the arts in Mann's time. What Leverkühn gives up is not just his own soul, it is the soul of music. As a novelist Mann always remained on the side of romantic tradition; he held on to chronological narrative, sentiment, and grandeur. His protagonist is an iconoclastic innovator, but he often rues what he has had to give up. He speaks nostalgically of the blending of the advanced and the popular (i.e., appealing) in the nineteenth century. The gulf that has opened between expressivity and appeal in the twentieth century must at some time, Leverkühn is made to say, lead back to older ways, to a time when music was only music. While this may strike us as pure nostalgia, it has some validity. The infinite progress in which we believe must eventually reach some limit. A real twentieth-century composer, Arthur Honegger, in a sort of quasi-autobiography writes, "A few years hence musical art as we conceive it will no longer exist. . . . No one any longer listens to music; they come to view the performance of a famous conductor . . ."[4] The key words are "music as we conceive it," of course, but history teaches us that no great art ever really goes back to one of its earlier incarnations.

The life and career of Leverkühn are metaphors for the rise of Nazi Germany and run parallel to it. Just the same, there is little external connection between the musical development of the protagonist and the events among which he lives. One of the common assumptions about art, namely, that it reflects current social conditions, is thus tacitly dismissed. Leverkühn is quite indifferent to political events, so self-absorbed that in view of what is happening, he is almost immoral. The narrator, Serenus Zeitblom, accepts his detachment. Although he himself is deeply troubled and repelled by

---

4.   Arthur Honegger, *I Am a Composer* (New York: St. Martin's, 1966): 14.

current events, he takes for granted that the preoccupation of genius is above conventional morality, that true morality is implicit in great art. Reality is not a factor in another sense. How do composers who are not also performers of some kind live if their music does not appeal to audiences? Leverkühn has no such concern; somehow he has enough money to live in comparative comfort, occupying himself first with his studies and then with composition. Real composers today take for granted that their music cannot support them, that they must teach, perform, or write for films in order to make a living. While it may be crude to raise the issue, the topic ought to rear its head when one considers the division between composer and audience that has developed in the short time in which composers have been independent of church and court.

There have been a few such fortunate composers, of course. Milhand's autobiography and Poulenc's published interviews make quite clear that both were financially independent.[5] Instead of feeling free to be radically avant-garde composers, however, both were quite concerned with the reception of their work, even if in the negative sense of taking pleasure in shocking their audiences. When Mann introduces an impresario named Fittelberg from Paris who vainly tries to tempt Leverkühn to make personal appearances there, Fittelberg counts on success achieved by means of scandal. Scandal is both "honorable and promising," he says, in fact, "*au commencement était le scandal.*"

Those phrases of Fittelberg are not openly expressed but they are implied in several of the autobiographies that have Paris as their focal point, not only Milhaud's but also Virgil Thomson's and others of that generation.[6] Milhaud tells us about his parents, his friends, his travels, his concerts, and his scandals without ever getting beneath the surface. His writing is rather detached, far colder than Leverkühn's is supposed to be. The latter's intellectual passion is more endearing than the facile superficiality of some real contemporaries. Milhaud even neglects to tell us very much about his "discovery" of polytonality. It seems to have been just an amusing game. Similarly, his account of the formation of the group known as "Les Six" gets no

5.   Francis Poulenc, *Moi et mes amis.* Interviews with Stéphane Audel, Paris and Geneva: Palatinei, 1963. Darius Milhaud, *Ma vie heureuse* (Paris: Belfont, 1974).
6.   Virgil Thomson, *Virgil Thomson* (New York: Knopf, 1966).

further than the making of cocktails and going out to dinner together. He tells us that he was greatly influenced by Cocteau's ideas in "Le Coq et l'arlequin" without being more explicit about them or why they affected him.[7]

Leverkühn and Milhaud represent the opposing edges of the gulf between attitudes to music in the twentieth century. On the one side stands the severely arrogant intellectual who considers only what he believes to be the rigorous pursuit of an inevitable inner logic or equally inevitable historical laws; on the other, the artist who feels that novelty is necessary but not if it costs losing the audience entirely. With someone like Milhaud one cannot really tell whether he has thought about this deeply, whether he is aware that he may be trying to rescue music from the alienation that even Leverkühn predicts. Virgil Thomson makes the difference national; the former type, essentially German, is repugnant to him, the latter, his own side, is French. This is a seductive oversimplification. No matter what their national origins, the Vienna school and the Stravinskys, Bartóks, and the Shostakovichs all held on to an inner vision which each pursued with iron consistency even if, like Stravinsky, they changed style several times.

Thomson is a far better writer than Milhaud, a professional who has produced much intelligent criticism. Nevertheless his autobiography is disappointing. For the most part it is a merely picaresque work skimming only the surface. Otto Luening's recent *An American Composer's Odyssey* continues in the same vein although he is wittier.[8] While Luening again fails our expectations by telling us nothing about creativity and I about artistic development, he does recreate an American life, a life that mirrors a mad era. He is neither Franco- nor Germanophile, even though his ethnic background is upper-class German. Luening's early years as a composer are tragic-comedy. A composer had no place in American life, one of the reasons why sooner or later all the aspirants went to Europe. A typical and very realistic American like Luening managed to eke out a living by performing in all sorts of settings, catering to wealthy

---

7.   Jean Cocteau, "Le Coq et l'arlequin," in *L'Appel à l'ordre* (Paris: Stock, 1948). The article was originally published between 1918 and 1926. I doubt that it is very widely known.

8.   Otto Luening, *The Odyssey of an American Composer* (New York: Scribner, 1980).

society snobbery in which there was little real understanding of
music, teaching in out-of-the-way colleges, etc., until a reputation,
as a teacher rather than a composer, lands him at a prestigious
university. He was helped no doubt by his unpretentious pragmatism,
utterly democratic and not very impressed by the traditions of the
Old World. One assumes that what is reflected in all of the American
autobiographies is the curious position of the artist in the early part
of the twentieth century, a society which, as Saul Bellow put it
somewhere, was "so raw that it was difficult for the artist to explain
his presence in it." Most of the Americans depict themselves as
either "regular guys" or, like Ned Rorem, hopelessly different, so
utterly out of place, that he might as well flaunt his differences with
naked candor, a kind of *épâter le bourgeois* not through music but by
confessions published as a series of diaries.[9] Composers' autobiographies used to be rare, and only a few were especially valuable.
Whatever their value, however, it never had anything to do with
self-justification and no composer attempted to depict himself as just
a regular guy. Earlier composers such as Grétry or Spohr took their
calling for granted. It is only megalomaniacs like Berlioz and Wagner
who flaunted their egos although neither apologized for it nor
attempted to justify himself.

Proportionally there are more autobiographies in recent times
than there were before, in itself a curious fact, since often the music
of the autobiographer is hardly known. What possesses such a man
as Luening or his publisher to issue an autobiography reaching a
readership that can hardly have heard more than a few of his works?
Even a Milhaud, some of whose music is played fairly regularly, is
represented in the repertoire by perhaps ten works out of many
hundreds. Apparently our hunger for biography is far greater than
our need for new music. We used to read biographies because we
wanted to know whether the person matched his work or whether
we could explain the mystery of great art. Now we seem to read
them for their own sake. Perhaps readers have come to the conclu-

---

9.   Ned Roren, *The Paris Diary of Ned Rorem* (New York: Braziller,
      1966); *The New York Diary* (New York: Braziller, 1967); *The Final
      Diary, 1961—1972* (New York: Holt, Rinehart and Winston, 1974);
      An Absolute Gift: A New Diary (New York: Simon and Schuster,
      1978).

sion that composers are far more interesting than their music precisely *because* the music leaves them cold.

Some modern autobiographies are quite good and very interesting. Luening's is one of the best and so is George Antheil's, though again, how many readers have ever heard Antheil's music?[10] Antheil is not a major composer perhaps because he is too astute an observer; he is too interested in others. All sorts of composers influence him, a disadvantage to someone with his facility or his flippancy. Not that he is too casual as an artist, but having the ability to laugh at oneself is not conducive to serious artistry. Yet Antheil is especially perceptive. "The truth of the matter is that we have just emerged [in 1945] from a stylistic period where style was everything and content nothing — in so far as human meaning is concerned. . . . And now, today, having passed through two wars in history, the human heart is beginning to find the music of this period singularly lacking."[11] The sentence reflects a kind of primitive insight, that of a man who writes as he speaks and who seems not to realize that style *is* content in music. (What he must have meant was "idiom" rather than style.) It is true that for a time novelty and originality took precedence over nearly every other element of music, and something is obviously amiss with the contributions that cannot find their way into the repertoire, a repertoire almost entirely made up of music written between 1700 and 1950. In the recent past it was the young who were on the side of the avant-garde, but young people have turned their backs on the old as well as the new, on tradition as well as innovation. They confine their interest in huge numbers to a kind of inchoate protest expressed in the facile rhythm and harmony known as Rock. It is too easy to blame this alienation on serious composers, but composers have left a vacuum not easy to fill. (Paradoxically, the universities which support many composers cannot always provide audiences.)

General readers are naturally more interested in the autobiographies of great composers than they are in *Kleinmeister* even if scholars regard biography primarily as the documentation of an era and its musical life. It is the minor composer, however, who has tended to contribute more information if only because he is not so

---

10.   George Antheil, *Bad Boy of Music* (Garden City, N.Y.: Doubleday, 1945).
11.   Ibid.: 356.

egocentric as to be blind to everyone else. Seen from this perspective there is probably no autobiography as valuable as that of Louis Spohr.[12] He was not an introspective man, and since he toured for much of his long life, he observed everything and reported it. That he lived in a period when attitudes were changing drastically adds even greater interest. At the end of his life he could no longer understand what was happening. Even the middle-period works of Beethoven were already beyond him in spite of his earlier admiration for the master. Berlioz, in his turn, regarded Spohr as totally irrelevant. A far more romantic writer, Carl Friedrich Zelter (1858– 1932), of greater historical interest as Mendelssohn's mentor than as a composer, seems to have come under the spell of the early romantic novel.[13] His autobiography imitates that kind of novel so effectively that his emphasis is on his development as a person and touches on his life as a musician only incidentally. He thus deprives us of the specific documentation we think we have a right to expect.

If in our time the two most important memoirists are Shostakovich and Stravinsky, it is not because they are the only major composers, they are the only major composers who wrote (or dictated) genuinely autobiographical books.[14] Shostakovich's melancholy story is of great interest in part because of the political environment in which he lived, while Stravinsky's too early autobiographical effort can almost be said to be callow. His is a recitation of events and persons written with consistent haughtiness that in his case is hardly justified; audiences had been more than sympathetic to his music ever since it came to their attention. That his autobiography comes closer to the character of the eighteenth-century type should not surprise us. He was drawn to the unsentimental attitude to their craft shared by

---

12.   Louis Spohr, *Lebenserinnerungen.*
13.   Carl Friedrich Zelter, *Darstellung seines Lebens,* edited by Johann Wolfgang Schottländer, Schriften der Goethe Gesellschaft, vol. 44 (Weimar: Goethe-Gesellschaft, 1931).
14.   Dimitri Shostakovich, *Testimony.* The Memoirs of Dmitri Shostakovich as told to Solomon Volkov. Translated by Antonia W. Bouis (New York: Harper and Row, 1980). Igor Stravinsky, *An Autobiography* (New York: Simon and Schuster: 1936). In a review in *Russian Review* (39 [1980]: 484ff.), Laurel E. Fay questions the authenticity of *Testimony.* There is no doubt that sections have been badly translated, sentences have been omitted, and some parts taken from previous publications of Shostakovich. In my opinion, however, this does not affect the general conclusions reached in this essay.

composers before the nineteenth century. He must have known better than to assume that nobody cared about his personal life, but he refused to cater to that curiosity. The merit of the several books he produced later in collaboration with Robert Craft lies in the skill of Craft's questioning which pushed Stravinsky toward some of the revelations his readers wanted although even then his guard never quite comes down.[15] Craft must have realized how inadequate the autobiography had been and did his best to supplement it by his questions. I know of course that Craft has been criticized for whatever editorial emendations he made and for his supposed purification of Stravinsky's literary style. There are those who do not consider these books authentic. When one reads all of them, however, one realizes that they have a higher authenticity, that whatever editorial judgment Craft may have exercised, the conversations and diaries share a consistent tone, a literary attitude that is for once matched by Stravinsky's music. Craft and Stravinsky have similarly acerbic styles and both seem to be enamored of words nobody else has even heard. Those words, the wit, and the willingness to be blunt resemble the writing of another Russian exile, Vladimir Nabakov. Stravinsky and Nabokov share their air of superiority, a haughtiness that may be characteristic of upper-class Russian intellectuals in exile who look down on us as if we were a lesser species. This is probably not because we do not write or compose well, but rather because we are not Russian intellectuals. It is certainly neither English nor American, neither polite nor democratic. Nabokov's dealings with himself are also untypical of writers who as a group tend to be less haughty than modern composers whenever they wax autobiographical. Perhaps the writer's craft is not so mysterious as that of the composer. Readers can understand how they do what they do and therefore writers are less reluctant to let the public look over their shoulders. Writers are also generally more tolerant of criticism than composers. They cannot refer vaguely to

---

15.   See also Igor Stravinsky, *The Poetics of Music* (New York: Vintage, 1947). I read freely in no particular order among the books jointly written with Robert Craft, namely, *Conversations with Igor Stravinsky* (London: Faber and Faber, 1958); *Memories and Commentaries* (London: Faber and Faber, 1960); *Expositions and Developments* (London: Faber and Faber, 1962); *Dialogues and a Diary* (Garden City, N.Y.: Doubleday, 1963); *Themes and Conclusions* (London: Faber and Faber, 1972).

their intentions and scold everyone who does not accept them. Nabokov is not one of the tolerant ones. Neither, for that matter, is Shostakovich who even as composers go presumes a great deal. In comparison to the intellectual Stravinsky he is a primitive.

In no way can one fit the presumed memoirs of Dmitri Shostakovich into the list of relatively bland recollections of his colleagues. For one thing, they make clear that Mann's use of the Faust-story is old-fashioned even if his devil has been modernized in several of his guises. The story of Shostakovich represents a new and very real Faustian bargain. Shostakovich and others like him may be said to have pledged their souls to live and function in their homelands, places that took a terrible toll but ultimately left them alone to live and function in relative comfort, though probably like Shostakovich, always afraid that their privileged status might end at any moment. But we cannot assume that the artist who is allowed to continue to work on those terms is merely a passive victim of circumstance. Most of the all-pervasive political systems of our time insist on collaboration, on lip-service. As Solzhenitsyn writes, "it [the state] demands of us total surrender of our souls [and] . . . participation in the general conscious lie."[16] Those who are forced into exile or rejected by such states are fortunate; they have to maintain their integrity.

The memoirs of Shostakovich raise many questions, the most important of which is whether they can be trusted. One cannot imagine that the transcriptions of Volkov's furtive interviews could have been invented by anyone but Gogol. Perhaps if Shostakovich had written or talked believing that he had the time and the liberty for what he needed to say, an entirely different book might have resulted. The members of his immediate family who have recently come West protest that the book is not authentic, a protest so far not supplemented by evidence. They may be unhappy because the composer's self-portrait is not flattering. Shostakovich reveals himself as an embittered egotist who tells the story of a joyless life without laughter and seemingly with little love. In any case, *Testimony* is less a book than it is oral history, the oral history of a man preoccupied by telling the world how it was for him in the Soviet Union rather than the story of his life as such. There is always in such oral

---

16.   Alexander Solzhenitzyn, *From Under the Rubble* (Boston: Little Brown, 1975): 25.

accounts a question of editorial intervention, and the translation into rather clumsily idiomatic English is not helpful. Shostakovich himself suspected that he was not telling it right. He thought he was talking too much about himself, and these memoirs were not about him, they were supposed to be about others. The others were to have come first and he was to have figured in his memoirs only tangentially.

Actually he does talk about others a great deal; there are many pages about his teacher Glazunov, other musicians, writers, poets, and even military men he admired, as well as about the vicious bureaucrats he had to appease all his life. Paradoxically, however, Shostakovich is right. He may be speaking of others but except in the case of Glazunov one never gets a sense of either objectivity or warmth; everything comes down to a defense of Shostakovich, his reactions to the state, Stalinism, oppression, official stupidity, bureaucracy, and, above all, fear. There seems to be little left for the musical historian.

Or so it seems at first reading. Ultimately every word, every sentence contributes something about music and to the portrait of the composer himself. It becomes evident, for example, that there is not a single work by Shostakovich that does not have a program or message. "The *Scherzo* of the *Tenth Symphony* is a portrait of Stalin. Of course there are other things in it, but that is the basis."[17] The *Seventh Symphony*, his single most widely publicized work, during World War II, he now tells us, was not about the siege of Leningrad at all; it was part of his own requiem. That is in itself not astonishing. But what is astonishing is his resentment of audiences who seem not to have understood. "I've heard so much nonsense about the Seventh and Eighth Symphonies. It's amazing how long-lived these stupidities are. ... The Seventh Symphony had been planned long before the war and consequently it simply cannot be seen as a reaction to Hitler's attack. I was thinking of other enemies of humanity when I composed the theme."[18] If a composer can be so literal about his own music one must wonder how well he believes he "understands" the music of others.

Stravinsky, on the other hand, claims that music says nothing extraneous to it except that it may represent our sense of time. And yet he cannot be taken at his word either, since he asserts elsewhere

---

17.   *Testimony*: 141.
18.   Ibid.: 136.

that Beethoven's late quartets are a statement about human freedom
or, as he at least implies, that while music may not make extra-musical
statements, it does speak to us emotionally. Both Shostakovich and
Stravinsky refer to psychoanalysis in ways that indicate an acceptance
of its premises, although Shostakovich believes that the underlying
basis for our deepest experiences is not sex, it is fear. Stravinsky not
only refers to a psychoanalytical book by Anton Ehrenzweig, *The
Psychoanalysis of Artistic Vision and Hearing*, he occasionally even
relates some of his dreams as if to challenge some psychobiographer
to explain their meaning or function.[19] Yet he also hopes that some
intellectual composer like Ernst Krenek would write about the
nature of music.

When one subsequently reads Krenek's essays, it gradually becomes clear that what Krenek has to say about music is quite similar
to Stravinsky's ideas about meaning or, rather, non-meaning.[20]
Krenek insists in several places that what music "means" cannot be
expressed by metaphor or analogy; it is inherent in music. Even to
describe a harmonic progression does not reproduce the actuality, it
is only description.[21] Musical thought (and presumably musical
feeling) is inherent in music.

> When the average listener is pleased by the music's reminding him of
> a moon-lit night on the seashore, the musician will express his delight
> at the delicacy of the harmonic process, the smoothness of modula-
> tion, the subtlety of the melodic curve. . . . The means of the musical
> creative process cannot be grasped directly in conceptual terms: that
> is, they are not basically accessible to the means of verbal language.[22]

Neither Stravinsky nor Krenek is saying that music expresses
nothing. Both mean that what it expresses can only be perceived
through music.

The reason Stravinsky does not deal with creativity is that he
found it difficult to observe even in himself. It may appear that the
two subjects, the meanings of music and creativity, have nothing to

---

19. Anton Ehrenzweig, *The Psychoanalysis of Artistic Vision and Hearing*
(New York: Braziller, 1965). See also *The Hidden Order of Art*
(Berkeley and Los Angeles: University of California Press, 1971).
20. Ernest Krenek, *Exploring Music* (London: Calder and Boyars, 1966).
21. Ernst Krenek, "The Ivory Tower," in ibid.: 157.
22. Ernest Krenek, "Basic Principles of a New Theory of Musical
Aesthetics," in ibid.: 131.

do with each other, but both Shostakovich and Stravinsky imply that they do. Krenek, it would seem, is begging the question when he says that music can only be explained through itself. If the author may draw on his own experience, he can say that music is quite self-sufficient. It is in itself moving without being a metaphor for anything else. Thus, for example, due writes has a great weakness for suspensions which touch him even in inferior music. Or in one Bach Sarabande in which the music has been moving along in even quarter and eighth-notes, two triplets suddenly appear and almost make due author gasp with their "emotional" impact. In another piece, an Allemande, the intensification of the rhythm achieved primarily by ever smaller sub-divisions of the beat gives him the illusion that he is playing louder and louder (on the harpsichord!) and with growing intensity of feeling. These effects are all perceived on purely musical grounds; they evoke nothing outside of the music itself. While what has been described may correspond to whatever ideas Stravinsky had about musical expressivity and certainly to what Krenek seems to be saying, it tells us nothing about how music works. It is only description. It must be this mystery that has given rise to modern attempts to find the psychoanalytical basis of music, to psychoanalytical biographies. Somehow whatever it is that affects some of us so deeply must have some deep roots. There is an urge to find those roots and thus to explain music and musicians. It must also be at the heart of the deep curiosity the more intellectual public has about composers, the curiosity that makes them want to read about their lives and their thoughts. Stravinsky suggests that what is sublimated in music, to use Freud's term, is our sense of experienced time, a concept also put forward by Susanne Langer and quite plausible. But fundamental as that experience is, psychiatrists cannot leave it at that, since it seems to a psychiatrist that even our sense of time must be a matter of a more basic process yet to be uncovered.

According to Ehrenzweig, who believes it is valid to reduce experience to its fundamentals, since these fundamentals have strong permanent effects on our psyche, the sense of time is felt very early in the tensions and expulsions of our digestions, in hunger and satiation. This is quite likely true, but whether that primitive sense of time should be stronger than gesture and motion, breathing and the sense of our time being finite, is doubtful, certainly in relation to esthetic experiences. All music, even the worst, may reflect these elemental physiological urges and their resolutions, but this can have little to do with the quality of experience, why some music is good, some bad. To reduce an artistic experience so drastically makes it ultimately meaningless.

It is really not so mystifying that with all his exploration of unconscious and pre-conscious forces in our psyche, Freud neglected the arts even though his theories were an outgrowth of romanticism and the arts should have had priority. Since the romantics had elevated music to the ideal expression of feelings, music should have figured more prominently in his explorations. But music is unanalyzable in a system that depends on verbal and visual imagery. (According to Theodor Reik, furthermore, Freud was not especially musical. Reik himself, in his book *The Haunting Melody* is largely preoccupied with texts or with musical associations that are not intrinsic to it.)[23]

There are several deeper problems with psychoanalysis when applied to music which neither esthetician nor analyst has wanted to confront. The first is the assumption that art is sublimation arising out of inner conflict. So far we have only scattered evidence that this may be so in music at all. In fact, if there is one thing I have learned from reading the autobiographies of composers written over two centuries, it is how early the compulsion to make music occurs even in pre-romantic musicians, when music was only music and not the expression of the composer's feelings, long before sublimation is likely to have been a factor. That the maturing artist incorporates conscious and unconscious experiences in his later work is undoubtedly true. Ultimately, however, what makes great art great, as many adolescents learn while trying to express their feelings, is not mainly feeling; it is form, skill, and invention.

To mention pre-romantic autobiographers leads to another realization about psychohistory. Whenever analysts bring examples to bear on their assertions, these come almost exclusively from the late eighteenth and the nineteenth centuries. True, that is when feeling became overt in music. But when we speak of the most fundamental human drives we cannot include only the obvious. If art is the product of conflict and sublimation, then it always was and is presumably so in all civilizations, not just ours. We cannot assume that this began at some late historical point unless we assert that art did not come to its true function until it began to wear its heart on its

---

23.   Theodor Reik, *The Haunting Melody* (New York: Farrar, Straus, and Young, 1953).

sleeve. The beginning of emotionalism in music happened around 1600 and was at first calculated for effect, i.e., to allow the audience to follow the inflection of a text and its emotional implications. Are we prepared to dismiss all previous music as "primitive" as our ancestors once did? If eighteenth-century theorists such as Mattheson and Heinichen catalogued the emotions and the musical devices appropriate to them, should Bach be heard as expressing himself (and his conflicts) or did he share the assumptions of his contemporaries? To anyone who had been struck by the emotional intensity of the recitatives in the *Coffee-Cantata*, which are appropriate to, say, the *St. Matthew Passion*, the question should cease to be relevant for Bach. It is certainly not grist for the mill of psychoanalysis.

There is no denying that composers themselves began to see their music as self-expression in the nineteenth century and that, partly as a consequence, we became fascinated by the men behind the music or even *in* the music. Our romantic interest is limited primarily to those who lived and worked during this expressive era so that there has been little sense of urgency to uncover the biographical data of, say, Josquin des Prez. Since he wrote before the subjectification of art, it is doubtful that if we discovered even as little about his personality as we know about Bach, it would change the way we hear his music. Josquin's music is simply not suitable for psychoanalysis, at least not as we perceive the music of the Renaissance.

None of this should be read as an objection to psychobiography per se. Rather it is an attempt to regain some perspective. Psychohistory has its uses in terms of explaining artists as persons and in responding to the inherent fascination they have for us. It may even shed light on motivation and on the psyche of the composer. The danger does not lie in the assumption that unconscious forces are responsible for music, but rather in the belief that "self-expression" is an inherent element of art, that there is no longer a place for the classicistic artist and that we are permanently locked into what Curt Sachs saw as the greater romantic cycle, a cycle that embraces our entire musical history.[24]

Maynard Solomon's *Beethoven* aroused considerable controversy in some circles, a controversy that was for once not based on rejection of the main part of his biography of Beethoven but on

---

24.   Curt Sachs, *The Commonwealth of Art* (New York: Norton, 1946).

admiration.[25] That a musicologist might object to the application of psychohistory to composition should come as no surprise.[26] But one of the participants in a forum dealing with this book advanced the theory that it is the hemispheres of the brain that in some lives keep the right brain from knowing what the left brain is doing.[27] The example cited in this response to Solomon is Beethoven's behavior and some of his unscrupulous acts which do not match his idealistic music. The classical persona should have been Wagner, of course, in whom the same division between life and art can be observed in an extreme manifestation.

The author is in no way qualified to discuss the scientific validity of the function of the hemispheres of the brain. It is interesting to me largely because if this interpretation were to achieve any status, it might keep us as-well as composers themselves from confusing the artist and his work. As long as music was not subjective, as long as it was craft, it probably did not cause confusion in the composer's mind. He was a mere mortal, no matter how gifted. Art was an idealization to which he need not aspire in his life. Not that such aspirations became universal. The rise in status of the artist in the nineteenth century either meant that he was beyond the morality of ordinary mortals or that he tormented himself over the difference between art and life. The latter tendency most likely underlies much of Mahler's and Shostakovich's torment and is reflected in their music. It is also reflected in Expressionism, in the assumption that art that overlooks ugliness and bestiality is falsification. We, the audience, have been shamed into accepting this tenet in principle even when we find that we do not willingly submit to art that becomes distinctly unpleasant.

Thomas Mann's Adrian Leverkühn starts out classicistically, rejecting emotionalism in favor of a highly intellectual game, a ritual. It is in one of his earlier works, the setting of *Love's Labours Lost*, that Holofernes seems to speak for him when he says that he has a gift, ". . . a foolish extravagant spirit full of forms, figures, shapes, objects, ideas, apprehensions, motions, revolutions: these are begot in the ventricle of memory, nourished in the womb of pia mater and

---

25.   Maynard Solomon, *Beethoven* (New York: Schirmer, 1977).
26.   See Siegmund Levarie, "Biography of a Composer," *American Imago* 36 (1979): 313ff.
27.   Jan Ehrenwald, "Hero and Anti-Hero," in ibid.: 301ff.

délivered upon the mellowing of occasion." One can imagine Mozart describing his creative impulse that way. But as Leverkühn matures and realizes the eternal consequences of his terrible bargain he turns romantic; his music becomes confessional to an extreme, so extreme that it no longer makes sense. It is a matter of interpretation whether Mann sees this as applying to the history of music, although in view of Leverkühn's nostalgia it is plausible.

While Shostakovich might have written much more wisely had he had time and the freedom to question himself, his relatively spontaneous dictation tells us a great deal about the composer in modern times. It does not matter whether he is conservative or radical; in the most interesting autobiographies of our time, the memoirs of Shostakovich and the collected biographical books of Stravinsky, the same problems keep coming up. The twentieth-century romantic and the twentieth-century classicist have come to a place where they must question the function of their art. It had not been a problem in the past.

Stravinsky is apparently seen by Shostakovich as a member of an older generation whom he can consider the greatest composer of our time without detracting from himself. But he makes him into a foreigner. Stravinsky, writes Shostakovich, cannot be considered Russian, he is French, and that, he implies, is not quite honest. It means that one trades in scandal and self-glorification, that one lets the Fittelbergs dictate the rules. Scandal, as far as Shostakovich was concerned, was the last thing he needed. In Russia scandal meant official disapproval; even one's friends would become afraid to talk to one.

Another composer of whom Shostakovich speaks with mild approval is Berg whose *Wozzek* he found admirable although he hastily denies that it influenced him at all. His contemporaries, those of his time who might be rivals do not fare well at all. Prokofiev, claims Shostakovich, did not even do his own orchestrations while Bartók is completely ignored. Perhaps the reason Bartók is overlooked by Shostakovich is his genuine rivalry. From the point of view of vulgar Marxist esthetics he had solved the problem with which Shostakovich was literally forced to deal most of his life. Bartók not only absorbed the "idiom of the people" in his music, he even managed to solve the formal problems of twentieth-century music with great originality and elegance, yet all the while remaining highly intelligible. (It is tragic-comedy that a sophisticated Hegelian esthetician like Adorno considered Bartók out of the historical mainstream which inevitably led to twelve-tone composition.) As far as Shostakovich must have been concerned on some subliminal level, not only did Bartók succeed in terms of socialist realism, he went into exile as well. At some point Bartók found the courage to leave an untenable situation to risk moving to a place where he was far less well-known than Shostakovich who could easily have lived on his American royalties. Unlike such cosmopolitans as Prokofiev, Stravinsky, or Nabokov, however, Shostakovich could probably not have functioned on foreign soil. We cannot imagine him in Beverly Hills or in the Russian Tearoom; he belongs to a wintry climate. And as if he like Leverkühn rued his bargain with the devil, it is not reflected only in the elegiac quality of nearly all of his late works, it is also expressed in the deep sense of guilt that turns his memoirs so bitter. The oral memoirs of Shostakovich seem more like a contemporary Russian novel written in exile than any novel a writer could invent.

Most of us would assume that had Schoenberg written an autobiography, it would have been highly intellectual. But the reader of his letters and essays comes away with the impression that Schoenberg's idealism, his cast-iron integrity, also involves a certain amount of self-deception. In his early letters to Kandinsky, for example, he claims to write almost automatically, even if it is difficult to imagine that a musician raised within traditional norms of sound, tonality, euphony, and the resolution of dissonance could free himself from such conditioning without a great deal of effort.[28] Later, in his essay, "Heart and Brain in Music," he protests that most of what he writes comes to him as spontaneously as it did to Holofernes.[29] It is not relevant, of course, how much intellect goes into an artistic work. One suspects that even a Haydn whose music on the surface seems to have come to him with utter ease must have thought about much of it a great deal or that Bach's improvisation was possible only because the rules of his art had become second nature. That Schoenberg did not carefully plan the applications and the working out of his tone-rows is not believable. It is not inherently

28.   Jelena Hahl-Koch, ed., *Arnold Schoenberg, Wassily Kandinsky: Briefe, Bilder und Dokumente einer aussergewöhnlichen Begegnung* (Salzburg/Vienna: Residenz, 1980).

29.   *Style and Idea; Selected Writings of Arnold Schoenberg* (New York: St. Martin's Press, 1975).

important whether what he says is true or not. It becomes interesting only because of the romantic implications. While Bach was accused of being too intellectual in the last few decades of the eighteenth century, this represented a crisis in the perception of music, not the implication that his creativity had failed him. That Schoenberg should have succumbed to the prevailing notion that art is inspired self-expression and thus became defensive tells us a great deal about our musical culture.

We should not be surprised that the way musicians understand themselves often leaves much to be desired, and even if ultimately the novelistic approach to biography is sometimes superior to most self-analysis, it cannot really cope with the wellsprings of creativity either. While metaphor and other niceties of language may ultimately describe better what makes composers what they are than either the composer himself or the psychoanalyst, the novelist is similarly limited because he cannot understand why he does what he does. Thomas Mann not only does not succeed in explaining how his protagonist became a composer, but his narrator does not even try very hard. Zeitblom speculates that Leverkühn's mother was musical even though she never played or sang, but ironically, the composer's first musical experience, learning to sing rounds, came from a stable-maid. It is not an explanation, since his musicality continued to lie dormant until much later when Leverkühn went to live with an uncle who was an instrument maker. There the boy avoided the seductive shapes and sounds of the wares but could not resist experimenting with modulation on the keyboard. Had Mann written the novel as purely the story of a composer he would have let his hero succumb right then and there. But Leverkühn somehow senses that music will ultimately destroy him; he fights its lure the way puritans might fight the attractions of the flesh, and, indeed, he loses that battle first. From the very beginning music appears to him as temptation; finally he leaves the study of theology to study music. This particular juxtaposition of the sacred and the profane that recurs throughout the history of our music here comes fully to the fore.

To a primitive psychoanalyst such as this writer, another element of artistic choice that must always have been present is implied. What really makes artists choose their profession seems to be a need to be loved. Most talented people get so much approval when they first exhibit their talent that it becomes a need, that it promises that kind of approval as long as they develop their gift. This is seemingly not a factor in Leverkühn's psyche. But that Leverkühn sacrifices ordinary love in order to reach the highest level of creativity is not just a solitary abberation. The romantic stereotype for one-hundred-fifty years has had to make his sacrifices. Poverty, early death, loneliness, or misunderstanding are presumed to be the price of genius. When his work is not understood or not properly understood, from the point of view of his original intention, the artist rages at the rejection. Even the most successful composers are not happy if acceptance does not come on their terms.

In terms of such primitive psychology, Adrian Leverkühn's reaction is arrogance; he pretends to himself that he does not need love, selling it to the devil in exchange for creativity. Until he begins to "break down," he never faces the question of his art in terms of audiences, apparently writing for himself or posterity and only reluctantly making a concession to audiences in his violin concerto which, however, is a deliberate travesty of such concertos. In most modern autobiographies we encounter similar attitudes. Either there is contempt for audiences for their musical obtuseness or the composer attempts to shock. More realistic composers such as Luening or Antheil seem not to expect much more than they received; the others, who include Stravinsky and Shostakovich, develop considerable bitterness even when that bitterness is not justified in terms of their reception. Somehow the assumption has grown that the public is musically stupid and against novelty in general. Everyone seems to have forgotten that not so very long ago the public wanted only novelty; they eagerly went to hear new works. Even the grand controversies such as that between the Brahmsians and the Wagnerites reflected an avid interest in such matters as the fact that composers like Beethoven or Chopin may have written what they were compelled to write but were pleased when audiences responded. Only Hindemith, probably speaking too soon to be understood, puts the rights of the audience into some realistic perspective. "As long as an effort [to listen] is made at all," he writes, "the listener has a moral right of existence."[30]

It may be too late. At this time only a small portion of the public wants to hear new music; the others ask for the same repertoire over and over again while the young refuse to bother with either. This is

---

30.   Paul Hindemith, *A Composer's World* (Cambridge, Mass.: Harvard University Press, 1952).

not true in the other arts or at least not to the same degree. Film is in the enviable position music was in the nineteenth century; it is an art that combines the innovative with the popular. Just as was the case with music in the nineteenth century, a large percentage of films is pure dross, but the more intellectually ambitious and the avant-garde filmmaker has his share of the audience.

One could not deduce this from autobiographies which for the most part can only corroborate or document what we already observe. What one can see, in fictitious as well as real lives, is an attitude on the part of composers that is not likely to reverse the situation.

Bibliography

Abert, Hermann. "Ueber Aufgabe und Ziel der musikalischen Biographie." *Gesammelte Schriften und Vorträge von Hermann Abert*. Edited by Friedrich Blume. Tutzing: Schneider, p. 562ff.

⸺. *W. A. Mozart*. Leipzig: Breitkopf und Härtel, 1919—21.

Adler, Guido. "Umfang, Methode und Ziel der Musikwissenschaft." *Vierteljahrschrift für Musikwissenschaft* 1 (1855) p. 5ff.

⸺. *Gustav Mahler*. Vienna: Universal, 1916.

⸺. *Wollen und Wirken*. Vienna: Universal, 1935.

Adlung, Jacob. *Anleitung zu der musikalischen Gelahrtheit*. Erfurt: 1758. Reprinted in *Documenta musicologica*, 1. Reihe, vol. 4. Kassel: Bärenreiter, 1953.

Alsop, Joseph. *The Rare Art Traditions*. Bollingen Series 27. Princeton University Press. New York: Harper & Row, 1982.

Ambros, August Wilhelm. *Culturhistorische Bilder aus dem Musikleben der Gegenwart*. Leipzig: H. Mattes, 1860.

⸺. "Fétis." *Bunte Blätter*. Leipzig: Leuchart, 1872, p. 141ff.

Angeloni. Luigi. *Sopra la vite, le opere ed il sapere di Guido d'Arezzo*. Paris: Author, 1811.

Antheil, George. *Bad Boy of Music*. Garden City, N.Y.: Doubleday, 1945.

⸺. *Bach Dokumente II. Fremdschriftliche und gedruckte Dokumente zur Lebensgeschichte Johann Sebastian Bachs, 1685—1750*. Edited by Werner Neumann and Hans-Joachim Schulze. Kassel: Bärenreiter, 1969.

⸺. *Bach Dokumente III. Dokumente zum Nachwirken Johann Sebastian Bachs*. Edited by Hans-Joachim Schulze. Kassel: Bärenreiter, 1972.

Badura-Skoda, Eva. "Probleme einer Dokumentar-Biographie Beethovens." *Bericht über den internationalen Musikwissenschaftlichen Kongress Bonn 1970*. Edited by Hans Heinrich Eggebrecht. Kassel: Bärenreiter, 1971.

Bailbé, Joseph-Marc. *Le Roman et la musique en France sous la Monarchie de Juillet*. Paris: Lettres Moderne Minard, 1969.

Baini, Guiseppe. *Memorie storico-critiche della vita e delle opere di Giovanni Pierluigi da Palestrina*. 2 vols. Rome: Societa tipografica, 1828.

Barth, Richard, ed. *Johannes Brahms im Briefwechsel mit J. O. Grimm*. Berlin: Deutsche Brahms-Gesellschaft, 1912.

Barzun, Jacques. *Berlioz and the Romantic Century.* 3rd ed. New York: Columbia University Press, 1969.

Becker, Carl Ferdinand. *Systematisch-chronologische Darstellung der musikalischen Litteratur von der frühesten bis auf die neue Zeit.* Leipzig: 1836. Reprinted, Hilversum: Knuf, 1964.

Benda, Franz. "Autobiographie." In, *Franz Benda und seine Nachkommen.* Edited by Franz Lorenz. Berlin: de Gruyter, 1967.

Berlioz, Hector. *Mémoires de Hector Berlioz.* Paris: 1870. Translated and edited by David Cairns as *The Memoirs of Hector Berlioz.* London: Gollancz, 1969.

Bertini, Guiseppe. *Dizionario storico-critico di musica.* 2 vols. Palermo: Tip. Reale di Guerra, 1814—15.

Bibliothèque Royale Albert Ier. *Catalogue de la bibliothèque de F. J. Fétis.* Brussels: C. Murquart, 1877.

Bingley, William. *Musical Biography.* London: 1814. Reprinted, New York: Da Capo, 1971.

Blume, Friedrich. *Johann Sebastian Bach im Wandel der Geschichte.* Musikwissenschaftliche Arbeiten, 1. Kassel: Bärenreiter, 1947. English translation as *Two Centuries of Bach* by Stanley Godman. London: Oxford University Press, 1950.

Boetticher, Wolfgang, ed. *Briefe und Gedichte aus dem Album Robert und Clara Schumanns.* Leipzig: Deutscher Verlag, 1979.

———. *Robert Schumann, Einführung in Persöñlichkeit und Werk; Beiträge zur Erkenntniskritik der Musikgeschichte und Studien am Ausdrucksproblem des neunzehnten Jahrhunderts.* Berlin: Hahnefeld, 1941.

Bombet. (See Stendahl.)

Borde, Benjamin de la. (See La Borde.)

Brendel, Franz. "Robert Schumann. Eine Biographie von Joseph Wilhelm von Wasielewski. Zweite Besprechung." *Neue Zeitschrift für Musik* 48 (1858), nos. 11—18.

———. "Robert Schumann mit Rücksicht auf Felix Mendelssohn-Bartholdy und die Entwicklung der modernen Tonkunst überhaupt," *Neue Zeitschrift für Musik* 22 (1845), pp. 63, 81, 89, 113, 121, 145.

Brossard, Sébastien. *Dictionnaire de musique.* Paris: G. Ballard, 1703.

Burney, Charles. *The Present State of Music in Germany, the Netherlands and United Provinces.* London: 1775. Included in *An Eighteenth-Century Musical Tour in Central Europe and the Netherlands.* Edited by Percy Scholes. London: Oxford University Press, 1959.

Cannon, Beekman. *Johann Mattheson, Spectator in Music.* New Haven, Conn.: Yale University Press, 1947.

Carpani, Guiseppe. *La Haydine, overo lettere sulla vita e le opere del celebre maestro Giuseppe Haydn.* Milan: Boccinelli, 1812.

Charlton, David and George Grove. "Wasielewski." *The New Grove Dictionary of Music and Musicians,* vol. 20, p. 227f.

Chissell, Joan. *Clara Schumann, a Dedicated Spirit: A Study of Her Life and Work.* New York: Taplinger, 1983.

Choron, Alexandre and François Fayolle. *Dictionnaire historique des musiciens.* Paris: Chimot, 1810—11.

Chrysander, Friedrich. *Georg Friedrich Händel.* 3 vols. Leipzig: Breitkopf und Härtel, 1858—67.

——. "Lodovico Zacconi als Lehrer des Kunstgesangs." *Vierteljahrschrift für Musikwissenschaft* 7, 9, 10 (1891—94) pp. 337ff, 249ff, 531ff.

Cocteau, Jean. "Le Coq et l'arlequin." In, *L'Appèl à l'ordre.* Paris: Stock, 1948.

Coover, James. *Music Lexicography.* 3rd ed. Carlisle, Pa.: Carlisle Books, 1971.

Cramer, Carl Friedrich. *Anecdotes sur W. G. Mozart.* Paris: Author, 1801.

da Ponte, Lorenzo. *Memorie di Lorenzo da Ponte.* New York: 1823. English translation by Elizabeth Abbott, edited by Arthur Livingston. New York: Orion Press, 1959.

Dahlhaus, Carl. *Between Romanticism and Modernism.* Translated by Mary Whittal. Berkeley: University of California Press, 1980.

——. "Christoph Graupner und das Formprinzip der Autobiographie." *Bachiana et alia musicologica. Festschrift Alfred Dürr zum 65. Geburtstag am 3. März 1983.* Kassel: Bärenreiter, 1983.

——. *Die Musik des 19. Jahrhunderts.* Neues Handbuch der Musikwissenschaft, 6. Wiesbaden: Akademische Verlagsgesellschaft Athenaion, 1981.

——, ed.*Studien zur Trivialmusik des 19. Jahrhunderts.* Studien zur Musikgeschichte des 19. Jahrhunderts, 8. Regensburg: Bosse, 1967.

David, Hans T. and Arthur Mendel. *The Bach Reader.* Rev. ed. New York: Norton, 1966.

Deiters, Hermann. "W. J. von Wasielewski, Ludwig von Beethoven." *Vierteljahrschrift für Musikwissenschaft* 5 (1888), p. 469ff.

Deutsch, Otto Erich. *Franz Schubert. Die Dokumente seines Lebens und Schaffens.* 2 vols. Munich and Leipzig: G. Müller, 1913—14.

——. *Mozart, die Dokumente seines Lebens.* Neue Ausgabe sämtlicher Werke, ser. 10, suppl. Kassel: Bärenreiter, 1961.

Dittersdorf, Carl Ditters von. *Karl von Dittersdorfs Lebensbeschreibung.* Leipzig: Breitkopf und Härtel, 1801.

Dlabač, Bohumir Jan. *Allgemeines historisches Künstler-Lexikon für Böhmen und zum Theil auch für Mähren und Schlesingen.* 3 vols. Prague: Hasse, 1815—18.

——. *Versuch eines Verzeichnisses der vorzüglichen Tonkünstler in oder aus Böhmen.* Materiale zur alten und neuen Statistik von Böhmen 7 & 12. Prague: 1788 & 1794.

Ehrenwald, Jan. "Hero and Anti-Hero." *American Imago* 36, p. 301ff.

Ehrenzweig, Anton. *The Hidden Order of Art.* Berkeley and Los Angeles: University of California Press, 1971.

—— The Psychoanalysis of Artistic Vision and Hearing. New York: Braziller, 1965.

Eibel, Joseph Heinz. Addenda und Corrigenda zu Mozart, die Dokumente seines Lebens. Neue Ausgabe sämtlicher Werke, ser. 10, suppl. Kassel: Bärenreiter, 1978.

Einstein, Alfred. Mozart. His Character and His Work. New York and London: Oxford University Press, 1945.

——. "Die deutsche Musiker-Autobiographie." Jahrbuch der Musikbibliothek Peters für 1921. Leipzig: Peters, 1922.

Eitner, Robert. Bio-bibliographisches Quellen-Lexikon der Musiker und Musikgelehrten vom Anfang der christlichen Zeitrechnung bis zur Mitte des 19. Jahrhunderts. 10 vols. Leipzig: Breitkopf und Härtel, 1900—4.

Eschenburg, Johann Joachim. Dr. Burneys Abhandlung über die Musik der Alten. Leipzig: 1781.

Fabroni, Angelo. Vita italorum doctrina excellentium. Rome: 1778—1805.

Farmer, Henry George. "British Musicians a Century Ago." Music and Letters 12 (1931), p. 395ff.

Federhofer-Königs, Renate. "Wasielewski als Düsseldorfer Konzertmeister und Biograph." Robert Schumann — ein romantisches Erbe in neuer Forschung (Robert Schumann Gesellschaft, Düsseldorf. Mainz. Schott, 1984.) P. 67ff.

——. Wilhelm Joseph von Wasielewski im Spiegel seiner Korrespondenz. Mainzer Studien zur Musikwissenschaft 7. Tutzing: Hans Schneider, 1974.

Fétis, François-Joseph. Biographie universelle des musiciens et bibliographie générale de la musique. 1st ed. 1835—44. 2nd ed. 8 vols. Paris: Firmin-Didot, 1866—68.

Fischer, Kurt von. "Organal and Chordal Style in Renaissance Sacred Music: New and Little-known Sources." Aspects of Medieval and Renaissance Music. Edited by Jan LaRue et al. New York: Norton, 1966. P. 173ff.

Forbes, Elliot. Thayer's Life of Beethoven. 2 vols. Princeton, N.J.: Princeton University Press, 1964.

Forkel, Johann Nikolaus. Allgemeine Litteratur der Musik. Leipzig: Schwiekert, 1792.

——. Ueber Johann Sebastian Bachs Leben, Kunst und Kunstwerke. Leipzig: Hoffmeister und Kühnel, 1802.

Franck, Wolf. "Musicology and Its Founder, Johann Nikolaus Forkel." The Musical Quarterly 25 (1949), p. 588ff.

Freud, Sigmund. Gesammelte Werke. Edited by Anna Freud, et al. 18 vols. Frankfurt a/M: S. Fischer, 1961—68.

——. Leonardo da Vinci. Translated by A. A. Brill. New York: Random House, 1922.

——. Moses and Monotheism. New York: Knopf, 1939.

Freytag, Gustav. *Gesammelte Aufsätze.* 2 vols. Leipzig: Herzel, 1888.

Gathy, August. *Encyclopädie der gesammten Musik-Wissenschaft.* 2nd ed. Hamburg: G. W. Niemayer, 1840.

Gerber, Ernst Ludwig. *Historisch-biographisches Lexikon der Tonkünstler.* Leipzig: 1790—92. New edition by Othmar Wessely. Graz: Akademische Druck und Verlagsanstalt, 1966—77.

———. *Neues historisch-biographisches Lexikon der Tonkünsler.* Leipzig: 1812—13. New edition by Othmar Wessely. Graz: Akademische Druck und Verlagsanstalt, 1966—77.

Gerbert, Martin. *Scriptores ecclesiastici de musica sacra potissimum.* 3 vols. Berli: 1784. Reprinted, Milan: Bolletino Bibliographico Musicale, 1931.

Germer, Mark. "Dlabǎc' Dictionary and Its Place in the Literature." *Fontes artis musicae* 28 (1981), p. 307ff.

Greitner, Aloys, ed. *Billroth im Briefwechsel mit Brahms.* Munich: Urban und Schwarzenberg, 1964.

Grétry, André-Ernest-Modeste. *Mémoires ou essais sur la musique.* Pluviôse: 1789. Reprint of 2nd ed., 3 vols. New York: Da Capo, 1971.

Guigard, Joannis. *Indicateur de Mercure de France 1672—1787.* Paris: Mercure de France, 1869.

Gyrowetz, Adalbert. *Biographie des Adalbert Gyrowetz.* Vienna: 1848. Reprinted in Lebensläufe deutscher Musiker von inhen selbst erzählt. Vols. 3 and 4. Edited by Alfred Einstein. Leipzig: C. F. W. Siegel, 1915.

Hahl-Koch, Jelena, ed. *Arnold Schoenberg, Wassily Kandinsky: Briefe und Dokumente einer aussergewöhnlichen Begegnung.* Salzburg/Vienna: Residenz, 1980.

Hanslick, Eduard. *Aus dem Tagebuche eines Musikers.* Berlin: Allgemeiner Verein für deutsche Literatur, 1892.

———. *Aus Meinem Leben.* 2 vols. Berlin: Allgemeiner Verein für deutsche Literatur, 1894.

———. *Geschichte des Concertwesens in Wien.* 2 vols. Vienna: Braumüller, 1869.

———. "W. von Wasielewski und Clara Schumann." *Aus neuer und neuester Zeit.* Berlin: Allgemeiner Verein für deutsche Literartur, 1900.

———. "Richard Wagner und Wendelin Weissheimer." *Aus neuer und neuester Zeit.* Berlin: Allgemeiner Verein für deutsche Literatur, 1900.

Hauser, Arnold, *The Social History of Art.* 2 vols. London: Routlege & Kegan Paul, 1957.

Hertel, Johann Wilhelm. *Autobiographie.* In, *Wiener musikalische Beiträge* vol. 3. Edited by Erich Schenk. Graz: Böhlhaus Nachf, 1957.

Heussner, Horst. "Nürmberger Verlag und Musikalienhandlung im 18. Jahrhundert." In, *Musik und Verlag. Karl Vötterle zum 65. Geburtstag.* Kassel: Bärenreiter, 1968.

Hildesheimer, Wolfgang. *Mozart.* Frankfurt a/m: Suhrkamp, 1977.

Hilgenfeld, C. F. *Johann Sebastian Bachs Leben, Wirken und Werke.* Leipzig: 1850. Reprinted, Hilversum: Knuf, 1965.

Hiller, Ferdinand. *Künstlerleben*. Cologne: Mont-Schaubergsche Buchhandlung, 1880.

———. *Mendelssohn. Letters and Recollections*. Translated by M. E. von Glehn. 2nd ed. London: Macmillan, 1874.

Hiller, Johann Adam. *Lebensbeschreibungen berühmter Musikgelehrten und Tonkünstler neuerer Zeit*. Part I (all published). Leipzig: Dykische Buchhandlung, 1784.

Hindemith, Paul. *A Composer's World*. Cambridge, Mass.: Harvard University Press, 1952.

Hitzig, Wilhelm. "Pariser Briefe. Ein Beitrag zur Arbeit des deutschen Musikverlages aus den Jahren 1833–1840." *Der Bär*, 1929/30. Leipzig: Breitkopf und Härtel, 1930. P. 27ff.

Hoboken, Anthony von. *Discrepancies in Haydn Biographies*. Louis Charles Elson Memorial Lecture. Washington, D.C.: Library of Congress, 1962.

Hoffmann, Carl Julius Adolph Hugo. *Die Tonkünstler Schlesiens*. Breslau: Aderholz, 1830.

Hoffmann, Ernst Theodor Amadeus. *Die Lebensansichten des Kater Murr*. Berlin: Reimer, 1820–22.

Honegger, Arthur, *I Am a Composer*, New York: St. Martin's, 1966.

Humperdinck, Engelbert. *Briefe und Tagebücher*. Edited by Hans-Joseph Irmen. 2 vols. Beiträge zur rheinischen Musikgeschichte, vols. 106 and 114. Cologne: Volk, 1975–76.

Jahn, Otto. *W. A. Mozart*. 4 vols. Leipzig: Breitkopf und Härtel, 1856–59.

Jones, Ernest. *The Life and Work of Sigmund Freud*. 3 vols. New York: Basic Books, 1953–57.

Kaiser, Georg, ed. *Sämtliche Schriften von Carl Maria von Weber*. Berlin and Leipzig: Schuster und Löffler, 1908.

Kahl, Willi. *Selbstbiographien deutscher Musiker*. Cologne: 1948. Reprinted, Amsterdam: Kunf, 1972.

Kandler, Franz Sales. *Ueber das Leben und die Werke des G. Pierluigi da Palestrina*. Leipzig: Breitkopf und Härtel, 1834.

———. *Cenni storico-critico . . . del celebre compositore Giuseppe Adolfo Hasse*. Venice: Picotti, 1820.

Kelly, Michael. *Reminiscenses of Michael Kelly*. London: 1826. Reprinted in 2 vols. New York: Da Capo, 1968.

Kiesewetter, Raphael Georg. *Guido von Arezzo, sein Leben und Wirken*. Leipzig: Breitkopf und Härtel, 1840.

King, A. Hyatt. *Mozart in Retrospect*. 3rd ed. London: Oxford University Press, 1971.

Köchel, Ludwig Ritter von. *Chronologisch-syematisches Verzeichnis sämtlicher Tonwerke Volfgang Amadeus Mozarts*. Leipzig: Breitkopf und Härtel, 1862.

Kossmaly, Carl and Carlo (pseud.). *Schlesisches Tonkünstler-Lexikon*. Breslau: E. Trewent, 1846–47.

Krenek, Ernest. *Exploring Music*. London: Calder and Boyars, 1966.

Kretzschmar, Hermann, "Lodovico Zacconis Leben auf Grund seiner Autobiographie." *Jahrbuch der Musikbibliothek Peters für 1910.* Leipzig: Peters, 1911. P. 45ff.

Krummacher, Friedhelm. *Die Überlieferung der Choralbearbeitungen in der frühen evangelischen Kantate.* Berliner Studien zur Musikwissenschaft 10. Berlin: Merseburger, 1965.

La Borde, Jean Benjamin de. *Essai sur la musique ancienne et moderne.* 4 vols. Paris: P. D. Pierres, 1780.

La Mara (Ida Maria Lipsius). *Musikalische Studienköpfe.* 5 vols. Leipzig: Schmidt, 1868—82.

Lacombe, Jacques. *Dictionnaire portatif des beaux-arts.* Paris: La Veuve Estienne, 1752.

———. *Dizionario portatile delle belle arte.* Venice: Remondini, 1768.

Landon, H. C. Robbins. *The Collected Correspondence and London Notebooks of Josephy Haydn.* London: Barrie and Rockliff, 1959.

———. "Haydn." *Die Musik in Geschichte und Gegenwart.* 16 vols. Kassel: Bärenreiter, 1956—79. Vol. 5, column 11ff.

———. *Haydn: Chronicle and Works.* 5 vols. Bloomington: Indiana University Press, 1976—86.

Laugier, Marc-Antoine. *Apologie de la musique française contre M. Rousseau.* Paris: n.p., 1754.

Leblond, Gaspar-Michel. *Mémoires pour servir à l'histoire de la révolution opérée par M. le Chévalier Gluck.* Naples and Paris: Bailly, 1781.

Ledebur, Carl Freiherr von. *Tonkünsler-Lexikon Berlins.* Berlin: Rauh, 1861.

Lenneberg, Hans. "Bach, Handel and Comparative Reputations." *Bach. The Quarterly Journal of the Riemenschneider Bach Institute* 12 (1981), p. 22ff. and 13 (1982), p. 17ff.

———. *Breitkopf und Härtel in Paris. The Letters of Their Agent Heinrich Probst, 1833—1840.* La Vie musicale en France au XIXe siècle 5. New York: Pendragon, in preparation.

———. "The Myth of the Unappreciated (Musical) Genius." *The Musical Quarterly* 66 (1980), p. 219ff.

Lesure, François, et al. *La Musique à Paris en 1830—1831.* Paris: Bibliothèque Nationale, 1983.

———. *Igor Stravinsky, Le Sacre du printemps. Dossier de Presse.* Geneva: Minkoff, 1980.

Levarie, Siegmund. "Biography of a Composer." *American Imago* 36 (1979), p. 312ff.

Liechtenthal, Pietro. *Dizionario e bibliografia della musica.* 4 vols. Milan: Fontana, 1826.

Liszt, Franz. *The Letters of Franz Liszt.* Edited by La Mara and translated by Constance Bache. London: H. Grevel, 1894.

——. *Gesammelte Schriften.* 4 vols in 2. Edited by Julius Knapp. Leipzig: Breitkopf und Härtel, 1910.

Litzmann, Berthold. *Clara Schumann. An Artist's Life.* 2 vols. Translated and abridged by Grace E. Hadow. London: Macmillan, 1913.

Lockwood, Lewis. *Music in Renaissance Ferrara, 1400—1505.* Cambridge, Mass.: Harvard University Press, 1984.

Loesser, Arthur. *Men, Women and Pianos.* New York: Simon and Schuster, 1954.

Lonsdale, Roger. *Dr. Charles Burney.* Oxford: Clarendon Press, 1965.

Lowens, Irvin. *Haydn in America.* Detroit, Mich.: Information Coordinators, 1979.

Lowinsky, Edward. "Musical Genius — Evolution and Origins of a Concept." *The Musical Quarterly* 50 (1964), p. 321ff and 476ff.

Luening, Otto. *The Odyssey of an American Composer.* New York: Scribner, 1980.

Mainwaring, John. *Memoirs of the Late George Frederick Handel.* London: R. & J. Dodsley, 1760.

Mann, Thomas. *Doctor Faustus.* Stockholm: Fischer, 1947.

Marpurg, Friedrich Wilhelm. *Historisch-Critische Beyträge zur Aufnahme der Musik.* 5 vols. Berlin: Lange, 1754—78.

——. *Critische Briefe über die Tonkunst.* 3 vols. Berlin: F. W. Birnstiel, 1760—64.

——. *Der critische Musikus and der Spree.* Berlin: Hande, 1749-50.

Mattheson, Johann. *Critica musica.* Hamburg: Author, 1725.

——. *Grundlage einer Ehrenpforte, woran der Tüchtigsten Capellmeister, Componisten, Musikgelehrten, Tonkünstler, etc. erscheinen sollen.* Hamburg: Author, 1740. Reprint ed. Max Schneider. Berlin: Liepmannssohn, 1910.

——. *Das neu-eröffnete Orchestre.* Hamburg: Author, 1713.

Marx, Adolph Bernhard. *Die Musik des 19, Jahrhundertd und ihre Pflege.* Published in English as, *The Music of the Nineteenth Century.* London: Cocks and Co., 1855.

Mendel, Hermann and August Reissmann. *Musikalisches Conversations-Lexikon.* 2nd ed. 11 vols. Leipzig: List und Franke, 1880—83.

Mendelssohn-Bartholdy, Felix. *Briefe.* Edited by Rudolf Elvers. Veröffentlichungen der historischen Kommission zu Berlin beim Friedrich — Meinecke — Institute der Freien Universität Berlin. Berlin: de Gruyter, 1968—.

Menke, Werner. *Das Vokalwerk Georg Philip Telemanns.* Erlanger Beiträge zur Musikwissenschaft 3. Kassel: Bärenreiter, 1942.

Meusel, Johann Georg. *Teutsches Künstlerlexikon.* Lemgo: Meyer, 1788.

Meyerbeer, Giacomo. *Briefwechsel und Tagebücher.* Edited by Heinz and Gudrun Becker. 3 vols. Berlin: de Gruyter, 1975—.

Milhaud, Darius. *Ma vie heureuse.* Paris: Belfont, 1974.

Milo, Massimo. "Verdi e Hanslick." *La Rassegna musicale* 21 (1951), p. 212ff.

Mizler von Kolof, Lorenz Christoph. *Neu-eröffnete musikalische Bibliothek.* 4 vols. Leipzig: 1739—54. Reprinted, 4 vols. in 3. Hilversum: Knuf, 1966.

Moore, Jerold Northrop. *Elgar on Record. The Composer and the Gramophone.* London: Oxford University Press, 1974.

Möricke, Edward. *Mozart auf der Reise nach Prag.* Prague: 1856. Reprinted, Wiesbaden: 1959.

Morrow, Mary Sue. "Concert Life in Vienna, 1780—1810." Ph.D. dissertation. Indiana University, 1984.

Moscheles, Felix, ed. and trans. *Letters of Felix Mendelssohn to Ignaz and Charlotte Moscheles.* Freeport, N.Y.: Books for Libraries, 1970.

Moser, Andreas, ed. *Johannes Brahms im Briefwechsel mit Joseph Joachim.* 2 vols. Berlin: Deutsche Brahms-Gesellschaft, 1921.

Nabokov, Vladimir. *The Defense.* Translated by Michael Scammell. New York: n.p., 1964.

Neefe, Christian Gottlob. *Lebenslauf.* Edited by Walther Engelhardt. Beiträge zur rheinischen Musikgeschichte 21. Cologne: Volk, 1957.

Nissen, Georg Nikolaus von. *Biographie W. A. Mozarts nach Original briefen* . . . Leipzig: Breitkopf und Härtel, 1828.

Osborne, James M. *The Autobiography of Thomas Whythorne.* Oxford: Clarendon Press, 1961.

Ostwald, Peter. *Schumann. The Inner Voices of a Musical Genius.* Boston: Northeastern University Press, 1985.

Parker, John Rowe. *A Musical Biography.* Boston: 1825. Reprinted, Detroit: Information Coordinators, 1975.

Pettler, Pamela Susskind. "Clara Schumann's Recitals, 1832—50." *19th Century Music* 4 (1981), p. 70ff.

Pirotta, Nino. *Music and Culture in Italy from the Middle Ages to the Baroque.* Cambridge, Mass.: Harvard University Press, 1984.

Pitoni, Giuseppe Ottavio. "Notizia de' contrapountisti e compositori di musica dall'anno 1,000 alla 1700." Unpublished manuscript. Biblioteca Apostolica Vaticana.

Pleasants, Henry. *The Music Criticism of Hugo Wolf.* New York: Holmes and Meier, 1979.

Pohl, Richard. *Hector Berlioz. Studien und Erinnerungen.* Leipzig: Breitkopf und Härtel, 1923.

—— (Hoplit). "Robert Schumann. Eine Biographie von Joseph von Wasielewski. Erste Besprechung." *Neue Zeitschrift für Musik* 48 (1858), no. 608.

Poulenc, Francis. *Moi et mes amis.* Interviews with Stéphane Audel. Paris and Geneva: Palatinei, 1963.

Praeger, Ferdinand. *Wagner As I Knew Him.* New York: Longmans, Green, 1892. Translated as *Wagner wie ich ihn kannte.* Leipzig: Breitkopf und Härtel, 1892.

Praz, Mario. *The Romantic Agony.* Translated by Angus Davidson. 3rd ed. Cleveland: World, 1963.

Rees, Abraham. *The Cyclopdedia or Universal Dictionary of Arts, Science and Literature.* 39 vols. London: Longman, Hurt, Rees, Orne and Brown, 1802—20.

Reese, Gustave. *Music in the Renaissance.* New York: Norton, 1954.

Reich, Nancy. *Clara Schumann, the Artist and the Woman.* New York: Cornell University Press, 1985.

Reik, Theodor. *The Haunting Melody.* New York: Farrar, Straus and Young, 1953.

Reilly, Edward R. *Gustav Mahler und Guido Adler: zur Geschichte einer Freundschaft.* Vienna: Universal, 1978.

———. *Quantz and his Versuch.* New York: Galaxy, 1971.

Rheinfurt, Hans. *Der Musikverlag Lotter in Augsburg.* Tutzing: Schneider, 1977.

Ritchie, Lawrence. "The Untimely Death of Samuel Wesley, or the Perils of Plagiarism." *Music and Letters* 60 (1979), p. 54ff.

Rochlitz, Friedrich. *Für Freunde der Tonkunst.* 4 vols. in 2. 3rd ed. Leipzig: Cnobloch, 1868.

Rolland, Romain. *Jean Christophe.* 4 vols. Paris: Ollendorf, 1905—6.

Rorem, Ned. *An Absolute Gift: A New Diary.* New York: Simon and Schuster, 1978.

———. *The Final Diary 1961—72.* New York: Holt, Rinehart and Winston, 1974.

———. *The New York Diary.* New York: Braziller, 1966.

———. *The Paris Diary of Ned Rorem.* New York: Braziller, 1966.

Rubinstein, Anton. *La Musique et ses représentants.* Translated from the Russian by Michel Delines. Paris: Heugel, 1852.

Ruhnke, Martin. "Telemann als Musikverleger." *Musik und Verlag; Karl Vötterle zum 65. Geburtstag.* Edited by Richard Baum and Wolfgang Rehm. Kassel: Bärenreiter, 1968. P. 502ff.

Sacchi, Giovenale. *Vita di Benedetto Marcello.* Venice: Zitta, 1789. Originally in Latin by Francesco Fontana. Pisa: 1787.

Sachs, Curt. *The Commonwealth of Art.* New York: Norton, 1946.

Sainsbury, John. *A Dictionary of Music and Musicians.* London: Sainsbury, 1825.

Sams, Eric. "Eduard Hanslick: The Perfect Anti-Wagnerite." *The Musical Times* 116 (1975), p. 867ff.

Schäffer, Boguslaw and Jan Steszewski. "Poland." *The New Grove Dictionary of Music and Musicians.* 20 vols. Edited by Stanley Sadie. London: Macmillan, 1980. Vol. 5, p. 26ff.

Schiedermeier, Ludwig, ed. *Die Briefe Wolfgang Amadeus Mozarts und seiner Familie.* 5 vols. Leipzig and Munich: G. Müller, 1914.

Schilling, Gustav. *Encyclopädie der gesammten musikalischen Wissenschaften.* 6 vols. Stuttgart: F. H. Köhler, 1835—37.

Schindler, Anton Felix. *Biographie von Ludwig van Beethoven.* 1st ed. Münster: Aschendorff, 1840.

Schlichtegroll, Friedrich. "Nekrolog auf das Jahr 1791." In, *Musiker-Nekrologe.* Edited by Richard Schaal. Kassel: Bärenreiter, 1954.

Schmid, Anton. *Christoph Willibald Ritter von Gluck.* Leipzig: F. Fleischer, 1854.

Schnoebelen, Anne. *Padre Martini's Collection of Letters in the Civico Museo Bibliografico Musicale in Bologna.* New York: Pendragon, 1979.

Schoenberg, Arnold. *Style and Idea.* New York: Philosophical Library, 1975.

Schubart, Christian Friedrich Daniel. *Schubarts Leben und Gesinnungen von ihm selbst im Kerker aufgesetzt.* 2 vols. Stuttgart: Gebrüder Mäntler, 1791—93.

Schumann, Robert. *Tagebücher.* Edited by Georg Eismann. Leipzig: Deutscher Verlag, 1975—.

Schumann, Robert and Clara Schumann. *Briefwechsel.* Kritische Gesamtausgabe edited by Eva Weissweiler. Vol. 1. Frankfort a/M: Stroemfeld/Roter Stern, 1984—.

Shaw, H. Watkins. "Extracts from Anthony a Woods 'Notes on the Lives of Musicians' Hitherto Unpublished." *Music and Letters* 15 (1934), p. 157ff.

Shostakovich, Dmitri. *Testimony: The Memoirs of Dmitri Shostakovich.* Edited by Solomon Volkov and translated by Antonia W. Bouis. New York: Harper and Row, 1980.

Siegmaister, J. G. *Ueber den Ritter Gluck und seine Werke.* Berlin: Voss'sche Buchhandlung, 1822.

Smith, Logan Pearsall. *Four Words, Romantic, Originality, Creative, Genius.* Society for Pure English, Tract 17, Oxford, 1924.

Solomon, Maynard. *Beethoven.* New York: Schirmer, 1977.

Solzhenitzyn, Alexander. *From Under the Rubble.* Boston: Little Brown, 1975.

Sowinski, Albert. *Les Musiciens polonais et slaves anciens et modernes.* Paris: Adrian Le Clère, 1857.

Spitta, Philipp. *Johann Sebastian Bach.* 2 vols. Leipzig: Breitkopf und Härtel, 1873—80.

———. "Ein Lebensbild Robert Schumann." In, *Sammlung musikalischer Vorträge.* Edited by Paul Graf Waldersee. Ser. 4. Leipzig: Breitkopf und Härtel, 1882. P. 1ff.

Spohr, Louis (Ludwig). *Selbstbiographie.* Kassel and Göttingen: 1860—61. Edited as *Lebenserinnerungen* by Folker Goethel. 2 vols. in 1. Tutzing: Schneider, 1968.

Stendahl, (Henry Beyle), pseudonym, Bombet. *Lettres écrits de Vienne en Autriche, sur le célèbre compositeur Haydn, suivie d'une vie de Mozart, et de considerations sur Métastase, et l'état present de la musique en France et en Italie.* Paris: 1814. Translated as *Haydn, Mozart and Metastasio* by Richard Coe. London: Calder and Boyars, 1973.

Stravinsky, Igor. *Chronique de ma vie.* English as *Chronicle of My Life.* London: Gollancz, 1936.

———. *The Poetics of Music.* New York: Vintage, 1974.

Stravinsky, Igor and Robert Craft. *Conversations with Igor Stravinsky.* London: Faber and Faber, 1958.

———. *Dialogues and a Diary.* Garden City, N.Y.: Doubleday, 1963.

———. *Expositions and Developments.* London: Faber and Faber, 1962.

———. *Memories and Commentaries.* London: Faber and Faber, 1962.

———. *Themes and Conclusions.* London: Faber and Faber, 1972.

Thayer, Alexander Wheelock. *Ludwig van Beethovens Leben.* For the complex history of his work, see Forbes, *Thayer's Life of Beethoven.*

Thym, Jurgen. "Schumann in Brendel's *Neue Zeitschrift für Musik* from 1845 to 1856." *Mendelssohn and Schumann.* Edited by John Finson and R. Larry Todd.

Tillet, Évrard du. *Le Parnasse françois*, Paris: J. B. Coignard, 1732. Supplements 1743 and 1755.

Tomášek, Jan Vaclov. "Erinnerungen." In, *Libussa 1845—1850.* Excerpts translated by Abram Loft in *The Musical Quarterly* 32 (1946), p. 244ff.

Tschulik. *Also sprach Beckmesser.* Vienna: Bergland, 1965.

Tyson, Alan. "Stages in the Composition of Beethoven's Piano Trio op. 70, #1." *Proceedings of the Royal Musical Assn.* 97 (1970—71), p. 2ff.

Ulybichev, Alexandr Dmitrievich. *Mozarts Leben, nebst einer Übersicht der allgemeinen Geschichte der Musik und einer Analyse der Hauptwerke Mozarts.* 3 vols. Stuttgart: A. Becker, 1847.

Vasari, Giorgio, *Le Vite de piu eccelenti architetti, pittori et scultore italiani da Cimabue al' tempi nostri descritte in lingua toscana.* Florence: Torrentino 1550. 2nd ed., Florence: Giunti, 1568.

Vetter, Walther "Gedanken zur musikalischen Biographik." *Die Musikforschung*, 12 (1959), p. 132.

Wagner, Richard. *Mein Leben.* Munich: List, 1963.

Walther, Johann Gottfried. *Musikalisches Lexikon.* Leipzig: 1732. Reprinted in *Documenta musicologica* 1. Reihe, v. 3. Kassel: Bärenreiter, 1953.

Wasielewski, Wilhelm Joseph von. *Aus siebzig Jahren.* Stuttgart and Leipzig: Deutsche Verlags-Anstalt, 1897.

———. *Robert Schumann.* Leipzig: 1858. Reprint of 1906 edition, Wiesbaden: Sändig, 1972.

———. *Schumanniana.* Bonn: Strauss, 1883.

Weber, William. *Music and the Middle Class.* New York: Holmes and Heyt, 1975.

Weinmann, Alexander. *Vollständiges Verlagsverzeichnis Artaria und Co.* Beiträge zur Geschichte des alt-wiener Musikverlags, Reihe 2, Folge 2. Vienna: L. Krenn, 1952.

Wieck, Friedrich. *Briefe aus den Jahren 1830—1838.* Edited by Käthe Walch-Schumann. Beiträge zur rheinischen Musikgeschichte 74. Cologne: Volk, 1968.

Winckler, Théophile Frédèric. *Notice biographique sur Jean-Chrysostome-Wolfgang-Théophile Mozart.* Paris: 1801.

Winterfeld, Carl von. *Johannes Gabrieli und sein Zeitalter.* Berlin: Schlesinger, 1834.

Zedler, Johann Heinrich. *Grosses vollständiges Universal-Lexikon.* 64 vols. and suppl. Halle and Leipzig: Zedler, 1732—54.

Zelter, Carl Friedrich. *Darstellung seines Leben.* Edited by Johann Wolfgang Schottländer. Schriften der Goethe-Gesellschaft. Weimar: Goethe-Gesellschaft, 1931.

Zentner. *Johann Friedrich Reichardt, eine Musikerjugend im 18. Jahrhundert.* Regensburg: Bosse, 1940.

INDEX

217